DICTIONARY OF YORKSHIRE DIALECT, TRADITION AND FOLKLORE

Dictionary

of
Yorkshire
Dialect, Tradition and Folklore

Arnold Kellett

Illustrated by Peter Kearney

First published in 1994 by

Smith Settle Ltd
Ilkley Road
Otley
West Yorkshire
LS21 3JP

ISBN   Paperback   1 85825 016 1
       Hardback   1 85825 017 X

British Library Cataloguing-in-Publication Data:
A catalogue record is available for this book
from the British Library.

Designed, printed and bound by
SMITH SETTLE
Ilkley Road, Otley, West Yorkshire LS21 3JP

Dedicated to the memory of my father, a real Yorkshireman.

Acknowledgements

Thanks are due first of all to my friend and former colleague Peter Kearney who, once again, has so readily supplied splendidly clear and illuminating illustrations to my exact and sometimes peculiar specifications (eg 'Dick's 'atband').

Special thanks to my wife, Pat, who has coped with card indexes and word-processing up to the very eve of our ruby wedding, when we should have been remembering Robin Hood's Bay.

Of the members of the Yorkshire Dialect Society who have given encouragement and advice, I would particularly like to thank Ruth Dent (chairman) and Stanley Ellis (secretary), as well as Irwin Bielby, Cedric Sellars, Bill Cowley, Jack Danby OBE, Ian Dewhirst, Arthur Kinder, Sydney Martin, Muriel Shackleton, Norman Stockton, and Peter N Walker. The unpublished word-lists compiled by N A Hudleston (East Riding) and Donald Barker (West Riding) have also been most useful.

Professor J D A Widdowson not only made me welcome at the Centre for English Cultural Tradition and Language at Sheffield University, but has also welcomed this *Dictionary* in his warmly supportive preface.

Others who have supplied material or helpful comments are: Rev B Abell (Official of the Peculier of Masham), Richard Beetham, Irwin Bielby, Peter Brears, the *Dalesman*, John Dent, Jean and Stanley Evans, Alan Hardill, Alan Hemsworth, Audrey and Peter Houlston, Andrew Kirkham, Vera and Brian McHugh, W R (Bill) Mitchell, Ian Porter, Dr Clive Upton, Richard van Riel and Julia Smith — as well as the staff of the reference libraries of Harrogate, Keighley, Leeds and York, and of various Yorkshire museums.

Author's Note

Lexicographers are not word-perfect, and, though I have cast my net as widely as possible, some items may have slipped through. Suggestions which may be useful for a future edition would be gratefully received, via the publisher.

Please note that both text and illustrations are copyright. Permission is required for reproduction, and acknowledgement of this *Dictionary* should be made when quoting.

Preface
by
Professor J D A Widdowson

As we approach the end of the twentieth century, we become increasingly aware that the past hundred years have seen unprecedented changes in virtually every aspect of English life. Developments in science, technology, education and communication are rapidly carrying our culture into a new and very different era. Older patterns of life and work have given way to new lifestyles and methods of production.

At the same time, however, the often bewildering pace of change has generated an interest in the past, in every aspect of our heritage, not least in the language and traditions which are central to the English way of life. This interest is often strongest at the local level, as people rediscover the history of their family, community or region, whether as individuals, or as members of the many societies and institutions which act as focal points for the study and enjoyment of the heritage in all its forms. The impetus for these investigations usually springs form the desire to locate oneself in time and space — to acquire a sense of belonging, especially to a particular locality. Identifying oneself with a specific place, to feel part of one's village, town, city or county, is central to the well-being of most people. Equally, a knowledge of language and tradition at both local and national levels lies at the heart of our Englishness.

In these changing times, it is therefore especially important to give the may different varieties of local language and tradition throughout the country the serious attention which they deserve. In his thought-provoking introduction to this new *Yorkshire Dictionary*, Dr Arnold Kellett rightly emphasises such an approach. At the same time, he draws attention to the sense of a proper pride in one's community and county arising from familiarity with local dialect and tradition, which link the present with the past and provide a felling of security and continuity. He is also very much aware of the erosion of dialect, and especially of its rich vocabulary, during this century, and encourages us to join him in documenting, understanding and participating in the language and traditions of the ancient county of Yorkshire. What is more, the material presented in the *Dictionary* draws very much on his own personal experience over a lifetime of enthusiastic interest in and observation of local usage and custom, from his early days in the Bradford area to his more recent research on Knaresborough. Above all, the introduction not only recognises the crucial inter-relationships between local language and folklore, but also that individual words and phrases are best understood in their full linguistic and social context. Many of the entries in the *Dictionary* are therefore exemplified by authentic quotations of actual spoken usage, which immediately give the reader the precise meaning and flavour of the word or phrase, often incorporating traditional humour for good measure.

The introduction is essential reading for all who are interested in English dialects. It presents an overview of the present state and future development of dialects, wherever they may be found, and readers can hardly fail to respond to the writer's staunch commitment to and enthusiasm for his subject. The introduction also sets out in some detail precisely what the *Dictionary* includes, and why. It concludes by offering a very useful and accessible summary of the historical background to English dialects in general, and to Yorkshire dialect in particular, along with an account of its study and use.

The *Dictionary* itself is an alphabetical listing of a judicious selection of words and pronunciations, phrases, customs, traditions and other items of specifically Yorkshire interest. It is a natural successor to Dr Kellett's admirable and highly popular book *Basic Broad Yorkshire* (1991; revised edition 1992). The alphabetical entries quickly lead the reader to individual items, but the temptation to read other entries on the same page immediately prompts one to browse, and it is here that the book reveals its less obvious delights: the informative summary accounts of calendar customs such as Barnaby Fair, barring-out, Carlin' Sunda, Collop Munda, Denby Dale Pie, Driffield Pennies, Fig Sunday, Fruttace Wednesday, Kiplingcotes Derby, Leggin' Day, Owd Bartle, Penny Hedge,

Rammalation Day, Rive-kite Sunda, Spanish Sunday, Spaw Sunday, Thomassing and Wilfra Feast; beliefs and legends; topographical features and their associations — Brimham Rocks, Cow and Calf, the Devil's Arrows, Dropping Well, Filey Brigg, Gypsey Race, Roseberry Topping, the Strid and Troller's Gill; and historical and/ or legendary characters — Blind Jack, Caedmon, Dick Turpin, Ludlam's dog, Mother Shipton, Robin Hood and Throp's wife.

There is a fascinating thread of local rhymes and sayings about certain Yorkshire villages and towns which runs through the book; these are part of the tradition of *blason populaire* which presents a stereotypical image of a locality and/or its inhabitants, often detrimental either to the locals or to neighbouring communities — see, for example, the entries for Austwick carles, Bedale, Castleford lasses, Heptonstall, Keighley kay-legged-uns, Leeds loiner, Ossett, Pudsey and Steeas (Staithes). The reader will also find a great deal of information on traditional Yorkshire food, as well as interesting entries on sport, sword-dancing and folk plays, among many other topics of interest. Twenty-eight entries under Yorkshire and Yorkshireman, occurring conveniently almost at the end of the alphabetical listing, help to round off the collection in resounding fashion!

It is the dialect items, however, which form the bulk of the entries, and here the reader will have a field day. The selection of pronunciations, words and phrases is both wide-ranging and revealing; either the individual entries are instantly recognised by readers well-versed in the dialects of one or more of the three Ridings, or the memory is jogged as words once familiar are suddenly recalled. Anyone unfamiliar with the dialects will find the glosses, explanations and examples clear and helpful, as they make their first acquaintance with hundreds of Yorkshire words, the provenance of which may go back to the Middle Ages, and in many cases to the period of Old English and Old Norse spoken in these areas more than a thousand years ago; some, like *brock* and *coble,* can even be traced as far back as the Celtic period — around 500 BC.

One particular reason for studying regional dialects is that they preserve the pronunciation, vocabulary, grammar and word order of earlier stages in the history of the language. The dialects were in existence some seven centuries before the rise of Standard English, those of the North being distinctive from the outset. In purely historical terms, then, their modern equivalents have the best credentials, not to mention their extraordinary richness and diversity. It is therefore very heartening to discover that, even on a rough count, well over 850 of the words and pronunciations in the *Dictionary* are to my knowledge in active current use. At least twice that number will be well within living memory at the present time, even though many of them refer to objects and activities which are obsolescent.

This suggests that we should be cautious in proclaiming the imminent death of the regional dialects. Many conservative speakers use these older forms in daily conversation, largely unheard by those who investigate and study these usages. What is more, the dialects are strongly maintained in other parts of the British Isles and Ireland, along with the Celtic languages which give the English regional speech of these areas a distinctively Scottish, Welsh or Irish flavour. But in England the steady erosion continues. Dialects are living entities — they cannot be preserved or kept alive artificially, they must be used if they are to survive. To paraphrase a well-known present-day slogan: 'This is your dialect. Use it or lose it!'.

As the author says in his introduction, it is important to record this material while it is still in active use and living memory. He adds that the purpose of the *Dictionary* is to support and encourage those who use and have an interest in dialect. This book is the first of its kind, and sets an example for others to follow. Now that Yorkshire has led the way, it would indeed be a major contribution to knowledge if similar dictionaries could preserve for posterity the dialects and traditions of every county in England. We must hope that others will take up the challenge.

J D A Widdowson
Centre for English Cultural Tradition and Language
University of Sheffield

Introduction

Why a *Yorkshire* dictionary? Surely these are days when we should be thinking in terms of Europe, learning to develop an international outlook free from narrow parochialism . . . Well, it is precisely as a reaction to the pressure to be European and cosmopolitan that I have written this book. By all means let us co-operate with other countries — but not at the expense of losing our national and regional identity!

The twenty-first century is likely to be one of increasing uniformity, and therefore monotony. Everywhere we see the signs of creeping standardisation. We are in danger of setting up what John Betjeman once complained of in architecture — 'international nothingness'. So we must do our best, it seems to me, to conserve the surviving local differences — all those things which add colour and vitality to the drab, overall sameness of the modern electronic world. In contrast to bland and boring internationalism, let us encourage the best kind of regionalism, with its distinctive speech, tradition and folklore. In the UK this means taking a pride in being Scots, Welsh, Irish, Manx, Cornish or whatever — and, in this case, in being Yorkshire.

It is true that Yorkshire folk have the reputation of being jingoistic and opinionated, a point neatly made in the jibe: 'You can always tell a Yorkshireman — but not much!'. Our excuse, I suppose, is that we inhabit by far the biggest county, generously endowed with scenery and heritage. But in providing Yorkshire with a dictionary all to itself, the first of its kind, I am not suggesting that 'the county of broad acres' is superior to other parts of the kingdom — only that it has something special that is worth preserving.

There is a sense of urgency about this contribution to conservation. Dialect and tradition in Yorkshire — as everywhere else — are under threat of extinction. As I have said in my previous book, *Basic Broad Yorkshire*, real dialect speakers are an endangered species and, all over the country, dialect, with its rich vocabulary and idiom, is being replaced by an attenuated 'regional speech', distinguished from Standard English mainly just by accent and intonation. As with words, so with traditions: regional and local trades, crafts, food, games, customs, sayings and all kinds of folklore are in many cases becoming something that only the oldest generation can remember.

How important it is, then, to pin down this elusive material while it is still comparatively recent, and in many instances vividly recalled, presenting it as systematically and comprehensively as possible in one volume. This has been my aim in compiling this *Dictionary* — to provide a reference book of Yorkshire heritage, not in the sense of scenery and historic buildings, but an alphabetical compendium of the life and lore of ordinary Yorkshire people.

To some extent this book is personal and autobiographical, even though it also has what I trust is scholarly objectivity. As might be gathered from the dedication, I owe so much to my West Riding childhood in Wibsey, Bradford, and many of the terms and phrases in the *Dictionary* are defined with the authority of family experience. For example, my grandfather was a **hurrier**, pushing coal wagons underground at the age of eight, later becoming a Bradford **woolsorter**, wearing the special apron known as a **brat**. My father started life at Salts Mill, then became one of the 'twelve apostles', making the famous Scott motorbikes. Teaching modern languages in what became North Yorkshire brought me into contact with a more rural vocabulary and lifestyle. Recent editing of the *Transactions* of the Yorkshire Dialect Society has meant familiarity with material from all over Yorkshire, and the meetings of the society have allowed me to listen to a wide range of fluent dialect speakers.

The bibliography gives some idea of the kind of works I have consulted, but the bedrock of this *Dictionary* is a lifelong enthusiasm for all things Yorkshire, and contact with a wonderful variety of Yorkshire folk. These have ranged from William Riley and 'Romany' in my youth, and more recently Wilfred Pickles, to all kinds of contemporary Yorkshire men and women with a lively interest in our cultural heritage.

As so many Yorkshire terms are not actual dialect, but linked with custom and tradition, it seemed fitting to include these as well. It soon became apparent that there was also an overlap with items of folklore and legend. The *Yorkshire Dictionary* therefore comprises:

1. Yorkshire dialect from all parts of the county

In certain cases, words or phrases are identified as WR (West Riding), NR (North Riding) or ER (East Riding), these being the standard identifications used by the Yorkshire Dialect Society. Where a word is associated with both North and East Ridings I have added NER. Note that these identifications only mean that the word seems to be particularly associated with the dialect area indicated, and that it may be used or understood elsewhere.

This leads to the point that a number of entries are not exclusive to Yorkshire, and may occur in other dialects (eg those of Northumberland, Cumbria or Scotland) or in Standard English. They appear simply because they are commonly used in Yorkshire, or used here in a special way.

Every effort has been made to include authentic Yorkshire dialect. 'Beware of imitations'! It is unfortunate that from time to time rather silly booklets are published purporting to give Yorkshire words and phrases, and yet they are full of mistakes and misunderstandings, one little 'dictionary' even giving words from Cockney rhyming slang as Yorkshire dialect! This kind of thing only brings discredit to Yorkshire, and the Yorkshire Dictionary is offered as a counterblast to those who treat dialect as something to be sniggered at. Our dialect can certainly be used most effectively for humour, but as a regional language it deserves to be taken seriously.

It must not be assumed that because a word or phrase appears in the *Dictionary* it is used, or even understood, in contemporary Yorkshire. I have included many obsolete items, mainly to cater for readers who may be puzzled by dialect appearing in historical material or literature, the latter including, for example, *Wuthering Heights* or the verse of John Hartley. No attempt has been made to show which words and phrases are still in use. In my experience the very moment I have decided that some dialect item has gone out of use, I am delighted to find somebody who uses it, or at least understands it.

Derivations have been added at the end of entries in most cases. Where they do not appear it is because they are either unknown or too obvious to need comment. Most of the etymology is supported by the authority of the books in the bibliography. In a number of cases, I have given my own suggestion of the derivation, sometimes after long deliberation. Derivations may look pedantic, but often they are of real interest, and explain why we have, for example, both **bairn** and **barn** for 'child'.

Like all dictionaries, this covers mainly lexical items, that is, vocabulary and associated phrases. Readers should consult the author's *Basic Broad Yorkshire* for details of grammar and idiom, and for samples of dialect prose and verse. It is, of course, essential to see and hear words in context, fully dressed, as it were, and not just in their almost naked isolation in a dictionary.

(NB Writers of fiction should be warned that they cannot simply lift out words and phrases from this *Dictionary* to put into the mouths of characters, for example. They would have to do careful local research to establish exactly in what period and in what locality the usage occurs.)

2. Traditional terms and phrases

These are not necessarily dialect, but are especially associated with Yorkshire. They come first from the principal categories of working life in the county: farming, fishing, woollen mills, coalmines and steel — not forgetting tourism, one of Yorkshire's oldest industries.

Then there are domestic items such as food, and all kinds of terms to do with housework, mainly from the harsh and thrifty days before the advent of labour-saving gadgetry. In addition, I have included forms of recreation once so familiar to Yorkshire people, from children's games such as **taws** to the weightier contests of **knur and spell** and **merrils**.

From the extensive vocabulary of technical terms used in farming, mills, mines, amongst coastal fishermen and in various trades and crafts, I have used the commoner items, mostly those likely to be encountered by the general public. For technical terms which do not appear here the reader should consult specialised glossaries and word lists, including those in the *Transactions* of the Yorkshire Dialect Society.

3. Folklore terms and names

These are either peculiar to Yorkshire or have a strong association with it. Sword-dancing, for example, is found elsewhere, but is part of our own heritage. Similarly, Robin Hood may be chiefly associated with Nottingham and Sherwood Forest, but so many places in Yorkshire are named after him that he is rightfully included.

Note that the names are mostly not historical figures (eg famous Yorkshiremen such as William Wilberforce), but those associated with folklore (eg Mother Shipton) and larger-than-life characters (eg Guy Fawkes) linked to a custom or legend.

Nor is it within the province of the *Dictionary* to include churches, abbeys, castles and topographical features — unless there is a special link with a tradition or dialect saying.

Historical Background

The *Dictionary* should at least dispel the notion that Yorkshire dialect is something merely quaint and comical, even a debased and slovenly kind of speech belonging to the ignorant. In this book the derivations alone will show that, on the contrary, Yorkshire dialect is an ancient and honorable form of speech, often far closer to the language of our ancestors than modern English. Again and again, in tracing the origin of a dialect word I have been struck by its similarity to the original Anglo-Saxon or Old Norse, the language of the Viking sagas. Even the French spoken by the Normans had its influence, and survives in dialect words that have no counterpart in Standard English.

Here is a simple outline of our early history which will serve to give the background to the words and many of the traditions which appear in the *Dictionary*. At the risk of oversimplification, I will first set out what I think of as the five linguistic invasions:

1. The Celts. From about 500 BC, Yorkshire was settled by the Brigantes, a fiercely independent tribe of the Ancient Britons. The Celtic language they spoke survives in certain topographical names (eg Penyghent, Chevin, Calder, Nidd), and possibly in the structure of sheep-counting numerals, but in only a few dialect words (eg **brock**, **coble**).

2. The Romans. (From 54 BC.) If the Romans had stayed long enough, the Celts would have ended up speaking their version of Latin (which is what happened in France), but in AD 410 they withdrew from Britain, leaving behind roads, forts, villas and artefacts — but no Latin words. (These came in much later, via the Normans.)

3. The Angles. (From the fifth century AD.) Once the Romans had withdrawn, the country was wide open to invasion and settlement by peoples speaking a Germanic language — the Angles in northern and central England, the Saxons in the south and west, with the Jutes in Kent.

The Angles divided their territory into two main kingdoms, in addition to East Anglia. These were Northumbria, literally 'north of the Humber', stretching from that river to Scotland, and Mercia, roughly what we now call South Yorkshire and the Midlands. At first all Yorkshire spoke the Northumbrian dialect, which is still the basis of NR and ER speech. Then the dialect of Mercia gradually spread into the WR, with the result that roughly north of Wharfedale we have NR and ER dialect, with 'about', for example, pronounced **aboot**, but to the south, in WR dialect, pronounced **abaht**. There are many other differences between NER and WR, including vocabulary. A friend whose name appears in the acknowledgements illustrated this by telling me that as a child when she went to one grandma in the WR she was given **spice**; when she went to the other grandma in the ER she was given **goodies** — both meaning 'sweets'. But the two areas have a great deal in common, and both retain more words from the Angles than we find in Standard English.

Though the speech of the Angles differed from that of the Saxons, the two were close enough for us to call their language Anglo-Saxon. As scholars now prefer to term this Old English, derivations from this have been shown in the *Dictionary* as OE. Sometimes the dialect word simply retains the sound of the Anglian speech (eg **blinnd** and **finnd** are pronounced with a short 'i' as in modern German). Sometimes what looks like a corruption actually preserves the older form (eg **ax** for 'to ask' was originally *acsian*). This is also

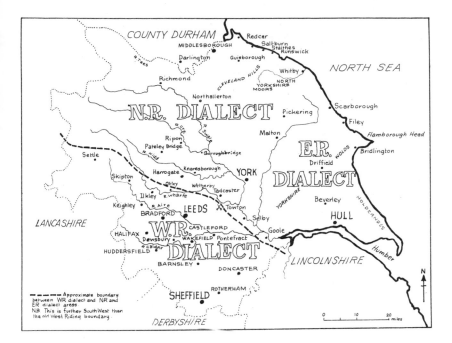

true of what seems like an ignorant misuse (eg **starved** for 'feeling cold' comes from *steorfan*, 'to suffer intensely' — not necessarily from hunger).

4. The Vikings. (From the ninth century.) These invaders came by two main routes. First, the Danish Vikings sailed up the Humber and captured York in AD 867, later dividing Yorkshire into the three Ridings. Then the Norwegian Vikings or Norsemen came into Yorkshire from the west, first settling in Swaledale, where place-names such as Keld, Thwaite, Muker and Gunnerside testify to a Norse origin.

The Scandinavian settlers not only added to our place-names and topographical terms (beck, fell etc), but gave many words still used in Yorkshire dialect, such as **laik** (to play), **laithe** (barn), **stee** (ladder) and **teem** (pour), and at the same time contributed to Yorkshire traditions.

5. The Normans. (From 1066.) The Normans were originally Norsemen who had settled in Normandy and came here speaking

French. At first this was used alongside English, that is, the language of the Angles modified by that of the Vikings. This meant there were often two words for the same thing. For example, whereas the English peasant spoke of a 'sheep', the Norman overlord would use the term *mouton*, later 'mutton'. Certain words from Norman French (shown in the *Dictionary* as Old French, OF) have survived in Yorkshire dialect, but not in English. For example, **arran** for 'spider' (cf modern French *araignée*). Other words retain the original Norman meaning, lost in Standard English. For example **buffit** is from OF *buffet*, not a sideboard, but a low stool.

By the time of Chaucer (d 1400), Old English and Norman French had coalesced to form Middle English. From the period of Caxton's printing press (1476) the dialect of educated Londoners gradually spread as the standard form of English, and the regional English spoken mainly by uneducated working folk was regarded as inferior dialect. By the eighteenth century it would have seemed only a matter of time before an increase in literacy and in the general education imposed a more-or-less uniform English on the whole population.

Dialect, however, was unexpectedly resilient, and had its champions. Most influential of these was Robert Burns (1759-96) who wrote inspired poems in the language of the people. There had already been publications of Yorkshire verse, such as the *Lyke Wake Dirge* and *A Yorkshire Dialogue*, and songs such as *The Yorkshire Horse Dealers* and *The Wensleydale Lad*. In 1815 a Knaresborough farmer, David Lewis, published poems in NR dialect, one on a frog he had accidentally killed with his scythe, obviously influenced by the poem Burns wrote on the mouse he disturbed.

In 1830, in Sheffield, the first of many almanacks appeared, most of them in WR dialect. These included prose as well as verse, and — together with public readings — did much to keep Yorkshire dialect alive during the rest of the nineteenth century, a period when education was increasingly establishing Standard English. As an example of the vigour and richness of Yorkshire dialect amongst working folk in the mid-nineteenth century, we have only to read the Haworth dialect of the old servant Joseph, so faithfully recorded by Emily Brontë in *Wuthering Heights* (1847).

Towards the end of the century the great academic friend of

Yorkshire dialect was Joseph Wright, Professor of Comparative Philology at Oxford. He had started life as an illiterate donkey-boy working in the quarries near Windhill, Shipley. When, through self-education and night-school, he became a linguist, and eventually a university don, he used his position to promote the study of dialect. He published a *Grammar of the Dialect of Windhill* and organised teams of researchers to compile the monumental six-volume *English Dialect Dictionary*, published in 1905 at his own expense, because no publisher was interested. This anticipated the *Survey of English Dialects,* to be based at Leeds University some fifty years later.

The committee which helped Professor Wright to collect written dialect material in Yorkshire formed the nucleus of the Yorkshire Dialect Society, founded in Bradford in 1897. Through its meetings and two journals the YDS, as it is usually known, seeks to strike the balance between serious academic interest in dialect and humorous verse and prose, both in written and spoken form. A similar objective is held by the more recent East Riding Dialect Society.

In the first half of the twentieth century, Yorkshire dialect continued to appear in Yorkshire novels by such writers as J S Fletcher, Edward Booth, William Riley, Phyllis Bentley and J B Priestley. Comic dialect tales regularly appeared in certain Yorkshire newspapers, such as the *Bradford Telegraph & Argus* 'Buxom Betty' series, and there were many amateur productions of plays and public readings and recitations in dialect.

In the second half of the century, though the *Dalesman*, for example, has continued to publish jokes and verse in Yorkshire dialect, and local radio has given dialect speakers a reasonable amount of time, there can be no doubt that real 'brooad Yorksher' is being used less and less by the general public.

The reasons for the decline of both dialect and tradition are all too obvious. In addition to the educational pressures already mentioned (and I see no reason why children should not be encouraged to speak dialect as well as Standard English), there is the comparatively recent factor of social mobility, with people moving around and settling in other parts of the country, so that Yorkshire, like all other parts, resounds to the speech of **off-comed-uns**. Allied to this are factors such as the desire to impress, either when seeking promotion or at some social gathering. Prejudice against dialect — so often confused with slang or slovenly speech — seeps in everywhere. When I recently asked a North Yorkshire tourist information officer how many in her rural area spoke dialect, she replied: 'Very few . . . They don't seem to feel it's right to use it, somehow.'

The non-stop outpourings of radio and television also have an adverse effect on both dialect and Standard English. Where Yorkshire dialect is included — in television dramas and soap operas — it tends to lack all authenticity and local character, and shows no understanding of the fact that speakers in an NR area, for example, would not be speaking with a WR accent. There are exceptions, however, and when a sensitive director works with an actor who speaks fluent Yorkshire it can come as a breath of moorland air.

The remarkable fact is that, in spite of all the pressures and prejudices, Yorkshire dialect is clearly going to live on into the twenty-first century. A minority of people will still speak it amongst themselves — with family and friends — even if it is only by using an occasional word or idiomatic phrase to express something for which there is no equivalent in ordinary English. And many more will understand it, and think with warm affection of the dialect used by the generation of their grandparents. Others will continue to listen to dialect readings and recitations, and read for themselves the now considerable collection of dialect writing, which includes some excellent poetry from each of the three main dialect regions of Yorkshire.

This *Dictionary* is offered as an encouragement to all such people. So many of the items in my collection of heritage material have gone for ever, because modernisation has made the objects or processes obsolete, along with the words describing them. In this respect I have felt like a curator assembling items to display in a kind of linguistic and cultural museum. Even so, these items can still be cherished, and where a word, phrase or tradition is still remembered with affection, it can always be revived.

Let us therefore make the effort to act while there is still time, passing on to the next generation the best and most characteristic things of Yorkshire. It may be something very simple, such as a dialect saying, or the singing of **Ilkla Mooar** (both with a good Yorkshire accent!), or the custom of eating *spice cake* with Wensleydale cheese, or supporting traditions like **Plough Sunday** or *pace egging*, and so on . . . Such things are never killed off. They simply die by default.

The *Yorkshire Dictionary*, I feel, has come in the nick of time, for things are changing with a bewildering rapidity. As I complete it I am aware that my grandchildren know far more about the hyped-up dinosaurs of 65 million years ago than they do about their Yorkshire forebears of the early twentieth century. Because that generation, too, is becoming extinct and fossilised, I have had to work fast. Research has been complex and frustrating, sometimes with a whole day spent in libraries and folk museums just to track down one or two terms, or an item to be illustrated. In other cases, a substantial amount of original research (eg on the Royal Maundy) has had to be compressed into a paragraph.

But it has been a labour of love. I am proud to be a Yorkshireman — and I trust that those who consult or browse through these pages will understand why.

Arnold Kellett
Knaresborough
1994

Pronunciation and Spelling

The only way to find out how dialect is pronounced is to listen to good dialect speakers or the various recordings available from the Yorkshire Dialect Society. The next best thing is to read dialect in the transcript used in linguistics, the IPA (International Phonetic Alphabet), in the YDS *Transactions*, for example. To simplify matters the IPA has not been used in this *Dictionary*, and only in a small number of cases has it been necessary to explain the pronunciation of a dialect word.

As a guide to the pronunciation of Yorkshire dialect in general the following points should be noted:

Vowels

These are mostly simple and 'broad', that is, not rounded into diphthongs, as in Standard English.

a is usually short, as in **brass** (not 'brahse' or 'bress'), **fatther, Ah**. (I)

ah is the usual way of writing the long 'a' sound, as in WR **abaht, claht, dahn, mahse, flahr** (flour, flower) etc.

ee often has an 'a' sound added — 'ee-a', as in **'eead, deead**, giving two separate syllables.

o when long, also has an added 'a' in older dialect, as in **booane**, *dooarstooane.* Nowadays this is more likely to be a simple unrounded 'o'.

aw often replaces 'o' in such words as **knaw.**

u when short is always pronounced as in Standard English 'put', never as in 'cut' 'shut' etc.

oo is always long, never short, as in Standard English 'book'. In earlier WR dialect this often has an 'i' added to give two seperate syllables in (eg) **booit, fooil, afternooin.**

ow in words like **owt, nowt** and **browt** is in most areas not pronounced like 'now', but more like 'aw-oo'. This sound is also used in S Yorks where a long 'o' would normally be used.

As a general rule a double consonant is used to show a short vowel. For example: **finnd** pronounced as in 'fit'; **oppen, ovver** or **ower** pronounced as in 'not'; **watter** pronounced as in 'cat'.

Consonants

These tend to be pronounced more emphatically, with subtle differences from Standard English. A Yorkshire person, for example, tends to use the voiced form of 's' in a phrase like *'e knew us*, when the last word is pronounced as 'uz' not 'uss'. In parts of the WR the 'r' is slightly rolled. In parts of the NER it is more like a West Country 'r', and pronounced in words like 'farmer'. Consonants almost universally dropped in Yorkshire dialect are 'h' and the final 'g', both shown in the *Dictionary* as an apostrophe (eg *'attock, carlin'*).

Glottal stops

Difficult for non-dialect speakers to imitate, these are mostly represented by *t'* (the) which is not actually sounded, but replaced by a brisk opening and shutting of the glottis at the top of the windpipe. So a phrase like **on t' bed** is pronounced neither as 'ont bed' nor as 'on bed'. Before a vowel, however, the 't' is usually sounded (eg **on t' end**).

Differences between WR and NER

These differences are reflected in many of the words and phrases in the *Dictionary*, and mainly concern vowels. Below are examples of many words which follow the same pattern:

Standard English	West Riding	North and East Riding
about	*abaht*	*aboot*
school	*schooil*	*skeeal*
don't	*dooant*	*deeant*
speak	*speyk*	*speeak*
coat	*coit*	*cooat*

In a few cases (eg *abaht, aboot*) both forms have been given in the *Dictionary*, but in most cases this kind of duplication has been avoided.

There are other differences between WR and NER, and variations within each dialect area. For example, in the Holme Valley district the usual WR vowel 'ah' is more like 'air', so *abaht* might be written *abairt*. Only the most puzzling cases have been given here. For example, *meyas* is the Holme Valley way of saying WR *mahse* (mouse). This part of the WR also tends to use a short 'a' in words like 'want', 'what' or 'wasp', where we would normally expect an 'o' sound. The WR also has an 'ee-ew' sound in words like 'music' which could be written *mewsic* or *meeusic*.

The final 'ed' is pronounced 'id' in most parts (eg 'started'), but in the southern WR (starting south of Halifax Road, Bradford) this sounds like 'e(r)d'. 'Boxes', for example, sounds like 'boxers'.

Some NER speakers soften 'd' and 't' before an 'r', so we have, for example, words sometimes written *dthroon* (drown), *sthranger* (stranger) etc.

This serves to illustrate the kind of variation found in Yorkshire dialect and explains why it is impossible to give definitive and universally-accepted spellings, as is the case in Standard English.

'Yorkshire', incidentally, is pronounced 'Yorksher', rhyming with 'teacher', *not* 'York-shire', rhyming with 'fire', or 'York-sheer', as in 'beer'.

Abbreviations

ER	East Riding
NR	North Riding
WR	West Riding
NER	North and East Riding
S Yorks	South Yorkshire
SE	Standard English
OE	Old English (ie Anglo-Saxon)
ON	Old Norse (ie the language of the Vikings)
OF	Old French (ie Norman French)
ME	Middle English (around AD 1400)
MHG	Middle High German
abbr	abbreviation
cf	compare with
esp	especially
lit	literally
pl	plural
prob	probably
pron	pronounced
qv	which see
var	variant

A

abaht about WR

aboon above; more than; up-stairs *aboon eighty year owd* (OE *on-bufan*)

aboot about NER (OE *on-butan*)

acker acre (OE *aecer*)

'ackled (see *hackled*)

addle to earn (OE from ON)

addled bad, rotten (esp of eggs); drunk (OE *adela* liquid filth)

addlins earnings, wages

adoot without; except, unless ER

afeeared afraid, frightened (OE *afoered*)

afooare before (OE *on-foran*)

agate going on; on the way, moving; occupied, busy with *gerr agate!*, get started! (ON *gata* way, street)

agee crooked, uneven, askew

ageean again; against, opposite (OE *on-gean*)

agen, agin (see above)

Ah (pron with short *a*) I; *Ah'm*, I am WR, *Ah's*, I am NER, *Ah s'll*, I shall WR

ah-whoa! bear right! (horse)

ahint behind (OE *aet-hindan*)

Ahr Mary's Bonnet title of a WR comic poem by John Hartley, so commonly learnt by heart that several variant versions of it are remembered. The original version appears in his *Yorkshire Lyrics* (1898).

'ahse (see *hahse*)

aht out WR

ahten out of WR

aiblins perhaps, possibly NER

ailment illness, disease (the standard term, esp WR)

Ainsty The Ainsty of York was an administrative area excluded from the three Ridings. When Richard II held his court in York in 1392 he raised York and thirty-five surrounding villages to the status of a county. It extended as far south as Tadcaster until 1837, when it became part of the West Riding. (See **Ridings**.)

'aigs (see **haigs**)

Aimbry, Aumbry Almondbury WR

Airedale Terrier type of dog bred by Thomas Foster of Bingley, Lower Airedale, from 1863 on-wards. At first called the Bingley Terrier, Foster suggested the name Airedale, which was first used at a National Dog Show in 1883. In 1900 he presented one of his early dogs, Bloss, as an exhibit for Cliffe Castle Museum, Keighley.

airt　direction, point of the compass, quarter

airtle　(see *ettle*)

Tetleys of Leeds dates from 1822, Theakstons of Masham (dating from 1827) named their Old Peculier ale after the **Peculier of Masham** (qv).

The Airedale Terrier — Bingley born and bred.

ale　formerly the standard term (OE *alu*) for an intoxicating drink based on malt. The term 'beer' has been in common use only since the sixteenth century, when it referred to ale made with hops. The oldest Yorkshire brewery is at Tadcaster, established in 1758 and run since 1847 by the Smith family, using the same well-water and original strain of yeast.

ale-posset　hot drink of ale and milk, sweetened and spiced

'ales　(see *hales*)

alicker　vinegar (ale, with OF *aigre* sour)

alley-strap　strap once wielded by overlooker to discipline workers in WR woollen mills as he walked the alleys between the looms.

All Souls Day　2nd November; formerly a time for soul-caking and the making of **Saumas loaves** (qv), in recent years the custom has survived only in the appearance of **guisers** (qv) at Stannington, near Sheffield.

'allack (see *hallack*)

'allidas holidays WR

allowance (see *lowance*)

alley-taw marble used in children's game, made of marble, pot or glass, but not metal (? from 'alabaster') (see also *blood-alley, dobby[1], taws*)

allus always

almanacks popular annual publications in Yorkshire dialect, mainly produced for the workpeople of the industrial West Riding. The first were the *Wheelswarf Chronicle* (1830) and the *Shevvild Chap's Annual* (1836), published by Abel Bywater. The *Barnsla Foakes' Annual an' Pogmoor Olmenack* by 'Tom Treddlehoyle' (Charles Rogers) appeared in 1843 and ran till the end of the century. Leeds issued *T' Frogland Olmenac an' Leeds Loiners Annual* (from 1852).The first of four published In Butley, *Dewsbre Back a' t' Mooin Olmenac*, appeared in 1861, then the *Leeds Tommy Toddles's Comic Almenack* (1862), and many more. The most successful was undoubtedly The **Clock Almanack** (qv) by John Hartley of Halifax.

alum one of Yorkshire's forgotten industries, established in the sixteenth century in the area between Scarborough and the Tees, where the red of alum shale can occasionally be seen. Alum mining, valued for its use in the preparation of parchment and as a mordant for dyes, was an important part of Yorkshire's economy until its decline in the 1870s.

amang among

amang-'ands with the help of each other

ammot am not *Ah ammot laikin'*, I'm not playing WR

an' all also; into the bargain *'e med a lot o' brass, an' all*

ananthers lest, in the event of, for fear of NER (*an* with OF *aventure*)

anent, anenst near, next to, side by side, opposite, in front of

anger-nail (see *nang-nail*)

'an'kercher handkerchief

anthers (see *ananthers*)

apiece each *two apiece*

'appen (see *happen*)

archery a strong tradition in Yorkshire, promoted by Roger Ascham (born at Kirby Wiske, near Thirsk) in his classic *Toxophilus, or The Schole of Shooting* (1545). The Society of Archers dates from the shoot for the 'Antient Silver Arrow' held at Scorton, near Catterick, in 1673. The Yorkshire Archers held their first meeting at Harrogate in 1793. (See *Scorton Arrow*.)

'ard on (see *hard on*)

'ardin (see *hardin*)

'ardlins (see *hardlins*)

ark chest; bin containing flour, kept in the kitchen, or feed for a horse (OE *aerc*)

Arkendale Arkengarthdale

arles money paid as an indication of good faith when striking a bargain (OF *arres*)

arran spider; spider's web (OF *araigne*)

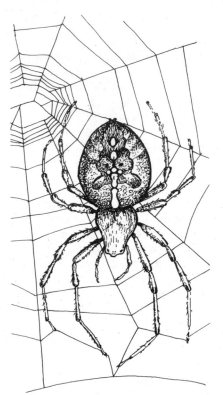

Arran or attercop.

arridge edge, ridge; projection on front of a horseshoe to prevent slipping (OF *areste*)

arrish field of stubble, following harvest (OE *erse*)

arrow-throwing competitive sport in the nineteeenth century amongst Yorkshire coalminers, who threw arrows between 240-300 yards, often before large crowds of spectators.

arse posterior; bottom or back (eg of a cart) (OE *aers*, ON *ars*)

arse-band harness round rear of horse when pulling a cart

arse-end bottom or tail-end of an object

arse-pocket back pocket

arsy-tarsy topsy-turvy

article person (used in a contemptuous sense), esp WR

arval bread kind of cake made to be eaten at funerals (see *funeral biscuits*) (ON *erfil*)

'arve! (see *harve*)

ash-nook (see *assenook*)

ask(er) newt; lizard (OE *athexe*)

askins (see *spurrins*)

'asky (see *hask*)

aslew not square or straight ER

ass to ask (OE *acsian*)

ass ash (OE *asce*)

assenook, assnook ashpan; space below grate; chimney corner

assle-tooth (see *axle-tooth*)

'as-ta? (see *hast-ta?*)

asteead instead (OE *stede* place)

aswint (see *aslew*)

at-after,-efter after, afterwards

'at that *all t' brass 'at wor on t' table*

'at hat

atta? are you? (var of *art thou?*)

attercop spider (OE *attorcoppe*, from *attor*, poison)

'attock (see *hattock*)

atwixt between (OE)

aud, auld old NER

aud-farrant old-fashioned

audit money money distributed by the Mayor of Richmond, resulting from a reduction in rent paid by the town since the fifteenth century, when a petition was made to Henry VI. First mentioned in 1576, the audit money now takes the form of a specially-minted token, 'the Richmond shilling'.

aum[1] elm-tree (OF *orme*)

aum[2] (see *awm*)

aumery cupboard, pantry (OF *almarie*)

Austwick carles simpletons associated with the village of Austwick, near Settle, of whom various tales are told, including one about them jumping into a pond to look for buried treasure because they thought a man drowning here had said *'t' best's at t' bottom!'*

'av(v)er (see *haver*)

Aw I (used by some writers of WR dialect, including Emily Brontë in *Wuthering Heights*, eg *Aw'm noan*, I'm not)

awd old NER

awd carlin sharp old woman (see *carlins*)

Awd Goggie female spirit who guarded orchards, esp after dark ER

Awd Man collective term for former generations of miners (used by Dales leadminers); sometimes also used for an exhausted vein of ore NR

Awd Nan witch reputed to have haunted Sexhow, Cleveland, who told a farmer where hidden treasure lay, but when he refused to share it, afflicted him until he died.

Awd Roy annual feast once held at Muker in Swaledale on the Wednesday before the 6th January, when it was the custom for local lads to beg for cakes, curd tarts etc.

Awd Scrat the Devil; person who never stops working NR

'awf a crahn, croon half a crown (2s 6d) WR, NER

awkerd awkward

awm oat-bread, made without yeast NR

awn (see *own*)

'awp'ny, 'ay-p'ny (see *hawpenny*)

'aw-porth, 'ay-porth (see *hawporth*)

awther either, each (OE *aeghwaether*)

ax to ask (OE *acsian*)

axins banns of marriage (see also *spurrins*)

axle-tooth molar, double tooth (ON *jaksel*)

ay! (pron as in day, sometimes written *eh!*) similar to 'oh!', used to express sympathetic agreement, surprise etc *Ay! What a shame!*, *Ay, dear!*

aye yes; *aye?* (said in a slow, questioning way), is that really so?

'azzled (see *hazzled*)

B

babbar dirt, esp faeces (said to a young child)

babby baby (probably closer to earlier forms such as *baban*)

babby-wark childishness

back'ards-rooad backwards

back back to move (a vehicle) in reverse (cf former custom of saying *'back! back!'* to a carthorse)

back-end autumn

back-endish towards the end of the year; the feeling that summer is over

backside bottom, posterior

back-word cancellation or postponement of visit, engagement etc *they've given back-word*

badger pedlar or corn trader, esp one using the **packhorse routes** (qv)

badly ill, sick *sh'wor feelin' badly*

baggin' snack eaten in the fields, esp during hay-making and harvesting (cf *drinkins*) (ref to carrying food in a bag)

baggy, bags term used when claiming, in children's games *bags ferrie!* (qv), I go first!

bahn going *Ah'm nooan bahn yonder*, I'm not going there WR

bahsen term of rebuke or abuse *thoo mucky bahsen* ER

baht without; except, unless **on** *Ikla Mooar baht 'at, Ah'm baht*, I haven't any (money) (OE *beutan*)

Bainbridge (see **hornblowing**)

bairn child (cf *barn*) (OE *bearn*)

bairt (see *baht*)

bait¹ to feed, offer food (ON *beit*, pasturage)

bait² packed lunch, usually carried in a *bait-tin* (see also *drinkins*)

bakst'n flat stone heated for baking, usually with fire underneath; circular iron plate with handle, used in baking over fire; moveable shelf in oven

balk headland in arable field where plough can turn; strip separating sections of land

balmy (see *barmy*, the correct spelling, because of its derivation from *barm*)

bam trick, practical joke NER

ban to curse, swear (ON *banna*)

band string, rope *man made o' band*, incompetent (ON *band*)

band-end makeshift, poor quality (job etc); worn out

band in t' nick (to keep) to keep a friendship etc ticking over (metaphor from mills where *t' band* had to be kept in the pulleys)

banter to tread noisily, heavily; to argue NER

bar[1] gateway in the walls of a city (York) (see **Micklegate Bar**)

bar[2] except *it's all ovver bar t' shahtin'* (OF *barrer*)

bare-gollie naked child (see *gollie*)

barf hill, esp when long and fairly low (OE *beorh*, ON *bjarg*)

barfan, barfin collar of a working horse (OE *beorgan*, to protect)

Bakst'n — an iron version.

barguest evil spirit in the form of a dog, pig or other animal, displaying teeth, claws and large flaming eyes, shrieking at dead of night. Sometimes it is said to be a portent of death, like a *guytresh* (qv). (See **Ivelet Bridge, Trollers Gill**.) (origin obscure, but cf

German *Berggeist* and Norwegian *berg* (mountain) and *geist* (spirit))

barkum (see *barfan*)

barley (see *barlow*)

barley-bairn child born too soon for conception to have taken place in marriage (perhaps derived from the fact that it could well have occurred during the harvest festivities)

barlow exempt, safe (truce word in children's games) (? OF *parler*)

barm yeast (OE *beorma*)

barm-cake bap, bread bun (associated with Lancashire, but also known in Yorkshire)

barm-pot pot, often sealed, in which yeast was stored; idiotic, silly person

barmskin oilskin apron worn by sea fishermen NER

barmy crazy (lit like *barm* or yeast, ie light and frothy)

barn child (ON *barn*) (cf *bairn*, derived from OE)

Barnaby Fair held at Boroughbridge on the Tuesday nearest the 22nd June, originally the Feast of St Barnabas (see below). Founded by a charter of Charles II in 1662, this was once a famous fair for cattle, sheep and hardware, but mainly horses, as indicated by the street named Horsefair (cf **Yarm Fair**). It is still well supported by gypsies and travellers.

Barnaby Neet night of the Feast of St Barnabas, 11th June. Before the calendar changes of 1752 this was the longest day, hence the saying: *Barnaby bright, Barnaby Bright, Longest day an' shortest night*. (See **Barnaby Fair**.)

Barguest, guytresh, padfoot . . . the terrifying spectral creature of Yorkshire folklore.

Barnaby Tarts lemon-curd tarts traditionally made for **Barnaby Fair** (qv) at Boroughbridge

Barnsla Feeast held the third week in August, a traditional holiday in the Barnsley area

Barnsley Chop very large chop, usually taken from a saddle of lamb. It is said to have first been served at the Kings Head (now the Royal Hotel), Barnsley, in 1849, and was on the menu when the Prince of Wales visited the town in 1933.

barrie-coat baby's or child's undergarment, esp of flannel; small coat (? F *barré*, striped)

barring-out custom formerly observed in parts of Yorkshire of schoolchildren locking the door and keeping the master outside until he granted them a holiday on **Shrove Tuesday** (qv), or on the Fifth of November, when *parkins* (qv) were then eaten by way of celebration.

Barrow Witch semi-legendary Driffield woman, real name Susannah Goor (1728-1826), with a reputation for fortune-telling and frightening children. Folklore claims she had an association with the Devil and the last seen of her was when she *'flew ower Driffield Church on a blazin' besom'*.

Bartle Saint Bartholomew; the name of fairs formerly held on this saint's day, 24th August (see **Owd Bartle**)

bass basket; straw matting, door-mat; workman's wallet or bag (eg joiner, plumber); pliable bag (eg for carrying fish)

bassock to batter, clatter, thrash soundly

bat straw left after sheaves have been threshed WR

bate to lessen, diminish (eg weather) *t' rain's batin'* (shortened form of 'abate')

bauk, baulk beam used in house-building or across a fireplace (see *rannel-bauk*); beam used for attaching horses to plough etc; (plural) wooden floor above cowshed

bauk to jib (of horse)

baumer (see *knur and spell*)

bawl to shout; to weep WR (cf *beeal* NER)

beam-mate term used by a weaver for the person working at the other side of the loom (cf *elbow-mate*) WR

Beamsley Beacon (see **Easter**)

beating the bounds customary walk or ride round parish boundaries, surviving especially' at Richmond, where it has been observed since Elizabethan times. Led by the mayor, with his Bellman and Cryer, it takes place every seven years and covers fourteen miles, the purpose being to check and confirm the boundaries. At one point the mayor is carried into the River Swale by the Water Wader to inspect a boundary stone. Formerly there was an annual circuit of all parish boundaries, sometimes involving little ceremonies such as bumping children on the boundary stones. (See **Rammalation Day**.)

beb a sip or drink (see *bub* for derivation)

beck stream (ON *bekkr*)

beck-ball traditional game forming part of the Maltby Festival, played at Maltby Crags, near Rotherham, in which four teams compete for three balls in a kind of free-for-all rugby across the beck.

Bedale This NR village has the traditional boast: *Bedale bonnets an' Bedale faces, Finnd nowt ti beat 'em in onny places*

bedoot without; unless NER

beeak to bake NER

beeal to shout; to weep NER (cf *bawl* WR)

beeant am not, isn't, are not ER

beeas, beeast cattle (this is the plural form, but *beeast* can be used in the singular) (OF *beste*)

beeastlins the first milk given by a cow after she has calved

beeasty puddin' dish made with rich milk of *beeastlins* (qv)

beel handle of cup or mug WR

beeld, beald (see *bield*)

beer (see *ale*)

bee's wine home-made alcoholic drink brewed by adding daily spoonfuls of sugar and ginger to a jar of water containing the yeast *Saccharomyces pyroformis*, which forms clusters moved about by the fermentation in a way suggestive of bees.

beet to repair, esp nets (OE *betan*)

Beggar's Bridge (see Lover's Bridge)

beggar's litany name given to the old prayer *'From Hell, Hull and Halifax, good Lord deliver us!'*. This prayer is said to refer to press-gangs and efficient law enforcement in Hull, but more particularly to the dangers of 'the furious river'. Halifax was dreaded because of the severe laws condemning cloth-thieves to an immediate beheading by its unique guillotine-style gibbet: *'They have a jyn that wondrous quick and well, Sends thieves all headless unto heav'n or hell'*. There is no evidence to support the theory that 'Hell' was originally Elland.

behint, behunt behind (OE *behindan*)

belder to bellow, roar (OE *bellan*)

belike probably NER

belk to belch (OE *bealcian*)

bellaces tongues of lace-up boots

bell-'oss horse wearing a bell, originally the one leading a line of pack-horses or horses carring ore from the leadmines; also used figuratively to mean a person who wants to have pre-eminence *as prood as a bell-'oss* NR

belled 'osses pair of horses harnessed side by side; children's game

Bellerby Feast old Whitsuntide feast at Bellerby near Leyburn, revived in recent years, which once had its own Sword Dance play (see **Besom Bessy**)

bellikin puppy NR

bellman The saying *'as well-knawn as t' bellman'* refers to the familiar appearance of the official who was appointed to make public announcements, alternatively known as the town crier. Ripon still maintains this ancient office, and the bellman rings in the market there every Thursday at 11am.

bellusses bellows; lungs (ie a double plural) (OE *blaest-belig*)

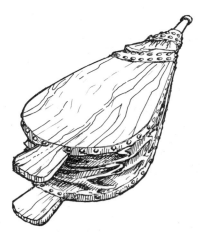

Bellusses — once found in every Yorkshire hearth.

bellringing In addition to the ancient art of ringing the changes, there are certain **bellringing** traditions associated with death. In some parts of Yorkshire it was the custom to give thirty strokes of the **passing bell** to indicate a man's death, twenty for a woman and ten for a child. In other parts it was *'three for a bairn, six for a woman, nine for a man'*, with an extra stroke for each year they lived. (See **Devil's Knell**.)

belly stomach; abdomen (OE *belig*)

belly-bun part of a harness round a horse's girth WR

belly-button-'oil navel WR

belly-wark stomach-ache (see *wark*)

belong to own; to come from *'e belongs t' mill, sh' belongs Skipton*

belsh (see *bolsh*)

belt to hit hard (from beating with a belt)

beltenger severe blow

benjy man's straw hat, with a low, flat-topped crown and broad brim (? from Benjamin)

benk bench, seat; stone working-slab (OE *benc*)

bensel, bensil to beat, thrash (ON *benzla*)

berries gooseberries (see **Egton Bridge**)

berril warble-fly, gad-fly

berryin' funeral (see *buryin'-brass, bid*)

besom (pron 'beezom') broom, esp of heather or twigs tied round stick (OE *besema*)

Besom Bessy female character, played by a man, in the **sword dance** (qv) plays, such as the one which is performed at Bellerby near Leyburn. Also known as *Besom Bet* or *Betty*, she was associated with **Plough Stots** (qv) along with *Blether Dick* (qv)

bethink to remember (used reflexively) *Ah've just bethowt missen*

betwaddled confused, usually because of drink

beuk, bewk book NER

Bevla Beverley

bezzle to squander, eat or drink greedily (OF *beziller*)

bid to invite to a funeral (see below) (OE *biddan*, to ask)

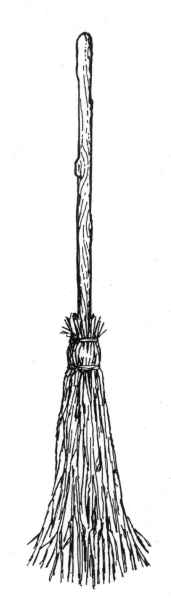

Besom, the traditional Yorkshire broom.

bidder person appointed to do the *bidding* for funerals (see below)

bidding invitation to attend a funeral, given either by the family or by specially-appointed bidders who would go round the village to inform those *bidden* or *bodden*. (See **funeral biscuits**.)

biddy louse

bide to stand, endure, put up with *Ah can't bide t' cowd, it 'll 'ave ter bi bidden* (eg pain); to stay (OE *bidan*)

bield shelter for sheep or cattle (OE *beldan*, to protect)

biggerstang scaffolding pole NER

biggin building (mainly in place-names, as Newbiggin)

billet coarse fish, associated esp with Flamborough, where the *billet-fishing* season extends from August to October.

billets game in which a *billet*, a small oblong piece of wood, is balanced on the end of a *billet-stick*, then thrown into the air and hit as far as possible. (cf *piggy* (qv))

Bill o' th' Hoylus End pen-name of William Wright (1836-97), a warp-dresser who lived at Hoylus End between Keighley and Haworth, and became well-known as a dialect poet and almanack (qv) publisher.

billy-biter bluetit ER

binds renewable timber fastened to ships to prevent damage to the hull

bink (see *benk*)

birk birch (OE *beorc*)

birl to pour out, esp drink WR

Bishop Blaise once well-known in Yorkshire as the patron saint of wool-combers. He was a fourth-century Armenian bishop, St Blasius, said to have been tortured to death by means of iron combs, hence the connection. Processions in honour of Bishop Blaise have been held on his feast day (3rd February) in places associated with wool, from Masham to Bradford, where there is a full-size sculpture of the saint at the entrance to the Bradford Wool Exchange. Inns have also been named after him, eg at Richmond.

bishopped confirmed (because a bishop officiated at confirmations) NR

bisslins (see *beastlins*)

bitin'-on a workman's mid-morning snack WR (see *drinkins*, *lowance*)

bitings grazing land

bitterstang (see *biggerstang*)

black-bright really dirty WR

black-clock black beetle (see *clock*)

black pudding kind of large sausage made from pig's blood, suet, meal etc. By no means confined to Yorkshire, but a traditional food here. In Cleveland, for example, it was the custom to eat **black pudding** on the first Thursday in Lent, hence the name **Bloody Thursday**.

Blades nickname of Sheffield United football club (from local cutlers, famous for steel blades)

blaeberry bilberry (ON *bla*, blue)

blag (see *bleg*)

blain stye, sore (on eye) (OE *blegen*)

blake sallow, yellow *as blake as beeswax* (ON *bleikr*)

blamed (see *blessed*)

blashment weak, sour (home-brewed) beer

blashy wet (weather), squally, with sudden heavy showers; sloppy and muddy after a thaw (var of 'splash')

blast bloodshot condition of the eye, such as is caused by grit WR

blate bashful

bleb blister, spot, weeping sore or anything which oozes (var of 'blob')

bleck thick and dirty grease (on bearings, axles, etc) (ON *blek*)

bleg[1] bream (Yorkshire coast fisherman's term) NER

bleg[2] blackberry (OE blaec)

bleg[3] to gather blackberries *we're bahn bleggin'* WR

blessed (pron as two separate syllables) damned (mild curse)

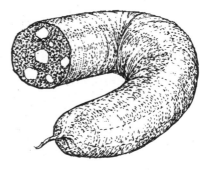

Black pudding.

Blessing the Boats annual service in Whitby Harbour each summer, first held in 1948

blether[1] bladder, usually of pig. Because used to store lard, this gave rise to the phrase *'as bald as a blether o' lard'*. When blown up and tied, blethers were commonly used as footballs.

blether[2] (see *bluther*)

Blether Dick character associated with **Besom Betty** and **Plough Stots** (qv) who wears strips of multi-coloured rags and carries a *blether* (bladder) fastened to the end of a stick, which he uses to keep the crowd in order.

blether-'eead fool (lit 'bladder' (ie empty)-head)

blether on to talk at length, talk nonsense

blether-skite gossip

blether-yed (see above)

blew blue (ME *blew*, OF *bleu*)

blewit a kind of edible mushroom (from bluish tinge)

Blind Jack nickname of John Metcalf, born in Knaresborough in 1717, blinded when six by smallpox. Although a legendary figure, most of what has been attributed to him is factual. Metcalf was a musician, sportsman, guide (at night and in fog), and undertook various enterprises, including pioneer work in road-building; the first of his 180 miles of turnpike was on the Harrogate to Boroughbridge road in 1765. He died at Spofforth in 1810.

blinnd (pron with short 'i') blind (OE)

blinnders blinkers, bridle to prevent horse from seeing sideways

blinndin rubble for foundation of a road ER

blish blister NR (OE *blyscan*, to redden)

blonk to sulk, scowl

blood-alley kind of *alley-taw* (qv) streaked with red (see *taws*)

Bloody Thursday (see black pudding)

blowed overwhelmed, staggered, damned *well, Ah'll bi blowed!* WR

blue-bob skimmed milk

Blue Pig name of an inn at Fagley, Bradford, said to be derived from an occasion when pigs were coloured blue because a workman had added 'dolly-blue' to the

John Metcalf, better known as 'Blind Jack', in 1795.

14

mixture when whitewashing the pigsty.

Blue Stots var of *Ploo Stots* (see Plough Stots). *Blue Stots* was the term used, for example, in Skelton-on-Ure, where the old mumming play was revived in the 1940s.

blunk (see *blonk*)

bluther to weep noisily

blutherment soft, slimy substance (eg mud) NER

boak (see *bauk*)

boar's head (see Bradford legend, Ripley)

bob bunch of flowers or fruit, eg cherries (see also *wessle-bob*)

bob a shilling (twelve old pence)

bobbin Bobbins were so familiar in textile mills that they gave rise to several expressions, including one perhaps referring to their neat, compact appearance when fully wound with yarn: *'as reight as a bobbin'*. On the other hand, if something is not working or running properly, it can be said (eg of late or irregular buses) *the' run on bobbins*. (Fr *bobine*)

bobbin-ligger textile worker replacing empty *bobbins* on a spinning-machine (see *ligg*)

bobby-dazzler (pron with emphasis on second word) something excellent, a person who is very smart etc

bobby-'oil police station

bocken to vomit, retch (ME *bolknen*)

bod-tentin' keeping watch and scaring off birds from fields of crops

bodden bidden

bog-eyed squinting; eyes heavy

with tiredness (said of someone staying up late) WR

bogey(-man) devil or evil spirit; nose-dirt (see also *bogie*)

boggart ghost, spectral spirit, esp haunting a particular place (? Celtic *bwg*, ghost)

boggle an evil spirit (var of *boggart*)

boggle-hole cave said to be inhabited by a *boggle* (qv) (eg Boggle Hole, Robin Hood's Bay)

bogie home-made go-cart, used by children, consisting mainly of a board with two pairs of wheels (eg from an old pram), the front pair being moved by a rope attached for steering. (See also *bogey*.) (var of *buggy*)

boke (see *bocken*)

bollie large steel marble S Yorks (cf *dobbie*; see *taws*)

Bolling Hall Ghost nameless female figure who is said to have appeared to the Earl of Newcastle at Bolling Hall on the eve of the second Royalist attack on Bradford in 1643. The citizens, who had protected their parish church with wool-sacks, were terrified that the earl, out of vengeance for the loss of his son, would order a massacre. The female ghost approached the sleeping officer, tugged at his bedclothes and wailed three times: 'Pity poor Bradford!'. Though Bradford was captured and looted, there was no undue bloodshed.

Bolliton Bridlington

bolsh, bulsh to bruise, knock a dent in; to kill by overfeeding

bon! damn it! dash it! etc ER (? from 'burn', ie in hell)

bonn to burn, esp ER

bonnet (see **Staithes**)

bonny attractive, esp of child or young woman; healthy-looking (said of someone recovering from an illness); plump, a little overweight (esp S Yorks) (OF fem *bonne*)

Bonny Napoleon Bonaparte (see *marrer ter Bonny*)

booan-idle extremely lazy

bool curved handle (eg of bucket)

bool, booler hoop, usually of wood, rolled along by children using a stick ER (see *hoop*)

boonder-stoup stone or post making boundary NER

boose division in cowshed, making a stall for a cow (?ON *bas*)

boose-stake post to which cow is chained (see *rudstake*)

Boroughbridge (see **Barnaby Fair, Devil's Arrows**)

bosh container round the belly of a blast furnace; circular tub of water used by cutlers for tempering blades

boskin partition between the *booses* (qv)

botch to beat up (eg eggs) NR

botchet mead; kind of ale made from honey

bottery elderberry bush. In NR folklore, elderberry brings bad luck because it is supposed to have been the tree from which Judas hanged himself. It should never be used to make a cradle, nor must it be burned indoors, or the Devil will sit on the chimney pot.

bottom to clean, tidy something thoroughly, esp a room *yon sittin'-room's nivver been bottomed* WR

bowdykite mischievous, unruly girl NER

bowel hole hole high up in wall of barn or stable through which hay is forked

bowl (pron as in owl) child's **hoop** (qv) (WR)

Bowling Tide Traditionally held on the 12th August, this was one of the most popular fairs in Bradford, and Bowling Tide Week became the official holiday week for Bradford millworkers.

bowster end part of pen-knife carrying the pin on which the blades turn

bowt bought

bowt bread bread brought from a bakery or shop, always regarded as inferior in the days when home baking was standard

Boxing Day So called from the custom of collecting alms and gratuities in a box, the 26th December is the Feast of St Stephen, and traditionally associated with sporting events. The Sheffield area has two groups of longsword dancers who perform on Boxing Day — one based on Grenoside, the other based on Handsworth, the latter dancers dressed in military tunics, originally used in the Light Dragoons of 1825. (see **sword-dancing**). The informal Flamborough Longsword Dance is also held on Boxing Day. Amongst recent traditions is the Knaresborough Tug of War across the River Nidd, held every Boxing Day since 1968.

brade to spread (gossip etc) NER

Bradford-by-the-Sea nickname

given to Morecambe, Lancashire, because of its popularity with holiday-makers from the WR, mainly Bradford.

Bradford legend In medieval times the inhabitants of the then small settlement of Bradford were said to be terrorised by a wild boar living in Cliffe Wood. A reward was offered for proof of its death. One huntsman tracked it down, killed it and cut out its tongue.

The boar on the Bradford coat-of-arms — without a tongue!

Another found the boar and cut off its head, which he brought into Bradford, claiming he had killed the animal — only to be discredited when the first man appeared with the missing tongue. The legend is enshrined in the Bradford coat-of-arms which includes a boar's head — minus tongue.

Bradford Whit Walk celebrated competitive walk on Bank Holiday Monday, following a circular route of thirty-one miles via Burley, Ilkley, Askwith and Otley Chevin, ending in Peel Park, Bradford. The winner receives the Hammond Cup, named after one of the Bradford businessmen who founded the walk in 1903.

braffin (see *barfin*)

braid¹ to make or mend nets or crabpots NER

braid² to be like, resemble, take after *sh' braids of 'er mother* (OE *bredgan*)

braidy foolish

brak broke, broken

Bramblewick (see **Robin Hood's Bay**)

brander, brandree (see below)

brandrith moveable iron frame to hold pans etc over a fire; gridiron (ON *brandr*)

A brandrith or brandree.

brandy-snap brittle, wafer-like biscuit, flavoured with ginger and brandy, traditionally sold at fairs, esp Hull Fair.

brant steep (OE *brant*)

brass money *wheeare ther's muck ther's brass* (OE *braes* — used in the sense of copper coins since the fourteenth century)

brass bands Brass or silver bands have long been an important part of Yorkshire musical tradition, a few tracing their origins to the military music of early volunteer bands (eg Knaresborough Silver Band), others based on woollen mills (eg Black Dyke Mills Band, Queensbury) or coalmines (eg Grimethorpe Colliery Band), or formed in places ranging from towns (eg Brighouse and Rastrick) to tiny village communities (eg Muker Silver Band in Swaledale). There are many competitions, including one each September in the natural acoustics of Hardraw Scar, Wensleydale, where a competition started in the 1880s was revived in 1989.

Brass or silver bands — a familiar Yorkshire sound.

brassock wild mustard, charlock (Latin *brassica*)

brat apron worn by WR textile-workers, mainly **woolsorters** (qv), when it extended from just below the chin to the floor, and was formerly chequered; any kind of home-made rather than bought from a butcher (OF *braon*)

bray to hammer, hit, beat, esp repeatedly (OF *breier*)

brazzent impudent, shameless *sh's nobbut a brazzen' trull* WR

brazzock (see *brassock*)

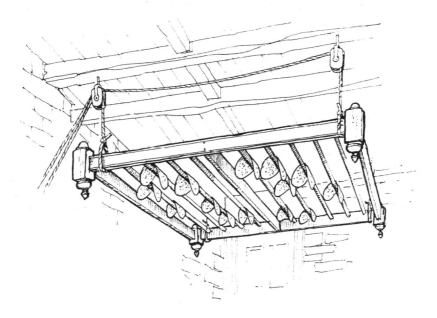

Breeadfleg or creel, with oatcakes hanging to dry.

apron; child's pinafore; a young child; piece of hessian tied on ewe's tail to prevent conception (? Celtic *brat*, cloth) (see *'ardin*) NR

bratted just turning sour (milk); clotted NR

braunge to boast WR

brawn boar; preparation of cold pig-meat in a mould, originally

breead-fleg wooden rack suspended from ceiling near fireplace. Originally it was used to dry **oatcake**, later to dry or air washing. Also known as a *creel* (qv). (For *fleg* see *flaik*.)

breeaks trousers, esp NER (OE *brec*)

brek to break (OE *brecan*)

brewis (see *browis*)

bribe short length of cloth, usually left-over or faulty piece (OF *bribes*, scraps)

bridal band bride's garter, formerly competed for in the Cleveland custom of young men racing from the church to the bride's home, where it was removed before she crossed the threshold — a trophy considered to bring good luck, esp in love.

Bridestones curiously-eroded rocks seven miles north-east of Pickering, the largest of which is known as the Pepper Pot

brig bridge; support for a sieve etc; projection of land into the sea (eg **Filey Brigg** (qv)) (ON *briggja*)

Brig o' Dreead bridge referred to in the *Lyke Wake Dirge* (qv) which the soul must cross on its journey to the next life.

Brimham Rocks These fantastically eroded rocks near Summerbridge, Nidderdale, have been given all kinds of fanciful names such as the Baboon's Head, the Idol Rock, the Druid's Coffin, the Dancing Bear etc, and there are several Rocking Stones. At 950 feet above sea level, covering 60 acres and weighing up to 500 tons, these curious masses of millstone grit are the subject of several legends, including that of an eloping couple who leapt from the Lovers' Rock but miraculously landed safely. It is now a National Trust site.

britch breechband (a horse's harness)

britches trousers (see *breeaks*)

broad Yorkshire This term was originally used to describe the size of the county, the largest in England, the county of broad acres (3,923,359 acres, often compared with the 3,566,840 letters in the Authorised Bible). Nowadays the term *'brooad Yorksher'* applies to Yorkshire dialect or accent.

broche, broitch steeple; spindle; instrument for enlarging hole; steel tooth of comb used in wool-combing WR (OF *broche*)

brock badger; larva in cuckoo-spit (from its supposed resemblance to a badger) *ti sweeat like a brock* ER (Celtic *broc*)

brod[1] kind of prodder used in making a *tab rug* (qv) and in thatching, when it is known as a *thack-brod* (see *thack*)

brod[2] to make (a rug) (ie by pricking through the bits of cloth to make a *tab rug* (qv))

broddle to poke, pick out, make holes in etc (var of 'prod')

brokken broken (OE *ge-brocen*)

Brontë Way forty-mile route designed to allow walkers to follow in the footsteps of the Brontës. Starting in the Spen Valley at Oakwell Hall, Birstall, it takes in the Red House, Gomersal, the birthplace at Thornton, the parsonage at Haworth, **Top Withens** (qv) and Wycoller etc.

browis *oatcake* (qv) steeped in boiling water then dipped in fat and served with broth (OF *broez*)

browt brought

broxy inflammatory disease of sheep, said to be caused by eating frosted grass

The Dancing Bear at Brimham Rocks.

Bruddersford fictional name for Bradford in J B Priestley's 1929 novel *The Good Companions*

bruff healthy, hearty in appearance

brummel bramble, blackberry

brummel-kite (see *bummel-kite*)

brummel-neeased having a purple, pitted nose popularly associated with too much drink NER (var of 'bramble-nosed')

brush term used for living together without being married *the' wer' livin' ovver t' brush*. The phrase is thought to be derived from the gypsy wedding-custom of the couple jumping over a brush. (See *daytal, tally*.) WR

brussen burst, bursting, esp of over-full stomach; broken; boastful, belligerent etc (OE *borstan*, burst)

brussen-guts glutton

brussen-gutted greedy

brust burst

bub to drink, esp of babies and children (? ME *bib*, Latin *bibere*, cf F *biberon*, drinking bottle)

buck cheek, impudence *none of yer owd buck!*

bucker leadmining term for a kind of flat hammer used mainly by women and boys to break ore into small pieces NR

buck-fan children's term for giving someone bumps, eg on a birthday WR

buck-stick[1] cheeky person, esp child WR

buck stick[2] driver or bat in *knur and spell* (qv)

buck-'ummer euphemism for hell *Well, Ah'll go ter buck-'ummer!*

buckth (see *bugth*)

bud but, however

buddle leadmining term for a low circular vat with a raised centre, used for the final stage of washing ore

budget large can for holding milk, sometimes shaped to be carried on back, held with leather straps like a rucksack (OF *bougette*)

buff-brat short-sleeved white smock worn by a *buffer* (see below, and also *brat*)

buffer girl who worked in the Sheffield area buffing or polishing cutlery etc at a wheel.

buffit small low stool (OF *buffet*, stool)

buffle-'eead fool (cf Dutch *buffel*, block-head)

buffs (see *blinnders*)

bug delighted; proud, conceited

bugth size, bulk (of a person)

buist (see *boose*)

bullace wild plum *as breet as a bullace* NER (? OF *beloce*)

bull-'eead tadpole; miller's thumb fish; tussock of grass (see below)

bull-feeace tuft or patch of coarse grass, spoiling a meadow

bull-front (see below)

bull-fullock mad rush *gannin' in bull-fullock*, to rush in without thinking (see *fullock*) ER

bull-toppin' (see *bull-feeace*)

bull week last week of work before a holiday WR (miners' term)

bullie to bowl, roll along the ground

bullie-beul child's **hoop** (qv)

bullspink bullfinch NR

bullstang dragonfly NER

bullstooane grindstone; *strickle* (qv)

bulltree elderberry bush NR (cf *bottery* qv)

bum-bailie bailiff employed to seek out debtors etc, fear of whom is reflected in the WR dialect verse: *'Ere dahn i' t' cellar-'oil, wheeare t' muck slahts on t'winders, We've used all us coil up, an' we'r reight dahn ter t' cinders: But if t' bum-bailie comes 'e'll nivver finnd us . . . '* (*bum* is said to be derived from the fact that the bailiff tapped people on the back)

bummelkite bumble bee; blackberry

bumper fifteen in some systems of **sheep counting** (qv)

bun[1] going; bound, certain *Ah'll be bun*, I'll be bound NER

bun[2] small cake

bunniwoodin' (see *chumpin'*)

bup (see *bub*)

burler person who picks out small pieces of thread, knots etc from newly-woven cloth in the textile trade, known as *burlin' an' mendin'* WR (OF *bourle*, tuft of wool)

Burning Bartle (see **Owd Bartle**)

Burnsall Feast From at least Elizabethan times it has been held each August at Burnsall, Wharfedale, the feast being in honour of St Wilfrid. Since the nineteenth century it has included the popular Burnsall Fell Race, in which runners race up to a cairn 1,345 feet above sea level and back.

burnt on overcooked and sticking to pan (cf *set on*) WR

buryin' brass money put aside, often as weekly savings in a burial club or friendly society, to pay for funeral expenses

Busby Stoop name of an inn at Sandhutton, so called because a coiner, Tom Busby, was hung in chains there in 1702 after being hanged for killing his father-in-law. His ghost is said to haunt the area, and the chair in which Busby slept after the murder was kept in the inn, the superstition being that anyone who sat in it would meet disaster or death. The chair is now in Thirsk Museum.

bust to burst; to break; broken

butt short piece of ploughed land in an irregularly-shaped field (cf *gore*)

butterscotch hard kind of toffee, enriched with butter, once particularly associated with Doncaster, where Parkinsons made their 'Celebrated Royal Doncaster Butterscotch', presenting Queen Victoria with a tin at Doncaster Races in 1851. (See also **Harrogate Toffee**.)

Buttertubs deep depressions in the limestone of the pass between Swaledale and Wensleydale, 1,700 feet above sea level. The name may simply refer to the shape of these water-eroded holes, but it has been suggested that it is because they were once used to cool down loads of butter being conveyed between the dales.

Buxom Betty The pen-name of Emily Denby (1890-1955) of Tong

Park, Baildon, who for almost thirty years wrote weekly stories in authentic WR dialect for the Bradford *Telegraph & Argus*. These homely and humorous tales of the Higginbottams and Nimbletongues enjoyed great popularity.

buzzard moth, esp nocturnal moth (from sound of wings)

buzzer standard term for steam hooter or whistle at a mill or factory calling people to work *all t' buzzers 'as gooan!* WR

by! exclamation of astonishment, disapproval etc, short for various expressions (see below)

by gow! by God! Good Lord! (var of God)

by gum! my word! fancy that! etc (euphemism for God)

by heck! dammit etc (euphemism for hell)

by lad! my word! NER watch it! etc WR

by shots! dammit etc WR

byre cowshed (OE *byre*)

C

cack-'anded clumsy; left-handed

cad man who took fish from boats to set out for sale on the quayside (esp Bridlington)

cadely in delicate health WR

Caedmon Yorkshire's earliest poet (circa AD 680) was an elderly cowherd working at Whitby Abbey who had a dream while asleep in a stable, inspiring him to sing about the Creation. St Hilda, the abbess, was so impressed that she admitted him as a monk. Of the many poems he wrote on passages of scripture the only one to survive is from the dream. In the Anglian speech of the Whitby area, the poem begins: '*Nu seylun hergan hefaenricaes Uard . . .* ' ('Now should we praise the Guardian of Heaven's Kingdom . . . ').

caff to give up, give in WR

caff-'earted cowardly, shy ER

caffle to argue, quarrel NER (cf MHG *keffeln*)

caggy-'anded (see above)

cagmag fatty, gristly meat; poor quality or unwholesome meat in general

cah-clap patch of cow dung WR

cahr to stay (quiet etc); to settle down, sit *cahr quiet — like the' do i' Birstall* WR(var of 'cower')

cainjy bad-tempered NER

cake-'oil jocular term for mouth WR (see *hoil*)

Cakin' Neet the eve of All Souls Day (2nd November), when it used to be the custom to distribute soul-cakes or *saumas loaves* (qv). Recently revived at Dungworth and Stannington, near Sheffield, when there are *guisers* (qv), but no special cakes.

Calderdale Way circular fifty mile route round the upper Calder Valley between Brighouse and Todmorden

calker clog-iron; hind part of horse's shoe

call (not to be confused with *kall* (qv)) to speak of somebody critically, find fault with; verbally abuse *sh' wor reight callin' 'im* (saying disparaging things about him) WR (? from 'to call names')

callit a scold; a contentious, nagging woman NER

Calverley Hall Scene of one of Yorkshire's best-known murders, this hall at Calverley, between Leeds and Bradford, is said to be

25

haunted by the ghost of Walter Calverley, who in 1604 stabbed his wife and two of his young sons to death. He was pressed to death by stones in York, and is said to have pleaded for a speedier end by calling out *'A pund more weight! Lig on! Lig on!'*. The ghost took the form of an angry figure holding a blood-stained dagger, sometimes riding a headless horse. The crime became the subject of *The Yorkshire Tragedy*, dubiously attributed to Shakespeare.

cam bank, slope; ridge (ON *kambr*)

cammeril (see *caumbril*)

canals Of particular importance in Yorkshire during the Industrial Revolution, artificial waterways were constructed by groups of labourers known as *navvies* (qv). They connected rivers, such as the Aire and Ouse (Selby), and the Don, Aire, Calder and Ouse (at Goole). Driffield and Market Weighton were linked with the Humber, and Pocklington with the Derwent. Vital links with Lancashire were made by the Leeds-Liverpool Canal (1773-1816), with its famous Five Rise Locks near Bingley, and with the 5,415 yards long Standedge Tunnel near Marsden. (See *legger, Tom Pudding*.)

candle auction (see **Hubberholme land-letting**)

Candlemas Church festival (2nd February) involving the symbolising of light (*Luke 2:32*) by the blessing of candles. Sometimes the occasion for fairs (eg at Ponte-

fract), and also for weather-lore, as in the saying from Hornsea: *'A Can'lemass crack, Lays monny a sailor on 'is back'*.

canned drunk, esp WR

cann'l, cannle candle (see also Candlemas) (OE *candel*)

canny careful, shrewd etc (but see *conny*)

canthrif gathering, group of people NR (cf Welsh *cantref*)

canty brisk, lively, cheerful, healthy

cap to surprise, astonish; to beat, surpass *'e wor reight capped; it caps owt* (OE *caeppe*, from Latin *caput*, head)

cappel brass nose-cap on clogs WR

cappil patch of leather over a hole in a shoe WR

cappin' surprising, remarkable

cap-steeans coping stones

Captain Cauftail leader of the team of Plough Stots (qv) NER

Captain Cook Yorkshire's most famous seaman, who became a legend in his lifetime. Born at Marton, near Middlesborough (1728), James Cook first went to school at Great Ayton, then worked for a grocer and haberdasher at Staithes. Here he is said to have been dismissed for theft — but he had simply taken a bright new shilling from his employer's money, and exchanged it for one of his own. This led to his move to Whitby, where he was apprenticed to the shipowner John Walker of Grape Lane, before going to sea and eventually embarking on his famous voyages of exploration,

Yorkshire's canals and mills — a once-prosperous combination.

his ships being designed on the lines of Whitby coal-ships. (See **Cook's Cottage**.)

carding process of disentangling wool following *scouring* (qv)

carker (see *calker*)

carlins dried peas

Carlin' Sunda fifth Sunday in Lent, when the traditional dish is *carlins*, or dried peas, steeped in water overnight, then fried in butter. The origin of the custom is said to be a shipwreck (one version says off Hunmanby Gap in Filey Bay), on the fifth Sunday in Lent, when a cargo of dried peas was washed ashore, the sacks bursting open because the peas had swollen in the water. The name is said to be that of the ship or her captain, but the association of peas with Lent is much older than this nineteenth century story, and *Carlin'* may be derived from Care Sunday, another name for this, officially called Passion Sunday, with reference to the sufferings of Jesus. (See **Lent**.)

carols (see **Christmas singing**)

carpet-weaving an important development of the WR textile industry, esp Crossleys Carpets of Halifax, the biggest carpet-makers in the world, who in the first half of the twentieth century employed up to 4,000 workers.

carr marsh; marshy woodland (ON)

carr land reclaimed low-lying peaty areas ER

carriage mester undertaker, funeral director (esp S Yorks)

carse cake brown bread WR (? from 'coarse')

case-clock a grandfather or grandmother clock

cast (see *rig-welted*)

Castleford lasses The girls of this WR town were traditionally complimented in the saying: *'Castleford lasses may weel bi fair, For they wesh i' t' Calder an' sind i' t' Aire'*.

cat-'aigs, cat-'awse haws, hawthorn berries NR

cat-collop cat-meat, offal

catchin' infectious

catchins children's chasing game, more commonly known as *tig* or *tiggy* (qv)

catie-cornered aslant, cockeyed

cat's eyes (see **eyes, cat's**)

catty (see *piggy*)

cauf (see *cawf*)

caumbril, cammeril slightly curved piece of wood with notches at each end, used by butchers to hang carcasses

Caumbril or cammeril.

caus'a, causey pavement or causeway WR; narrow paved trackway NER (OF *chaucie*)

cauven having calved

cawf[1] calf NER

cawf[2] small boat formerly kept in a *coble* (qv) for hauling fishing- (see also *bogey*)lines etc NER

cawf-'eead fool

cawf-licked hair sticking up or out awkwardly and persistently

cawker (see *calker*)

Cawood Feast legendary dinner of gargantuan size said to have been provided by George Neville at Cawood, near Selby, when he became Archbishop of York in 1464. The 2,000 cooks are supposed to have prepared 1,000 sheep, 100 oxen, 2,000 pigs, 5,500 venison pasties, 4,000 rabbits, and many thousands of chickens, quails, peacocks etc. Dessert included 5,000 custards and 4,000 tarts, with unlimited ale and wine.

cazzans pieces of cattle dung formerly dried for fuel

ceead (see *kedd*)

chafin'-dish (see *chover*)

chakky-pig familiar name for a pig (cf 'pussy-cat') WR

chalter-'eeaded pig-headed, empty-headed (from *chalder*, cauldron) (OF *chaudron*)

chamber bedroom, upper room (OF *chambre*)

champion excellent, outstandingly good

chap man, esp one who is unknown to the speaker

chapil 'at-pegs pegs, originally of wood, in the vestibule of chapels, where the congregation hung hats and coats. They were so prominent that they gave rise to the description of someone staring (usually in astonishment): *"er eyes stuck aht like chapil 'at-pegs'* WR

chapil spice (see *pew spice*)

charver friend or mate; lad (Romany *charvo*, boy)

chat something very small, eg *chat-haddock* NER

chats[1] small potatoes, esp fried whole WR

chats[2] catkins, 'pussy willow'; seeds of sycamore etc NER (cf F *chatons*, kittens)

chaumin'-dish (see *chover*)

chavvle to chew, gnaw, nibble (OE *ceafl*)

checker checked, esp of **brat** (qv) worn by **woolsorters** (qv)

cheddy-yow! call to sheep being brought down from the fell, to come closer NR

cheese (see *Cotherstone, Coverdale, Swaledale, Wensleydale*)

cheese-cake (see *curd tarts*)

cheg to chew NR

cheggle to cut roughly or badly (eg grass) NR

chelp to chatter, talk loudly, answer back (var of 'chirp') WR

chesford mould used in cheesemaking, equipped with a sinker to press down the cheese

childer children (ME *childer*, from OE *childra*, genitive pl)

chimla, chimley chimney (OF *cheminée*)

chine pig's backbone, sometimes stuffed with parsley etc, esp ER (OF *eschine*)

chip-'oil fish and chip shop, an essential component of every

Chesford — a mould used in cheese-making.

Yorkshire community (see **Harry Ramsdens**)

Chippendale name synonymous with some of the best furniture in eighteenth-century England (eg at Nostell Priory and Harewood House) made by the cabinet-maker Thomas Chippendale (1718-99), born in Otley, where his statue can be seen.

chippy¹ starling (? var of *shepster* (qv))

chippy² short for *chip-'oil* (qv)

chizzock (see **curd tart**)

chocolate Yorkshire has made a major contribution to the popularity of chocolate, mainly through the York firms started by Joseph Terry, an apothecary who joined the confectioners Bayldon and Berry in 1767, and Joseph Rowntree, who came from Scarborough to start a 'Grocers and Provision Merchants' in the Pavement, York, in 1822, taking over from Tukes

who had made chocolate since 1725. Thorntons, originally a Sheffield firm selling **toffee** (qv), are also producers of quality chocolate.

choil indentation in a blade where cutting edge joins *tang* (qv)

choil it to clear off, leave in a hurry (Sheffield)

choirs Choral singing is an important part of Yorkshire tradition, with choirs and glee clubs all over the county. In the recent past many chapels and some churches regularly staged performances of oratorios, notably Handel's *Messiah*. The famous Huddersfield Choral Society was founded in 1836, and there are many long-established choirs (eg Bradford Old Choral) and annual choral gatherings, two to raise money for hospitals — at Holmfirth (since 1882), and Mapplewell near Barnsley (since 1887). (See also **Filey Fisherman's Choir**.)

chonce chance, esp WR

chonce bairn (see below)

chonce-'un an illegitimate child

choop rose-hip (cf Norwegian *kjupa*)

choose-'o whoever, no matter who

choose-'ow whatever happens; no matter how

chover small iron fire-basket with three legs, used to heat a *bakst'n* (qv) etc (OF *chauffoir*)

Christmas (see following entries, also **Devil's Knell**, **horseshoe**, *Kersmass*, **lambswool**, **mistletoe**, **turkeys**, *waits*, *wassailing*, *wessle bob*, **Yule** etc)

Christmas Crack The annual gathering of the Yorkshire Dialect Society, featuring dialect verse, prose and traditions associated with a Yorkshire Christmas. (See *crack.*)

Christmas Pie The traditional Yorkshire **Christmas Pie** consisted of an elaborately-decorated crust containing a rich assortment of poultry, mainly goose, but often also turkey, chicken, partridge, pigeon, woodcock etc, together with seasoning, spices and butter. These pies were sometimes enormous, and so renowned they were exported to various parts of the kingdom.

Christmas singin' carol singing, going round from house to house. Many places in Yorkshire have traditions involving the singing of Christmas carols, including pubs in the Huddersfield

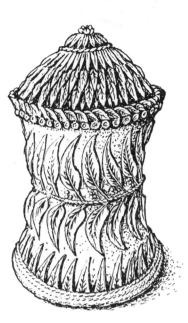

Yorkshire Christmas Pie.

area and in Worral and Stannington, near Sheffield, where they sing carols to old tunes by local composers, such as John Foster and John Hall, a Sheffield blacksmith who died in 1794. Carol singing in Yorkshire is also associated with traditional songs such as 'Hail, smiling Morn!' and 'Christmas Bells', the latter in several different versions. (See also *waits.*)

chubbin' (see *chumpin'*)

chuck to throw *it's chuckin' it dahn* (raining heavily) WR

chuffed very pleased, delighted

chuffed off displeased, disillusioned

Chover.

chump short, thick piece of wood used as fuel; fool (?combination of 'chunk' and 'lump')

chumpin' to go *chumpin'* is to collect chumps for a bonfire (see Plot, *proggin'*)

chunter to grumble, mutter, esp at length *'e chuntered a bucketful*

cinder tea folk remedy for stomach problems and bringing up a baby's wind, consisting of sweetened water into which was placed a red-hot cinder from the fire.

cinders coke (OE *sinder*, dross)

clack gossip, slanderous talk

claes, clais (see *cleeas*)

clag to stick, clog, esp of food when chewed

claggy sticky (see above)

claht[1] to clout, hit WR (ME *cloute*)

claht[2] cloth (eg *dish-claht*) WR (OE *clut*)

claht-'eead fool WR (lit 'cloth-head')

clame to spread, esp butter on bread; to smear with anything sticky (OE *cloeman*)

clammed (see *clemmed*)

clammin'-oil a place where animals were kept before being slaughtered WR

clap[1] to apply quickly, esp the hand; to set, slap, put down quickly etc *clap t' lid on it* (ON *klappa*)

clap[2] patch of cow-dung

clap-benny the action of a baby clapping its hands together, supposedly in gratitude for something given (from 'clap for a penny')

clapbread kind of *havercake*

(qv), so called because the dough was *clapped* or thrown onto a board or *bakst'n* (qv)

clap-cowd cold, said esp of food which has been allowed to go cold

clark to scold; to marry, mostly in figurative sense of joining two ends of yarn together

clart to smear, daub, esp with mud or something sticky (sometimes incorrectly spelt as *'clout'* (qv)) *all clarted up*, covered in mud, dirt

clartment false or flattering talk ER

clarty smeared with dirt; dirty, sticky

clashy stormy, wet weather; muddy NER

clatter to slap, strike with the open hand WR

clavver to chatter NER

clawk to scratch, claw

clawm, cloam to clutch, grab; to touch in a wheedling sort of way WR

cleak to grasp, seize (ME *cleken*)

cleckin' gossip, back-chat

cleeas clothes NER

cleat[1] coltsfoot, sometimes used to make *cleat wine*

cleat[2] small piece of iron (eg worn on shoes) ER

cleg horse-fly (ON *kleggi*)

clemmed parched with thirst; starving (OE *beclemman*)

clemmy small stone NER

clep stick with hook on end for hooking fish on board

cletch family of young (eg children, chickens) (ON *klekja*)

cleugh mill-race; sluice-gate NER

Cleveland Bay breed of horse originating in the Cleveland Hills in the NR, probably as a result of breeding thoroughbreds with carthorse mares. Usually light or dark bay, with black mane, legs and tail. Renowned for their staying-power and general usefulness, **Cleveland Bays** have been used for working on the land, as coach-horses (including the royal coaches) and as hunters.

clew ball of yarn

clews (see *clowse*)

click to catch; become friends, esp couple who start courting *Click 'od o' yond!*, Catch hold of that! (cf *cop on* (qv))

climm to climb

clinch to lift with winch and chains (fisherman's term NER)

clint shelf of rock, part of rock between the *grykes* (qv)

clip¹ to shear (sheep)

The Cleveland Bay — a fine, all-purpose breed.

Cleveland Way walk of 108 miles from Helmsley to Filey, established in 1969 by Alan Falconer, who named it after an early trading route.

clip² to embrace (see *clipping*)

clipping The old custom of 'clipping the church' involved the congregation standing all round the outside of it and joining hands as a blessing is asked on the church — usually at the patronal festival. Though it has died out, *clipping* has recently been revived at St Oswalds, Guiseley, and St Peter's at Tankersley near Barnsley. (OE *clyppan*, to embrace)

clock beetle

Clock Almanack The best-known of all the **almanacks** (qv) in Yorkshire dialect, this was published in Halifax from 1865 until 1957, sometimes selling 80,000 copies annually. It was edited by John Hartley (1839-1915), who wrote much of the material himself, including both comic and serious verse, and prose such as 'Seets i' Lundun' and 'Grimes' Trip to America', based on his own experiences. The name *The Original Illuminated Clock Almanack* was given by the founder, Alfred Wilson, whose hatter's shop in the Corn Market, Halifax, had a well-known illuminated clock over it.

clocker hen with chicks (OE *cloccian*, to cluck)

clock-making Yorkshire was once renowned for its clock-makers, who were found not only in cities and towns such as Leeds, Huddersfield, Wetherby and Northallerton, but in the country, in villages such as Askrigg, Settle, Haworth and Pateley Bridge. The industry flourished mainly during the late eighteenth and early nineteenth centuries. Most famous was self-taught John Harrison (1693-1776), born near Pontefract, whose ship's chronometers

dramatically improved the accuracy of navigation.

clog wooden-soled shoe, sometimes fitted with **clog irons** underneath. Formerly the standard footwear of working people in Yorkshire, they are still made at Hebden Bridge by the firm Walkleys *t' third generation goes back ter t' clogs*, ie returns to poverty. (See *patten*.)

clog, lime-burner's extreme thirst is conveyed by the phrase *as dry as a lime-burner's clog*

clog ageean to recover health and return to normal working life WR

clog on to keep going

clogs, to pop to die *t' owd lad's popped 'is clogs*

cloise enclosure, field (OF *cloistre*)

clomp to tread heavily, make a noise when walking (cf Dutch *klomp*, wooden shoe)

clonk to hit (on the head) WR; to *clomp* (see above)

cloot (see *clout*)

closit outside toilet; walk-in cupboard (ME from OF *clos*)

clough ravine, steep-sided valley (OE *cloh*)

clout cloth; blow (see *claht* WR, the NER equivalent being *cloot*)

clowse lock on a canal, sluice (ME *clowse*, originally pl)

clowter horse that is a good worker ER

clubby, clubster stoat NER

clumpst cold (eg of feet) NR

cob¹ to pick clean (an apple core) WR

cob² to strike ER

cob³ lump, esp of coal

cob[4] fit of sulking *get a cob on* (cf *mawk*)

cob'anded left-handed ER

cobble-tree bar of plough to which the *swingle-tree* (qv) was fastened; bar forming a link between the harnesses of two working horses

cobby neat, shapely, rounded ER; cheerful, lively *as cobby as a lop* NER

coble (pron 'cobble') Traditional fishing boat, with a high prow and stern, typical of the Yorkshire coast, esp Filey, used for fishing up to roughly fifteen miles offshore. (See *yawl*.) (Probably of Celtic origin, cf Breton *caubal*.)

cock[1] heap of grass, ready to spread to make hay

cock[2] best fighter or player (esp in boy's games) *cock o' t' midden* WR

cock-spade a type of narrow-bladed spade used for digging **peat** (qv)

The clog, once the standard footwear for young and old.

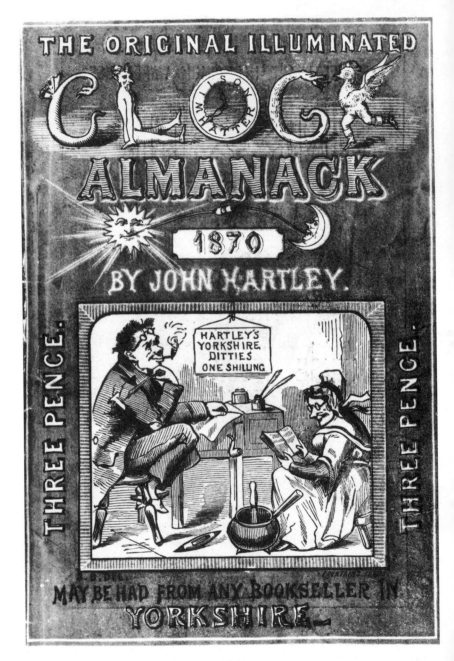

THE ORIGINAL ILLUMINATED
CLOCK
WILSON HATTER
ALMANACK
1870
BY JOHN HARTLEY.

HARTLEY'S
YORKSHIRE
DITTIES
ONE SHILLING

THREE PENCE.

THREE PENCE.

MAY BE HAD FROM ANY BOOKSELLER IN
YORKSHIRE.

A coble, beached and with its tiller detached; the characteristic Yorkshire fishing boat.

cock-stool poisonous toadstool NR

cocklety not firmly placed (eg a ladder)

cocklety-bread former children's game in which they swung each other round to a rhyme and made actions with their hands as though kneading bread.

cod¹ pod, husk (OE *cod*)

cod² to kid, deceive

codder leader of a press-forging team in the steel industry WR

coddle to stew (eg fruit); to roast; to pamper, over-nurse

The Clock — *John Hartley's best-selling almanack.*

cuddy-'anded left-handed

coggers lumps of compressed snow under shoes or **clogs** NR

coil coal, often used in pl (eg *put some coils on t' fire*) WR

coil-leader coal-man WR

coil-'oil coal-house WR

coit coat WR

coke (see *cowk*)

cokes cinders, esp WR

collier coalminer WR

collier-cahr squatting on one's haunches to have a conversation (as colliers were supposed to do in the pit) WR

collier Munda day taken off work, usually Monday, as this was said to be when miners were most likely to be absent from the pit WR

collop thick slice or lump, usually of ham or bacon; thick slices of potatoes, fried (? ON, cf Swedish *kalops*)

Collop Munda the last Monday before the start of Lent, when it was customary to use up items of food, esp *collops* of bacon or ham, fried with eggs

collywobbles attack of stomach pains, with diarrhoea, caused by nervousness (combination of 'colic' and 'wobble')

come thi ways (in)! come in! (with the implication of a warm welcome). Formerly this greeting was used all over Yorkshire, but it is now most likely to be heard in the NR, esp around the Yorkshire Dales.

Compo character in the TV series *Last of the Summer Wine*, set in the Holmfirth area (see also **Kompo**)

common-ossity person of coarse or vulgar behaviour, bad taste, etc (cf *funny-ossity*)

Congregationalism Though not as common as **Methodist** (qv) chapels, those built by the Independents or **Congregationalists** feature in many Yorkshire villages, esp in the Dales. Following the Act of Uniformity (1662) the Nonconformists, as well as the later Methodists, were typical of the independent spirit of Yorkshire people.

conkers horse chestnuts; the children's game played by hitting and attempting to smash a *conker* suspended from string. Popular in Yorkshire, but not confined to the county. In NR formerly called *conquerors*, but as the game was originally played with snail shells, the word is probably derived from OF *conque*.

conny small and neat, nice, attractive

conny-west shy, bewildered, secretive (said to be derived from Connie West, a woman noted for roaming the streets of Bradford in a furtive manner)

Cook's Cottage No longer to be seen in the village of Great Ayton, where **Captain Cook** (qv) went to school, this cottage belonging to his family was demolished stone by stone in 1935, and taken to Australia, where it was rebuilt in the Fitzroy Gardens of Melbourne. Though it has been widely publicised as where James Cook lived, it was not built by his father until 1755, and James had moved to Whitby in 1747. The most that can be said is that he may have seen it, or even stayed there, on a return visit.

cooper maker of wooden casks and barrels (ie one holding thirty-six gallons). The craft survives at Samuel Smiths Brewery, Tadcaster, and Theakstons Brewery, Masham, where there is a traditional initiation ceremony for a **cooper** after serving his apprenticeship. After he has made a hogshead (fifty-four gallons) he is placed inside, and his workmates pour over him a **'cooper's mixture'** consisting of old beer, wood shavings, soot etc, then roll him round the yard, after which he is accepted as a journeyman-cooper.

Cooper, Harry (see **Market Weighton Giant**)

cop to catch *tha'll cop it!* (be in trouble), *cop 'od an' stick!* (grab hold and hang on!) (? OF *caper*, to seize)

cop-coilin' (see *chumpin'*)

cop on to become friends with someone of the opposite sex (cf *click*)

copper¹ boiler used for heating water for washing clothes

copper² policeman (see *cop*)

copper-'aws poppies (from 'copper rose')

cordwainer shoemaker. The term is obsolete, except for its use by guilds. (OF *cordoanier*)

corf, corve basket or container for coal, formerly pulled or pushed along by the *hurrier* (qv) in a mine

Corn Law Rhymer nickname of Ebenezer Elliott, born at Masborough, near Rotherham, whose political verses helped to bring about the repeal of the Corn Laws in 1846.

cot knot or lug of hair

Cotherstone cheese soft farmhouse cheese made on the northern fringe of Yorkshire in the Barnard Castle area

cotter to strike heavily WR

cottered, cottery tangled, matted (eg of hair)

Cottingley Fairies Allegedly featured in photographs taken in 1917 at Cottingley, near Bingley, by Elsie Wright and her cousin Francis, these 'fairies' were taken seriously by many people, including Sir Arthur Conan Doyle, who published the photos in the *Strand* magazine in 1920. Though for many years Elsie maintained they were genuine, she finally confessed that the fairies were simply cut-out cardboard figures.

courtin' close friendship preparatory to engagement and marriage *'tha's been a-cooartin' Mary Jane!'* WR

courtin' cake kind of sandwich cake traditionally made by girls for their boyfriends

Coverdale cheese traditional farmhouse cheese, made at the Kirkby Malzeard factory

Cow and Calf name of two rocks on the edge of Ilkley Moor, once with a third rock known as 'the Bull', which was broken up for building stone towards the end of the nineteenth century. (See **Rombald**.)

cowk¹ core of an apple (see *cob*)

cowk² coke

A cask, product of the cooper's age-old craft.

cowle to rake, pull towards oneself

cowle-rake rake used for cleaning out ashes and soot, esp under an oven *cowlin' it in* (said of somebody making money)

cowls stems of dried or partly-burnt heather, gathered for fuel

cow-lady ladybird

cowpie fireside stool NR

cowter blade in front of plough-share (var of coulter, OE *culter*)

Cowthorpe Oak once famous as the oldest and largest oak tree in the UK. Situated at Cowthorpe, near Wetherby, it had, by 1829, reached 45 feet high and 60 feet in circumference, with branches up to 50 feet in length. The trunk was hollow and had standing room for forty people.

crack friendly conversation (see **Christmas Crack**)

cracked said of milk on the point of going sour

crackit low stool

crake crow (ON *kraka*)

crambazzled prematurely aged through drink and dissolute life NR

crammely tottery, unsteady, stiff-jointed, awkward NER

crammocky (WR equivalent of *crammely* (qv))

cran measure for fish (37 gallons)

cratch wooden fireside chair (OF *creche*, crib or hay-rack, because chair has rails)

Craven Heifer famous beast whose name and picture can be seen on several inn-signs, and from 1817 on notes issued by the Craven Bank. It was bred in 1807 at Gargrave by the Rev William Carr, incumbent of Bolton Abbey Church. The heifer weighed over a ton, was 11 feet 2 inches long and had a 10 feet 2 inches girth.

cree to simmer; to partly cook grain or rice (esp in oven)

creeak¹ to creak, croak (ME imitative)

creeak² crow; crook (see *crake*) NER

creeaked crooked *as creeaked as a dog's 'ind-leg* NER (ON *krokr*, hook)

creel frame with wooden rails, used for carrying hay etc; alternative name for *breead-fleg* (qv), a frame suspended from the ceiling (cf *flaik*)

creep hole hole made in a **drystone wall** (qv) to allow sheep to pass through (cf *thirl*)

crewkt (see *creeaked*)

cricket Yorkshire has long been associated with some of the finest cricket in the kingdom, with clubs being founded as early as 1784 (Heworth, York), 1796 (Hallam), 1815 (Knaresborough) and 1820 (Otley). The first county match was played against Norfolk in 1833. The first Roses game was at Sheffield in 1849. Amongst Yorkshire's cricketing traditions are the Black Hats versus White Hats match each May Day at Ilkley, and the Scarborough Cricket Festival, held in early September, and the various Test Matches and county matches held at Headingley, Leeds. The highest number of wickets taken was by

A cratch, the traditional Yorkshire fireside chair.

41

Wilfred Rhodes (4,187), with 240 in one season (1900). The greatest number of centuries scored was by Herbert Sutcliffe (112) between 1919 and 1939.

cripple-'oil   (see *creep hole*)

croggie   ride on crossbar of a bicycle

cronk   to crouch, esp huddled up (eg by fireside)

croose   proud, confident, boastful NR

crowdy   gruel of oatmeal and water, sweetened with treacle or sugar; broth thickened with oatmeal

crozzle   to wrinkle, wither, esp by heat; to burn to a cinder; to cake together as with burning

coals   *'e likes 'is bacon crozzled* WR

cruck   curved timber used as framework of a building

crud   curd

cruddle   to curdle, congeal

cuddy   donkey; hedge sparrow NER (? pet form of Cuthbert)

cuddy-'anded   left-handed NER

cuddy-wifter   a left-handed person NER

cufter   young rascal WR

cundef, cundith   drain under road NR (? var of 'conduit')

cup and ring   mysterious markings on boulders of millstone grit found most commonly in Yorkshire, mainly on the moors above Ilkley, Addingham, Burley and

A typical cruck-house, showing the curved timbers, with a settle by the fire.

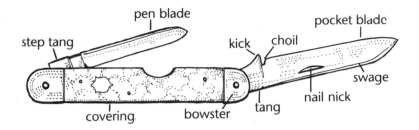

A pen-knife or flat-back, typical of the Sheffield cutlin' trade, and its various parts.

Baildon. Thought to date from the Bronze Age, they mostly consist of an indentation in the centre of a ring. Suggested explanations range from good luck symbols to territorial marking, but the mystery remains.

curd tart kind of cheese-cake, consisting of pastry filled with a mixture of curds, cream and currants etc, flavoured with nutmeg. These were traditionally begged for at Slingsby, **Redmire** (qv) and Muker (see **Awd Roy**), and in Holderness on **Plough Monday** (qv). In some places they were associated with Whitsuntide, or made for fairs, as at South Cave, near Hull.

curfew evening bell tolled to indicate the time for fires to be extinguished, a custom introduced by the Normans, and still observed by Ripon Cathedral and Trinity Church, Richmond. (OF *couvre-feu*)

curn currant, esp WR

cush! cush up! come here! (said to cows)

cushat ring dove NR

cushy-cow lady ladybird

cussen overcast, gloomy

cussen-muck mounds of grit and waste made by quarrymen

cut¹ canal

cut² (see *knur and spell*)

cutlin' manufacture of cutlery, particularly synonymous with Sheffield WR, esp S Yorks (see *bowster, buffer, flat-back, jimp, little mesters, makker, nicker-pecker, swage, swarf, tang, yaller-belly*)

cutten cut (past participle)

cutter to talk softly NR

cycling The Cyclists' Touring Club has a close association with Yorkshire, having been founded at Harrogate in 1878, and having held an annual church service at Coxwold (Coxwold Sunday) since 1927.

D

dacky pig ER
daffle to stun, stupefy
daffly confused, senile
daft silly, foolish (OE *gedaefte*, mild, meek)
dag[1] (see *deg*)
dag[2] piece of coarse material worn round hand when hauling in fishing lines NER
dahn on an indication of disapproval or suspicion *Ah'm dahn on 'im* WR
dainsh dainty, fussy, particular
Dalesbred type of sheep, commonly seen from the southern side of Wensleydale to the south of the county, with a black face and white blotches at each side of the nose (cf **Swaledale**)
Dalesman This renowned monthly magazine of Yorkshire life and lore, originally called the *Yorkshire Dalesman*, was first published in 1939, with Harry J Scott as editor. From 1968 until 1988 it was edited by W R Mitchell.
dander to shake, tremble
Darby and Joan This popular term for a devoted old couple is said to have originated in the early eighteenth century as a reference to a blacksmith and his wife of Healaugh, Tadcaster.
dasher comb with large teeth NR
dashery housework NR
dateless crazed, witless (esp with age)
dawgy soft, flabby, underbaked (bread) WR
dawk depression or flaw in the surface of something WR
dawks hands
dawky left-handed; over-dressed
dawn fluff, bits of wool etc (? var of 'down')
daytal-man labourer or other kind of worker paid by the day, once a common practice on Yorkshire farms ('day' with 'tally')
deck to give up, give in, either in the face of too much work, or when there is too much food on the plate or there is no appetite for it *Ah s'll 'ev ter deck* WR
dee to die (ON *deyja*)
deea to do NER
deeaf deaf WR
deear door NER
deeath death *'e looked like deeath wahrmed up*
deg to sprinkle (ON *doegva*)
deggin'-can watering can

A Dales shepherd, with a yowe and her lambs.

delf   quarry (ME *delf*)

delf rack   plate rack on a wall at the height of a picture-rail (from glazed earthenware made at Delft in Holland)

delver   quarryman WR

demmock   diseased spot on vegetables WR

Denby Dale Pie   the unique tradition of baking a gigantic communal meat-pie in the WR village of Denby Dale. First baked in 1788 to celebrate George III's recovery from a bout of insanity, the second pie celebrated the victory of Waterloo in 1815. The pie to commemorate Queen Victoria's Golden Jubilee in 1887 stank to high heaven when it was cut open, and was so badly decomposed it had to be buried in quicklime — though a week later the local ladies made a 'Resurrection Pie'. On the 3rd September 1988 a bicentenary pie was shared by 50,000 people, after the arrival of a procession of fifty floats from the village of Scissett. It contained 6,600 lb of beef, 6,600 lb of potatoes and 1,500 lb of onions — all fresh and tasty.

deng   damn (mild curse)

deng   (see *ding*)

Dent   (see **knitting**)

despert   very, extremely, eg *despert strang* NER

dess   truss, block (of hay or straw) NER (cf Icelandic *hey-des*, hayrick)

devil   (see *dule*)

Devil's Arrows   three prehistoric monoliths (originally with a fourth) between Boroughbridge and Roecliffe, so named because of the legend of the Devil attempting to destroy Aldborough by throwing them at it, saying: *'Boroughbrigg keep oot o' t' way, For Aldboro toon I'll ding doon!'*

Devil's Knell   the tolling of the bell 'Black Tom' at All Saints Church, Dewsbury, on Christmas Eve. The bell is said to have been presented by Thomas de Soothill in the fifteenth century as a penance after he had murdered a servant. The bell is tolled from midnight every Christmas Eve, each single toll representing a year since the birth of Christ. The idea is to celebrate the defeat of the Devil and to keep him at bay for the coming year.

Devil's Punchbowl   name given to the Hole of Horcum, an enormous depression in the highest part of the North York Moors (1,490 feet) near the Pickering-Whitby road. Folklore has two theories for its origin: it was scooped out by the Devil (a nearby bend in the road is known as the Devil's Elbow); or it was made by **Wade** (qv) the Anglian giant, who dug up handfuls of earth which he used to make nearby Blakey Topping and Wade's Causeway.

dialect readings   The public reading of Yorkshire dialect, mainly dialect poems, has been (along with the **almanacks** (qv)) an important way of keeping it alive. Its heyday was in the second half of the nineteenth century when enthusiastic WR audiences gathered to hear John Hartley of

Dibble's Bridge

Dick Hudson's

Halifax reading, for example, his own *Bite Bigger*, *A Hawporth* and *Ahr Mary's Bonnet*, or Ben Preston of Bradford movingly reading his *Come to thi Gronny, Doy*.

Dibble's Bridge bridge near Burnsall in Wharfedale, over a stream called the Dib, which according to legend was built by the Devil for a medieval shoemaker, Ralph Calvert, of Thorpe-sub-Montem. In May 1975 a coach

crashed through the parapet, killing thirty-one passengers, the worst accident of its kind in Britain.

Dick Hudson's The generally-accepted name of the Fleece Inn, High Eldwick — for countless hikers 'the gateway to the moors'. Situated opposite the starting point of a popular walk over Ilkley Moor, this inn became famous for its food, notably ham and eggs.

The Devil's Arrows between Boroughbridge and Roecliffe.

'Dick' or Richard Hudson, following his father, was publican from 1850 to 1878, when his son John took over until 1893. The inn was rebuilt in 1900.

Dick Turpin semi-legendary Essex highwayman, tried and hanged in York in 1739 for various crimes, including murder. His famous ride to York on Black Bess in order to establish an alibi is a myth based on a similar exploit by John Nevison or 'Swift Nick' in 1676, who, having committed a robbery at Gadshill at 4 am, reached York at 7.45 pm the same day. Dick Turpin was credited with Nevison's feat by W H Ainsworth in his novel *Rookwood* (1834). (See **Swift Nick**.)

Dick's 'atband   (see *queer*)

dicky¹   louse

dicky²   rickety, shaky, tottering

dill   to soothe, dull (pain) (ON *dilla*, but also perhaps related to the carminative herb dill, OE *dile*)

ding   to hit, esp heavily, knock, throw violently (to the ground) (? ON, cf Danish *daenge*)

dip   hot bacon-fat, dripping (in frying pan)

do   occasion, event; state of things *a reight good do*, *a bit of a do*

dobber, dobby   a pot marble, esp a large one, when it is described either as a *pot dobby* or an *iron dobby* (see *alley-taw*, *taws*)

dobby   den, home-base in children's games (S Yorks)

dock pudding   traditionally eaten on the fifth Sunday in Lent, or Passion Sunday, hence the plant's name of *passion dock*. This is not the same as the dock used to relieve nettle stings (see right), but is sweet dock (*Polygonum bistorta*). **Dock pudding** is made from the young leaves, together with nettles, onions and oatmeal. It is usually fried with bacon and served with potatoes. The tradition is especially associated with the Calder Valley, and competitions for the best *dock pudding* have been held at Hebden Bridge and Mytholmroyd.

'Passion dock' (bistort) used in dock pudding.

docken the common dock (*Rumex crispus*) or broad-leaved dock (*R obtusifolius*), the crushed leaves of which are the traditional cure for nettle-stings, when rubbed onto the affected area: *'In docken, oot nettle, Deean't let t' wahrm blood settle'* NER (OE *docce*, *doccan*)

dockener tool for prising out dock roots

doctor local name (mainly S Yorks) for butterfly with white wings, spotted black, presumably one of the cabbage white species

dod to cut off, esp dirty bits of wool from sheep

doddins bits of wool, usually dirty

doddy cow or bull without horns (see *hummelled, polly¹*) (ME *doddan*)

doff to take off, undress (ME do off)

doffer textile worker taking fitted *bobbins* (qv) from the spinning machine

dog-whipping former custom observed on St Lukes Day (18th October) of whipping stray dogs in the streets of York and Hull. (See **Whip-ma-whop-ma-gate**.)

doit to become forgetful or confused, to slip up in some way associated with getting old *nay lad, tha's doitin'* WR (var of 'dote')

doits fingers (OF *doigts*)

doll up to dress up, use make-up etc *sh's all dolled up* (cf *donned up*)

dollop lump of something soft, large shapeless mass (cf Norwegian dialect *dolp*)

dollum jumbled heap WR

dolly¹ strong wooden implement rather like a four-legged stool on a long handle, for *possing* (qv) and stirring washing, originally called a *possing-dolly* (? from resemblance to figure of a doll)

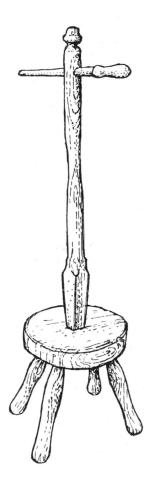

A dolly, essential washday equipment.

EVERY HOUSEWIFE SHOULD USE

Donkey stone derives its name from this brand.

dolly² log kept in a cutlery grinder's trough to adjust level of water in relation to grindstone

dolly³ wheel of discs used in polishing

dolly-posh left-handed

dolly tub wash tub in which *dolly* or *posser* (qv) is used

Dolly Varden an over-dressed woman (sometimes written **Dolly Vardy** or **Farden**) referred to in the WR phrase *'all donned up like Dolly Varden'*. (From the character in the Dickens novel *Barnaby Rudge*.)

don to put on (clothes)

Doncaster (see **butterscotch**, **railways**)

donkey stone yellow or white stone used for colouring *dooarst'ns* (qv), from the tradename 'Read's Donkey Brand'

donnakin earth closet, *privy* (qv)

donnat naughty child

donned up dressed up, very smart (see **Dolly Varden**)

dooad fool, simpleton WR

dooady overdressed person

Dooady familiar form of George WR

dooadge to handle food in a messy way (said of children) WR, S Yorks

dooaf dough WR

dooar-'oil doorway WR

dooar-st'n doorstep. Traditionally, esp in the industrial towns of the WR, housewives took pride in cleaning their doorsteps and windowsills, using a special *scahrin' stooan* (qv) or **donkey stone** (qv)

dook to immerse in water NR

doot to doubt; to suspect, be afraid that *Ah doot it'll rain, Ah doot t' aud meeare's boun ti dee* NER

dornton (see *drinkins*)

dorp carrion crow

doss to sleep in rough or makeshift circumstances eg *doss dahn*

dossel straw ornament on top of thatched roof or stack ER

dossn't dare not NER

dother to dirty, esp with mud or anything sticky *all dothered up* WR

douce pleasant, gentle (OF)

dowdy-cow ladybird NR

dowly gloomy, miserable; poorly, in low spirits

dowp (see *dorp*)

dowter daughter

doy dear, darling; term of endearment addressed to a young child WR, esp Bradford area (possibly a var of 'joy' influenced by 'dear')

doz term used of over-ripe corn, from which the grain is easily shed, when it is said to be *dozzin' oot* ER

Dracula The much-publicised connection of Count Dracula with Yorkshire is entirely fictional, and derives from Bram Stoker's novel *Dracula* (1897), written shortly after Stoker and Henry Irving were on holiday in Whitby, which provided a setting for part of the novel.

Dragon of Wantley legendary beast whose death at the hands of 'More of More Hall', a knight in spiked armour, was celebrated in a ballad (1699) and a comic opera by Henry Carey (1737). 'Wantley' has been identified as Wortley near Rotherham, but the original verse may be an allegory referring to the lawsuit between Sir Frances Wortley and the parishioners of Penistone.

drape (see *dreeap*)

drat! euphemism for to damn *drat it!, drat yond cat!* etc

drate to drawl, talk monotonously

dratted damned, cursed

draw well well from which water is drawn by a bucket, as distinct from a spring with a surface well *as deep as a draw-well* (used figuratively) WR

drawk to saturate

dree wearisome, melancholy *it's a dree neet*

dreeap cow not giving milk

Driffield pennies New Year custom of children scrambling for pennies and other coins, sometimes first heated on a shovel, thrown into the air by Driffield shopkeepers, traditionally to the chanting of the rhyme: *'Ere we are at oor toon end, A shoolder o' mutton an' a croon ti spend.'* The origin is obscure, but the custom may have been started by itinerant traders.

drinkins break for refreshments, esp by agricultural workers in the fields, usually in the afternoon, the morning break sometimes being called *t' forenooin drinkins* (cf *lowance*, *minnin'-on*)

droondid drowned NER

Dropping Well petrifying well adjacent to the River Nidd, Knaresborough, where water drips over a rockface, impregnating suspended porous objects with a calcareous, stone-like deposit. First described by John Leland in 1538, who made no mention of **Mother Shipton** (qv), later said to have been living near the well at this time.

dross-stay place for keeping grit for roads WR

droy dry, thirsty (S Yorks)

druffen drunk (? ON *drukkin*)

druft breeze ideal for drying washing on the line, or cloth on a tenter (qv); thirst *Ah've getten a reight druft on*, I'm very thirsty WR (? OE *drugath*, drought)

Druid's Altar popular name of a large rock near Bingley with extensive views; also a small group of stones on the fells between Masham and Grassington.

Druid's Temple name of a folly, like an imitation Stonehenge, at Ilton, near Masham, built by William Danby of Swinton Hall in 1820.

Drummer Boy The legend of the **Drummer Boy of Richmond** is linked with **Potter Thompson**

(qv). This boy, aged twelve, is said to have been sent by soldiers in search of treasure under Richmond Castle, because he was small enough to get through a hole leading to an underground passage. They heard him beating his drum as he went in the direction of Easby Abbey. Then it stopped, and the boy was never seen again — though his drumbeat can still sometimes be heard.

drumming well the name of the well at Harpham, ER, from which a ghostly drumming was said to forecast the death of a member of the local St Quinton family, one of whose ancestors is said to have knocked a drummer boy into the well.

drystone walls These walls, constructed without mortar, are characteristic of the Yorkshire landscape, esp the limestone walls of the Dales. Most are double walls, joined by throughs and packed with infilling, built to last by craftsmen skilled in *t' rack o' t' ee* (qv). (See *rood*.)

dub puddle, pool

dubbler bowl for kneading bread

ducks¹ (see *faggots*)

ducks² featured in the WR saying jokingly applied to places such as Pudsey, Wibsey, Cleckheaton, Drighlington and Dewsbury: *'wheeare t' ducks fly back'ards ter keep t' muck aht o' the'r een'.*

duffy too light and dry (hay) NR

duggly kind of hip flask used by coalminers WR

Duke of York The hill up and down which old Duke Frederick

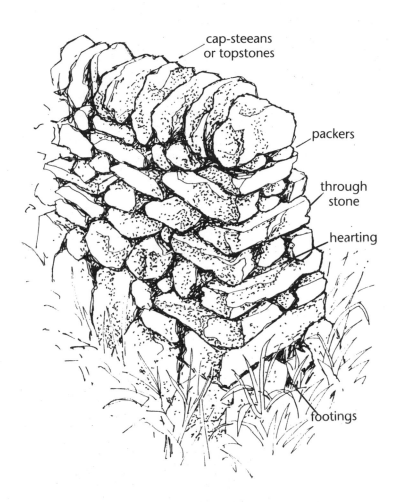

cap-steeans or topstones

packers

through stone

hearting

footings

Drystone walling, a time-honoured craft.

marched his 'ten thousand men' in the old song is said to have been the mound in Allerton Park (near the A1, north of Wetherby), on which stands the eighteenth century folly known as the Temple of Victory.

Duke of Wellington's infantry regiment dating from 1702, which has traditionally recruited in the WR. Around 1782, when it became the First Yorkshire (WR) Regiment, the soldiers became known as the **Havercake Lads** (qv).

dule machine for separating and cleaning wool, or for tearing apart material in the preparation of *mungo* (qv) and *shoddy* (qv) (from the teeth, said to be like those of a *dule* or devil)

dunch nudge, bump

dundy-coo (see *dowdy-cow*)

dunnock hedge sparrow (? from its dun colour)

durn doorpost, gatepost (cf Norwegian *dyrn*)

dursn't dare not WR

E

'eark(en) (see *hearken*)

'eart-sluffened (see *heart-sluff-ened*)

East Riding Dialect Society founded in 1988 in Driffield, where most of its meetings take place and from where a quarterly newsletter is issued. Similar in objectives to the county-wide **Yorkshire Dialect Society** (qv).

East Yorkshires name of an infantry regiment originally formed in 1685, which later recruited in East Yorkshire, and fought under General Wolfe in the taking of Quebec.

Easter Though the name is borrowed from the Anglo Saxon goddess of spring, *Eastre*, Easter Sunday is celebrated as the anniversary of the Resurrection of Jesus in all churches, including Beverley Minster, where early on Easter morning the choir proclaims it by singing hymns from the top of the north-west tower — a tradition started in 1876 by the organist and choirmaster Dr A H Mann. It was once the custom to climb some height, such as Beamsley Beacon, near Ilkley, to see the sun rise on Easter morning. (See also **Lent, pace egg**.)

Easter baking In addition to simnel cakes (qv), various kinds of home-made cakes and biscuits are traditionally made in Yorkshire at Easter, including hot cross buns (once sold hot in the streets) for Good Friday; special biscuits were formerly baked in Whitby, with holes in the centre so they could be strung up and hung from the ceiling. In other parts of Yorkshire it is still customary to bake **Easter biscuits**, which are thick and rich, with dried fruit and candied peel.

Ebbing and Flowing Well This well, at the foot of Buckhaw Brow near Giggleswick, is said to ebb and flow between six to eight times a day. Folklore claims that good fortune comes to anyone who sees the rare 'silver thread' in the water (a spiral of trapped air) and that the origin of the well is that a nymph, pursued by a satyr, was changed by the gods into the well whose ebbing and flowing commemorates her sighs and tears.

'eck! (see *heck!*)

Gooseberries being weighed at Egton Bridge Show.

ee! expletive expressing surprise, annoyance, etc especially when used on its own: *Ee! What wor that?*. It is also used to give emphasis to a statement: *Ee, she was thin!*

ee eye

'eeam (see *heeam*)

'eear tell (see *hear tell*)

eeasins eaves of a house or stack

'eead head

een eyes WR (OE *eagan*)

ees eyes NER

efter after (also see *at-efter*)

eggs (see **Pace eggs**)

Egton Bridge Show Yorkshire's unique Gooseberry Show, dating from the founding of the Egton Bridge Old Gooseberry Society in 1800. Held on the first Tuesday in August, around thirty prizes are awarded, including those for the heaviest six gooseberries, some of which can weigh up to two ounces.

eh? (pron with short 'e') what? (ie What did you say?)

eigh (see *ey!*)

elbow-mate term used by a weaver for the person working at the next loom on the other side of the gap or alley (cf *beam-mate*) WR

eld, elder as soon *Ah'd as eld do baht as pay yon price* WR

elder cow's udder, sold in tripe shops (see **tripe**)

elderberry (see *bottery*)

eldin, eldrin kindling, firewood (ON *elding*, fire)

elicker (see *alicker*)

ellam outhouse, shed

eller elder tree (OE *eldra*)

ellers alder wood (OE *aler*)

elsin shoemaker's awl (cf Dutch *els*)

'elter (see *helter*)

emmot ant (OE *aemete*)

end-irons pair of moveable iron plates used in fireplaces to reduce size of fire

eneeaf enough NER

'engments (see *hengments*)

'en-'oil chicken run

enoo, enow for the present; just now; shortly; presently NER (abbr for *e'en now*)

enough sufficiently cooked; *t' carrots aren't enough* (ie still hard)

esh ash tree (OE *aesce*)

'esp (see *hesp*)

'es-ta? have you? (var of *hast-ta?*)

etten eaten

ettle to intend, aim, attempt (ON *aetla*)

evverin' (see *ivverin'*)

ey! (pron as 'eh-ee') hey!; interjection to express surprise or call attention to something

ey up! (pron with emphasis on second word) look out!

ey (see *ay!*)

eyes, cat's The life-saving reflectors invented by Percy Shaw of Halifax are said to have been inspired by gleaming tramlines on his way home from Queensbury late at night

eyt (pron as 'eight') to eat (OE *etan*)

F

Factory King the nickname of Richard Oastler (1789-1861). Born in Leeds, and living at Fixby Hall, Huddersfield, where he was steward, he attacked 'Yorkshire slavery' in the woollen mills, and in 1830 started a campaign which eventually led to the Ten Hours Act, improving conditions for working women and children. In this he was helped by Michael Sadler, MP for Aldborough.

faddy fussy, particular

fadge to ride at the slowest pace a horse can trot NER

faggots moulded dish with jelly on top made by pork butchers from left-overs; also known as *ducks* (qv)

fahl (see *foul*)

fain very pleased (to); gladly *Ah'm fain an' glad ter see yer*

fair really, completely (with adjective), eg *fair capped*, really surprised

fairs (see **Barnaby, Bowling Tide, Hull, Lee Gap, Scarborough, South Cave, Wibsey, Yarm**)

fairish considerable NER

faith tea meal, esp organised by churches and chapels, dependent on diners bringing their own food and pooling it (cf **Jacob's join**)

fan found (OE *fand*, past tense of *findan*)

fansome conceited; charming, pretty NER

fantickles freckles NR (? from ferntickles)

Farndale daffodils A springtime tradition for many thousands is to visit the beautiful profusion of wild daffodils along the wooded banks of the little River Dove in Farndale, in the North York Moors. Said to have been introduced by medieval monks, the daffodils may flourish here simply because conditions are ideal.

farrier smith who shoes horses; horse-doctor, vet

fashion to to bring ones-self to; have the impudence to *Ah couldn't fashion to ask 'im ter do it fer nowt* (OF *fachon*)

fast short (of), stuck (for) *Ah'm fast fer a bit o' band* (OE *faeste*)

fat rascals small, round sconelike cakes, containing currants and almonds, once esp associated with Whitby and the Ship Inn at Saltburn.

fatther (pron with short 'a') father WR

fatty cake small, round pastry-like cake, made of lard, butter, flour and sugar (see *fat rascals, Gayle bannock, sad cake*) WR

fause shrewd, cunning

favver to resemble, seem to be like *sh' favvers 'er mother* WR (var of 'favour')

fawd-yard (see *fold-yard*)

Fawkes (see **Guy Fawkes, Plot**)

feeared (see *afeeared*)

feast, feeast local fair, annual public holiday eg *Barnsla Feeast* (qv) (OF *feste*)

felk wood forming the rim of a wheel

fell[1] hill, esp of rough moorland (ON *fjall*)

fell[2] to knock down, cut down; finish (eg a warp) *Ah could 'a' felled 'im!* (said by somebody who has been angered by another), *sh's felled a warp* WR (OE *fellan*)

Fellsman Hike the earliest challenge hike in the North of England, started in 1962 by Don Thompson of the Brigantes (Brighouse District Rover Crew). The route from Ingleton to Threshfield covers sixty miles of gruelling terrain, including Ingleborough and Great Whernside. Hikers compete for the Fellsman Axe.

felly[1] (see *felk*)

felly[2] to swagger, boast WR

felon sore place, whitlow; *rewel* (qv)

Felon Sow The **Felon Sow of Rokeby**, NR, was notorious in the sixteenth century for killing swineherds, until it was eventually

destroyed on the orders of the Greyfriars of Richmond.

felted hidden; confused, matted, entangled

femmer slight, light, weak *as femmer as a musweb* (qv) NER (ON *fimmer*)

fend to manage, cope, provide (from 'defend')

fendable good at management, efficient

fent remnant or odd piece of cloth (OF *fente*, from *fendre*, to split)

ferrie first, in children's games (cf *foggie*) (var of 'first')

fest penny (see *God's penny*)

fetch to bring; to give (a blow) *'e fetched 'im such a claht* (see also *fotch*) (OE *feccan*)

fettle[1] to fix, repair, deal with; put coal on (fire) etc; prepare, clean, tidy etc (OE *fetel*)

fettle[2] condition, state of repair *i' good fettle*

fettler textile term for cleaner of looms and machinery

fettlin' day cleaning day, usually Friday, when the house was made spick and span

feyt to fight (OE *feohtan*)

feyther father

fezzon to seize greedily NER

fick to struggle, jerk, flicker, give a slight kick

Fig Sunday name once used for Palm Sunday, when figs were traditionally eaten (possibly because of the fig tree referred to in the Gospels).

Filey Brigg rocky promontory forming the northern limit of Filey Bay, according to legend built by the Devil in an attempt to bridge

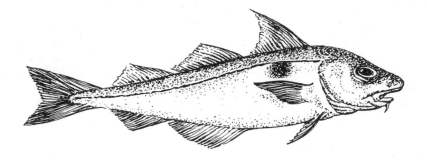

A haddock, with the Devil's legendary fingermarks, made off Filey Brigg

the North Sea. When he dropped his hammer into the sea he grabbed a haddock by mistake, and the marks on the fish are said to be the Devil's thumb- and finger-marks.

Filey Fisherman's Choir This choir of men wearing traditional fishermen's *ganseys* (qv) originated in 1823 in a mission amongst the hard-drinking, hard-swearing Filey fishermen by John Oxtoby. His many converts avoided pubs, never went to sea on Sunday, and toured the county singing mainly hymns in Primitive Methodist chapels. Though inactive after the Second World War, the choir was revived in 1960, and with its less abstinent offshoot, the Harmony Group, continues to raise money for charity.

finger poke finger stall

finnd (pron with short 'i') to find (OE *findan*, pron similarly)

Fire Mountain name sometimes given to Ingleborough because beacons and bonfires have so often been lit on its 2,373 foot summit (see **Three Peaks**)

fire-point poker (see also *poit*)

fire-poking An old Yorkshire superstition is that it is bad luck to allow anyone to poke a fire until they have known the householder for at least seven years.

first-fooit man who is the first to enter a house after midnight to herald in the New Year. Traditionally he is dark-haired and carries a piece of coal to symbolise good fortune. (See also *lucky-bod*.)

fishing Whereas Yorkshire rivers have always provided anglers with excellent sport, both for trout and grayling, and for coarse fishing, coastal and deep-sea fishing has been an essential source of livelihood. Though now greatly diminished, and in some places extinct, the dialect and traditions associated with fishing linger on. (See *coble*, Filey, *flithers*, *Steeas*, *yawl*.)

fish-'oil (see *chip-'oil*)

fit ready, prepared *art-ta fit?*, are you ready? WR

fitch seed pod of the plant vetch *as full as a fitch* (var of 'vetch')

Five Sisters Window beautiful stained-glass window in the North Transept of York Minster, according to legend presented by five maiden sisters. Charles Dickens, who visited York in 1838, elaborated on the legend and turned it into a story he included in *Nicholas Nickleby*. In this he described how when the youngest sister, Alice, died, five windows were made, each based on a design embroidered by the sisters.

fizzog face WR (var of 'physiognomy')

flacker to flutter, tremble (ME *flackeren*)

flags, flagstooanes paving or floorstones (ON *flaga*)

flahr flower; flour WR (both from OF *flor*)

flaid, flait frightened

flaik, fleeak hurdle, railings (ON *fleki*)

flannel cake kind of thin drop scone served hot with jam and cream

flappy-sket flirtatious girl ER

flat-back pocket knife, esp those made in Sheffield. The term was originally applied to cheap knives where the parts were not ground or finished separately. (See drawing on page 43.)

flat-cake large, plain, homemade teacake

flawn custard, baked in a pastry case (OF *flaon*)

flaycraw, flaycreeak scarecrow

flaysome terrifying

fleck-lenny chaffinch ER

fleet[1], flet fire, glowing embers

fleet[2] floor, inner room (OE *flet*)

fleet[3] to skim milk

fleg (see *flaik*)

flegs (see *flags*)

flep, flipper to blubber (with special reference to quivering of lower lip) (ON)

flig to fly (OE *fleogan*)

fligged fledged, with feathers

flipe[1] brim of hat, edge of cap

flipe[2] to fold a piece of cloth from the loom

flirt to flick (eg a marble) with finger and thumb WR

flish blister NR

flit to move house, move away (ON *flytja*)

A flaycrow, flaycreeak or mawkin.

flite to bawl, quarrel, reprimand, jeer (OE *flitan*)

flither limpet. Limpets once formed an important part of the economy of the Yorkshire coast, as they were extensively gathered for bait, esp by the *flither-pickers* of Staithes who combed the rocks as far as Robin Hood's Bay, for example, earning the gibe: *'Steeas yackers, flither-pickers, 'errin'-guts fer garters!'*

Flithers.

flittermouse bat (cf German *Fledermaus*)

flooats ends of wool not properly stitched (when a shuttle passes over the threads of the warp, instead of between) WR

flooer flower; flour NER (both from OF *flor*)

floss-docken foxglove

floudby cold and wild (weather) NR

flower friendly form of address *nah then, mi owd flower!* (cf *luv* (qv)) (parts of WR)

flowtered excited, flustered NR

fluff to break wind silently WR

fluffin kind of *frumenty* (qv) made with barley instead of wheat

flummox to bewilder, confuse

flup to hit WR (var of 'flip')

fluther to shudder, tremble

fodderum (see *fother-gang*)

fog a second crop of grass which follows mowing (see also York-shire Fog)

foggie first, in children's games (cf *ferrie*)

foil's fooit coltsfoot WR

foisty musty, mouldy, esp in taste (OF *fuste*, from word for wine or beer cask)

fold-yard enclosed area adjacent to farm or cowshed

fond foolish; having an affection (for) (? ME *fon*)

fond-pleeaf (see **Plough Stots**)

fooaks people NER

fooarced certain (to), eg *Is 'e fooarced ter bi theeare?*, Is he sure to be there?

foob to puff or bubble up NR

foomart stoat; polecat

football Ever since the days when lads too poor to afford a ball kicked around a *blether* (qv), football has been one of Yorkshire's most popular games, with Sheffield Football Club (founded around 1857) said to be the oldest in the world. By 1862 Sheffield alone had fifteen association football clubs, and Sheffield Wednesday is the oldest club in the Football League, which Yorkshire clubs joined from 1892. Many clubs have well-known grounds (eg Leeds United's Elland Road), and popular nicknames. (See **Blades**,

Owls, Terriers, Tigers, Tykes, and also **rugby**.)

foot-cock small heap of grass ready for spreading to make hay, made by using one foot and a hay rake

for all in spite of the fact that *'e supped nowt, for all 'e wor thirsty*

for-'and in front (with work etc)

force (see *foss*)

Foresters The Ancient Order of Foresters Friendly Society traces its origins to a meeting of Royal Foresters at Knaresborough in 1745. The first official meeting was in 1790 in Leeds, with the opening of Court No1. 'Forestry' spread all over the world in the Victorian period, and still maintains its ritual and symbolism, donating to various charities, as well as looking after the welfare of its members.

forenooin morning WR

forkin'-robin earwig NER (see also *twinge*, *twitch-bell*)

forra'd forward

foss waterfall, eg Janets Foss near Malham and Mill Gill Foss at Askrigg (ON *fors*, Danish *fos*)

fost first *fost o' t' sooart*, the first of its kind

fotch (see *fetch*)

fother to feed (stock) (var of 'fodder')

fother-gang space above cattle stall from which hay could be lowered; passageway in front of stalls (ON *fother*)

fotherley early (of grass etc) NER

fo'tnit fortnight

fo'ty (pron with short 'o') forty

fo'ty-legs centipede WR

foul ugly, grim-looking (OE *ful*)

fowd yard (see *fold-yard*)

fower four

fowerdy, fowerty, fowaty forty; fourth man in a team or on a farm

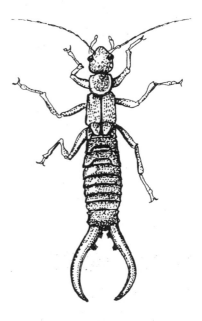

Forkin'-robin, twinge or twitchbell.

fowk(s) people WR

fowt fought

fra, frev from

frame to get organised, set about a task; to show promise (OE *framian*, to be helpful)

frame thissen! pull yourself together and get on with the job!

frammled upset, disjointed

fratch to argue, disagree, quarrel

freeten to frighten

Ancient frith stool in Beverley Minster.

fresh¹ new *Owt fresh?*, Any news? (OF *fresche*)

fresh² slightly drunk (cf German *frech*, cheeky)

fret mist or fog coming in from the sea (cf *harr*)

frith stool stone chair used by those seeking sanctuary. There are two in Yorkshire, the best known being on the right of the altar of Beverley Minster. It is believed to have been provided by King Athelstan some time in the tenth century. Any debtor or criminal sitting here could claim sanctuary, and be given food and lodging for thirty days. If the canons could not obtain pardon, the person could become a **frithman**, forfeiting possessions and taking an oath of obedience to the minster and the town. There is another **frith stool**, rather interestingly carved, in Sprotbrough Church, near Doncaster. (OE *frith-stol*, peace-chair)

Fritter Thursday (see Fruttace Wednesday)

frock dress (more commonly used in dialect than SE)

frosk frog (OE *frosc*)

frost sharp small stones stuck in horse's shoe

fruggan curved rake for use under an oven (OF *fourgan*)

frumenty, frumety Christmas dish consisting of a kind of thick porridge made from crushed hulled or pearled wheat (whole grains), which is *kibbled* (qv) and soaked overnight, and is then *creed* (qv) in milk with sugar or treacle, and spices like cinnamon, cloves or nutmeg. In some parts of Yorkshire a **frumenty bell** used to ring from churches in the early evening as a signal for the **frumenty** to be cooked. It was usually served in individual bowls on Christmas Eve, and accompanied by **Yule cake** or **spice cake** (qv), **pepper cake** (qv), apple pie etc. (OF *froment*, wheat)

Fruttace Wednesday old name for Ash or **Hash Wednesday** (qv) when it was the custom in certain parts of Yorkshire, such as the Craven and NER, to cook *fruttaces* or fritters, made of flour, eggs, apples, dried fruit and spices. (Sometimes this took place the following day, hence the name **Fritter Thursday**.) Possibly linked with the pancakes eaten the previous day, the custom is curious, as Ash Wednesday was the start of the fast of Lent. (*Fruttace* seems to be a var of 'fritters', perhaps influenced by 'fruit'.)

fruzzins bits of woollen or cotton thread, fluff

fud waste, refuse, esp from a loom WR

fuddle treat, time of self-indulgence, eating chocolates etc; annual works outing, usually to seaside

fufflement finery, showy clothes

fuggy (see *foggie*)

full up¹ having had sufficient to eat

full up² tearful, overcome with emotion

fuller's earth kind of clay used in *fulling* (qv)

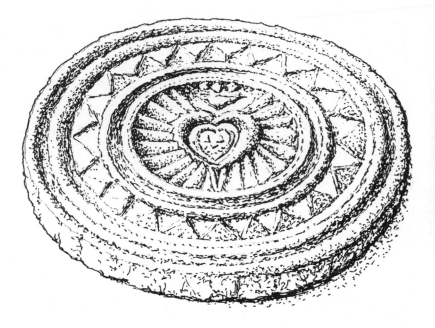

Funeral biscuit.

fulling process of washing woollen fabric, then squeezing and rolling it, to increase the fabric's density

fullock sudden rush; blow, punch *they cem oot all of a fullock* NER, *a fullock o' watter from t' tap* WR (see *bull-fullock*)

fun found (OE *funde*)

funeral biscuits Like funeral cakes or *arval bread* (qv), these were made for the mourners, and sometimes distributed as soon as they arrived. In the Dales they were usually a kind of shortbread flavoured with caraway seed, and stamped with a design, often heart-shaped. **Funeral biscuits** made by confectioners were enclosed in printed wrappers bearing appropriate verses from funeral hymns.

funny-ossity person of strange, quirkish behaviour (cf *commonossity*)

fust first

fuzz-ball puff-ball fungus

fuzzock donkey

G

gab¹ mouth (of animal) (var of *gob* (qv))

gab² to gossip indiscreetly, tell tales

gadge man, fellow (Romany *gorgio*, man who is not a gypsy)

gaffer foreman, boss

gailker tub used for brewing (cf *gulleyvat*)

gain quick (way), near (ON *gegn*)

gain-'and near at hand

gait (see *gate*)

gale beer beer made from sweet gale or bog myrtle NR (OE *gagel*)

gallock-'anded left-handed

gallocker left-handed person

gallowa small horse (under fifteen hands), pony (from the Galloway region of Scotland)

gallusses braces for trousers (double pl, var of 'gallows')

gammashes gaiters, sometimes covering leg as well as foot NER

gammerstang an immoral or wanton girl or woman NR

gammy lame, injured (esp leg)

gan, gang to go NER (OE *gangan*)

gang gallery in a leadmine NR

gansey jersey, pullover. The *gansey* is the typical attire of the Yorkshire coast fisherman, and is traditionally home-knitted. In the past most *ganseys* were knitted in Scarborough, and were of such a distinctive style that as recently as the Second World War a sailor lost at sea was identified by his Scarborough *gansey*. (From Guernsey, cf Jersey.)

Gaping Ghyll The best-known and most awe-inspiring of Yorkshire's many pot-holes, this is a cavern inside Ingleborough, with a waterfall dropping 365 feet into a chamber 460 feet long and 100 feet wide.

gantry platform, scaffolding, footbridge; wooden stand for beer barrels; structure supporting cage hoist at pit head (OF *gauntier*)

gap-steead gap in wall, fence etc

garl matter forming in corner of eye WR

garnet (see *mungo*)

gaston lively, high-spirited (eg child or pony) WR (? corruption of F *gascon*)

garth small grassed enclosure adjoining a house; plot of land on which liquorice was grown in Pontefract area (ON *garthr*)

garthangle pole with a prong at the end for hauling fish on board NER

gat got (ME, from ON *geta*)

gate street, way, eg *'Aht o' t' gate!*, Get out of the way!; manner; common pasture; aisle between looms in a mill; gallery in a coalmine; also used in compounds such as Kirkgate, 'the way to the church', Briggate, 'the way to the bridge', etc (ON *gata*)

gaum heed; common sense *Tak no gaum on 'im!*, Pay no attention to him! (ON *gaumr*)

gaumless stupid, lacking in common sense

gauve to stare

gauve-Andrew simpleton

gauvin'-tahme twilight (from the idea of staring, straining the eyes)

gauvison (see *gauve-Andrew*)

Gayle bannock kind of *fatty cake* (qv) with currants, made at Gayle in Wensleydale, and once the staple food taken to work by local quarrymen.

gavlock crowbar, lever (OE *gafeluc*)

gawback (see *gavlock*)

gawby fool, dunce; sometimes applied humorously to particular places, eg *'a Wibsa Gawby'*, *'a Pudsa Gawby'*

gawfer kind of thin biscuit or teacake, often made square and marked by lines of *gawfer-mould* (cf F *gaufre*, waffle)

gawk (see *gowk*)

gawky left-handed

gawm (see *gaum*)

gawp to gape, stare (ON *gapa*)

Gavlock.

gawp-'eead stupid person

gawpin handful; as much as can be held in both hands held together

Gawthorpe Coal-carrying Competition Easter Monday event held at Gawthorpe, near Ossett. Started by local miners in 1963, the race involves carrying a hundredweight sack of coal over an uphill course of nearly a mile.

gearing harness for horse pulling a cart

gee (back)! turn right! (to horse)

gee up! faster! (to horse)

gee whoa! bear left (to horse)

geean gone NER

geeas goose NER

gems (pron with hard 'g') glasses or spectacles WR

gerr away! get away! (in the sense of 'stop pulling my leg; I don't believe you')

Gerston Grassington

getten got

gev' gave

gey very; considerable NER

ghyll, gill deep and wooded ravine, often with waterfall, eg **Troller's Gill** (qv) (ON *gjel*)

ghosts So many towns and villages in Yorkshire have local ghost stories that it is impossible to list more than a few famous ones. (See *barguest*, **Bolling Hall**, **Calverley**, *guytresh*, *padfoot*, **Skull**.)

giants (see **Rombald**, **Market Weighton**, **Penhill**, **Wade**)

gi'en given

gill (pron 'jill') in Yorkshire this is half a pint, not the standard quarter pint (OF *gille*, water pot)

gillbox part of a spinning frame for thinning slivers of flax or wool preparatory to spinning (named after the Gill family of New York Linen Mills, Summerbridge, near Harrogate)

gillyvat (see *gulleyvat*)

gilt young sow (ON *gyltr*)

gimmer young female sheep, esp before it lambs, and between the first and second shearing (ON *gymbr*)

ginnel narrow passage between buildings or walls *'e couldn't stop a pig in a ginnel* (said of a bow-legged man) (see **snicket**)

gip¹ to retch, to feel like wanting to vomit

gip² to gut and clean fish NER

gippy starling

gird attack of pain or dizziness; fit, spasm

girn to grin, pull a face (var by metathesis of 'grin')

gitten (see *getten*)

give over! gi'e ovver! stop! (whatever you are doing)

gizzened over-full, choked, esp with emotion

gizzern throat (OF *gesier*)

glass-alleys marbles made of glass (see *dobby*, *taws*)

glave cold and shivery (weather) NR

glazy oilskin coat (Yorkshire coast fisherman's term)

glazzoner sharp blow, esp across the eyes

glee to squint WR

gleg glance, quick look, peep

gleyd tight-fisted, greedy and wilful (child) WR (? OE *gleda*, hawk)

glishy, glisky very bright (of sky), esp if thought to forecast rain

glocken to start to thaw NR

gloppened, glottened astonished, flabbergasted (ON *glupna*)

goaf miner's term for space left after coal has been dug out

gob mouth (? Celtic *gob*, beak)

gobby loudmouthed, gossipy WR, esp S Yorks

gobsmacked speechless

gobstopper very large sweet, hard and globular, changing colour as different layers are sucked away

God's penny small sum paid at a hiring fair or *stattis* (qv)

gog short piece of wood used for killing fish and removing hook NER

goiker (see *gallocker*)

goit channel of water (OE *geotan*, to pour)

gollie baby bird without feathers (see *bare-gollie*)

gollop to swallow greedily (var of 'gulp')

gommeril fool

gooan gone WR

goodies sweets NER (cf *spice*)

Goodies title story of the collection of humorous ER tales by the Rev W F Turner (1912).

gooise goose WR (OE *gos*)

gooise-gobs, -gogs gooseberries (see Egton)

gool(d)ans, gow(d)ans (see *cowls*)

gore odd corner of ploughed land (see *butt*); piece of cloth inserted in a garment (OE *gara*, triangle of land)

gorister cut of beef between neck and brisket

Gormire lake below Whitestonecliff, both places the subject of legends. Like **Semerwater** (qv), Gormire is said to have a town submerged beneath its waters, yet it is also supposed to be bottomless. (See **White Mare Crag**.)

gormless (see gaumless)

gossie gosling

goulders (see *cowls*)

gow (see *by gow!*)

Gowcar lilies reference to the jibe about Golcar, Huddersfield: *'Gowcar — wheeare t' lilies comes thru!'*

gowd gold WR

gowk cuckoo (see *huntin' t' gowk*) (ON *gaukr*)

gowlans, gowldens marigolds; buttercups NER

gowldy yellowhammer

gowled up stuck together (eg eyelids)

gowpen (see *gawpin*)

goz, gozzle to spit

graave to dig (in some areas used in the sense of to turn over earth with a spade, as distinct from 'dig', ie to break up earth with a mattock or pick) (OE *grafan*)

graavin'-fork long-handled fork for digging up sandworms NER

gradely excellent (rather more common in Lancashire dialect, but also in southern WR around the Pennines)

grain prong of a fork; branch of a tree; branch of a stream (ON *grein*)

grand excellent, greatly admired

grater to grate

greck weakest of a litter of pigs (see also **recklin**)

greean (see **groine**)

greeave (see **graave**)

Green Howards name in official use from at least 1747 for the infantry regiment of Col Charles Howard. As there was also Lt Gen Thomas Howard's regiment, to avoid confusion the regiments were named after the colour of their uniform collar-facings — 'Buff' and 'Green' Howards. Whereas the **Duke of Wellington's** (qv) are associated with the WR, the Green Howards have strong links with the NR and ER, including a museum at Richmond.

greet to weep NR

gressins stairs

grewp (see **groop**)

greys grey peas, served hot at pie and pea shops etc (see **carlins**)

grey slates typical Yorkshire roofing — slabs of stone, not slate

grid bicycle

griming a sprinkling or light covering of snow

Grimshaw of Haworth Many anecdotes are told of the eccentric vicar, the Rev William Grimshaw (1708-62), such as how he drove his parishioners to church with a horse whip, his zeal increasing his congregation from a dozen to 1,500. 'Mad Grimshaw' did much to support John Wesley and **Methodism** (qv) in the WR.

grindle bar, rail

grindle-cowk grindstone worn too smooth for grinding, but put to various other uses

grindle-stooane grindstone

grip[1] (see **groop**)

grip[2] deep trench dug for the cultivation of liquorice in the Pontefract area

gripe fork, usually with three prongs, used esp for turning soil, lifting and spreading manure (OE *gripan*)

Grisedale pie potato pie said to have been made at a farmhouse in Grisedale, Wensleydale, which was forgotten for six months. Even though the potatoes had sprouted it was put on the table, hence the saying that something or somebody would turn up again *'like t' Grisedale pie'*.

groine[1] snout (of pig)

groine[2] to cut grass, esp with sickle or scythe

gronfeyther grandfather

growler jocular term for **stand pie** (qv) or pork pie WR

grooin (see **groine**)

groop drain in a cowshed (ON *grop*)

grouse shooting one of Yorkshire's best-known traditional sports, the season opening on the Twelfth of August. There are many square miles of grouse moors, and the oldest shooting surviving butts, on Rushworth Moor, date from 1830.

grum severe, angry, grim

grund ground (OE *grund*)

grundid buried, underground (in hibernation) *as 'ard as a grundid tooad*

guide-stoup old form of milepost and guide-post consisting of a tall stone (see **stoup**)

Guide-stoup.

guider sinew, muscle; short rod used to move and control a *hoop* (qv); rope for steering *bogie* (qv)

guilp thin liquid

Guisborough Priory Augustinian priory, founded in 1129, to which legend ascribes an underground passage leading to a chest of gold, guarded by a raven capable of turning into the Devil.

guisers *mummers* (qv) taking part in Halloween traditions such as *cakin' Neet* (qv) and various Christmas and New Year events, whose faces are blackened or disguised, hence the origin of the term.

gully large-bladed knife

gulleyvat vat for brewing ale

gum (see *by gum!*)

gumption common sense

gurning contest of pulling faces (see *girn*)

gurt big (var of 'great')

guttle to guzzle, eat greedily

guy effigy, esp when paraded round by children ('A penny for the guy!') and then burnt on a bonfire. The term comes from the first name of the notorious Yorkshireman, Guy Fawkes, now one of the most overworked words in the English language, mainly in the USA, where it can refer to any person, male or female. A *guy* is not burnt at St Peters School, York, where Guy Fawkes was a pupil, nor usually at Scotton, where he lived, and in former times *guys* were not burnt in certain other places, such as Wakefield. (See **Guy Fawkes, Plot.**)

'Guye Fauxe of Scotton, gentilman', here seen in Spanish guise as a conspirator.

Guy Fawkes Yorkshireman who unwittingly originated one of England's most colourful traditions. He was born in York in 1570, educated at St Peters School, and brought up a Protestant. When his widowed mother remarried, Guy moved with her and his sisters to Scotton, near Knaresborough, where he became a convert to the Catholic faith. His experience as a captain in the Spanish army led to the plotters using him to position thirty-six barrels of gunpowder under the House of Lords, with the intention of destroying James I on the 5th November 1605. He was arrested on the 4th, tortured in the Tower, and hung, drawn and quartered on the 31st January, 1606. (See **guy, Plot**.)

guytresh evil spirit, esp an apparition that is a portent of death, said to be a terrifying figure with eyes as big as saucers. Mainly WR (eg the **Horton Guytresh**) but there is, for example, the NR **Goathland Guytresh**, said to appear as a huge black goat with blazing red eyes and horns tipped with fire. (See *barguest*.)

Gypsey Race the name of a stream near Wharram-le-Street in the Yorkshire Wolds, eventually flowing into Bridlington harbour. It is said to flood as a portent of scarcity or disaster, as it is supposed to have done before each of the World Wars. (Origin obscure, but cf F *eaux gypsées*, water containing gypsum.)

H

Haas, Hahse Hawes in Wensley-dale

hacker to hestitate (cf *ocker*)

hackle clothing *i' good 'ackle*, in good form

hagg division of a wood, esp on a rugged bank; part of wood to be felled, marked out by *hagg stakes* (ON *hagi*)

haggle to hail (OE *hagolian*)

hag mist thick mist or fog

hagworm snake; adder NER

hahse house (see *house* for special usage) WR

hahsummivver however WR

haigs haws (OE *haga*)

hales handles of a plough NER

half-timer child who worked for half a day in the mill and spent the other half in school. This became illegal in 1922.

Halifax gibbet This guillotine-style form of execution was so feared it was referred to in the prayer known as the **beggars' litany** (qv). The original blade, an axe head weighted with lead, is preserved in the Bankfield Museum, and in Gibbet Street there is a replica of the machine.

Halifax legs one leg which is shorter than the other through walking on steep hillsides (jocular term)

Halifax Thump Sunda Sunday following the 24th June, the traditional start of the annual fair known as **Halifax Thump**.

hallock to idle, dawdle

Hallowe'en The Eve of All Hallows or All Saints' Day in Yorkshire, as elsewhere, was once marked by customs connected with belief in witches, ghosts and prediction. It was sometimes called *Nutty-crack Neet* from the custom of throwing pairs of nuts in the fire. If they burned together it was a sign of married happiness; if they cracked and flew apart, the opposite was true. The tradition of playing tricks has largely been transferred from the 31st October to the 4th November. (See **Mischief Neet, Cakin' Neet, saumas**.)

halsh loop, knot (esp round neck)

hames curved pieces of wood or metal fastened to or placed over a horse collar, to which traces are attached; horse collar

hanch to snatch at, attempt to bite ER

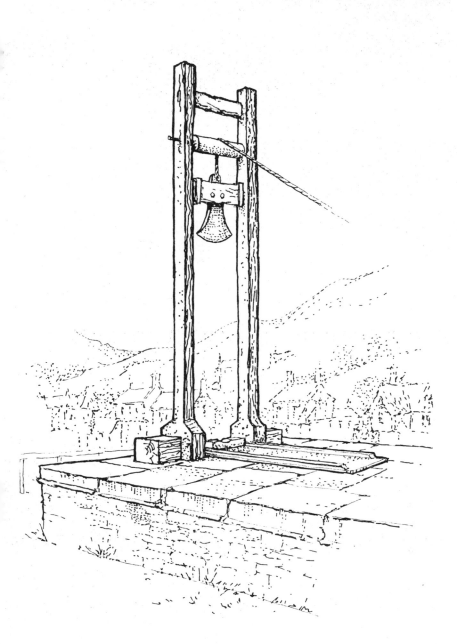

The Halifax gibbet: 'From Hell, Hull and Halifax, good Lord deliver us!'.

hand of glory grisly device used by burglars to bring them luck, help to open locks and put the inhabitants of the house to sleep.

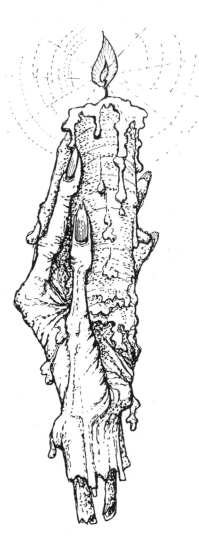

Hand of glory.

The hand was supposed to be taken from the corpse of a criminal on the gibbet. It was embalmed and dried in the sun, its fingers bent to hold a candle made from tallow and human fat. The flame was to be extinguished by pouring on blood or skimmed milk. Legends concerning the hand of glory come mostly from the NR (eg Danby Dale).

hand-runnin' following on, in succession *three days 'and-runnin*

Handale Serpent fiery, dragon-like creature of Handale, NR, which according to folklore preyed on local women until it was killed by a youth in armour named Scaw.

hangments (see *hengments*)

handsel money given to strike a bargain or bind a contract; the using of something for the first time (ON *handsala*, bargain)

hap to wrap, cover

happed tucked in (bed) (see *happins*)

happen¹ (almost always *'appen*) perhaps *'appen they've got lost*

happen² to have something happen to one *'e's 'appened an accident* (ON *happ*, chance, luck)

happen on to come across

happins covering, esp bed-clothes; substantial covering of snow

hard on (pron with emphasis on second word) fast asleep

hardin coarse, brown linen, esp used for making *brats* (qv)

hardlins hardly NER

harr¹ mist, foggy drizzle (cf Dutch *haere*)

harr² hole in stone carrying spikes on which a door turns (OE *heorr*)

harrier cross-country runner or walker, esp when member of team or club

Harrogate (see Harrogate Toffee, spa, Stray)

Harrogate Headache caused by the fumes of hydrogen sulphide rising from the water of the Old Sulphur Well or **Stinking Spaw** (qv)

Harrogate Toffee kind of butterscotch, made in Harrogate by the firm of John Farrah since 1840

Harry Ramsdens Now world-famous for its haddock and chips, this establishment at White Cross, Guiseley, started when Harry Ramsden first sold fish and chips here in 1928 from a 10 foot by 6 foot wooden hut. He opened a restaurant in 1931, then in 1936 an exact replica adjoining it, and doubled its size in 1968. With a million customers a year, it has become one of Yorkshire's best-known institutions. (See *chip-'oil*.)

Hart Leap Well spring near Richmond where a hunted deer is said to have died after making a prodigious leap, the subject of a poem by Wordsworth.

harve! turn left! (to horse)

harvest customs The harvest festival, with churches and chapels decorated with flowers, fruit and vegetables, is a comparatively recent tradition, dating from a revival of **Lammas** (qv) in Cornwall (though later in the

year) in 1843. Of great antiquity, however, are the customs of the **kern supper** (qv) and the **mell supper** (qv). A 'Harvest of the Sea' is held at Flamborough each October.

Hash Wednesday name mistakenly given to Ash Wednesday, because of the confusion between 'ash' (from the custom of the priest marking foreheads with ash) and 'hash', the latter dish sometimes being made on this day from previously-cooked mutton. In some parts of Yorkshire it was the tradition to make fritters on this day. (See **Fruttace Wednesday**.)

hask rough, dry, esp of throat; deteriorated condition of woollen garments after being incorrectly washed; also used to describe hard water, cold and dry weather etc

haslet cold form of finely-minced pork, with cereal and seasoning etc, in a veil or skin (OF *hastelet*)

hast-ta? have you?

hatch lower half of divided door (see *heck*)

hattock a *stook* (qv) of sheaves of corn, traditionally twelve, with a covering made of two sheaves to keep off the rain

hauf, hawf half

haugh hill, usually steep

haust cough, cold on chest

haver (pron with short 'a') oats (ON *hafre*)

Haverah legendary one-legged man to whom **John of Gaunt** (qv) is supposed to have granted as much land as he could hop round on the longest day — the result of which was **Haverah Park**, near

Harrogate, in which are the ruins of a hunting lodge called John of Gaunt's Castle.

haverbread kind of oatcake made from a stiff dough, then rolled out and cooked on a *bakst'n* (qv) (see *oatcake*)

havercake (see **haverbread**)

Havercake Lads nickname given to soldiers in the **Duke of Wellington's Regiment** (qv), many of whom came from Yorkshire and were known to eat oatcake. From about 1782 it was the custom of recruiting sergeants to go round with a **havercake** stuck on the point of a sword, persuading men to join and take the king's shilling.

hawp'ny halfpenny (see *spice*)

hawporth halfpence-worth

hay-mow, -mew place where hay is kept in a barn

hay ride (see **Walkington Hay-Ride**)

hay-timin' haymaking (see *footcock, hub, mew* etc)

hazzled roan, dappled (eg *leet-'azzled*, if white predominates) NER

hear tell to hear (information), gather (that) **Ah '*ear tell they've flitted*, I hear they've moved**

heark(en) to listen to *'eark at 'im!* (OE *heorcian*)

heart-sluffened heartbroken, very upset

Heavy Woollen District area round Dewsbury, Batley and

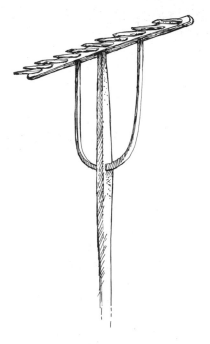

Typical rake used at hay-timin'.

Morley formerly associated with the manufacture of carpets, blankets, *mungo* (qv) and *shoddy* (qv).

heck! euphemism for hell

heck rack, railings, esp in a stable, cowshed etc, where hay is kept; frame across river for controlling fish (eg **salmon heck**); upper half of a hatch door (OE *hec*)

heckle to dress flax by combing out and splitting the fibres with a special kind of comb called a **heckle** (var of **hackle**, from OE *haecel*, related to 'hook')

Havercake Lads being recruited, a havercake stuck on the sword.

heckler flax dresser

heeaf part of moor apportioned to flock of sheep NER

heeam home NER

heed to mind, take notice *nivver 'eed*, never mind

heft handle of knife or tool *nivver judge a blade bi t' 'eft* (OE *haefte*)

hefted equipped, furnished *weel-'efted wi brass* (qv)

helter knot, ravel, confusion

hengments a mild curse, usually in the exclamation of astonishment: *what the hengments!* (from hangment, hanging)

hennot haven't

Heptonstall The Pennine village was the subject of the leg-pulling verse, probably by Halifax people: *'Halifax is built o' wax, Heptonstall o' stooane; I' Halifax ther's bonny lasses, I' Heptonstall ther's nooan.'* (See **Octagon**.)

Hepworth Feast said to date from 1665, when the village of Hepworth, near Holmfirth, was delivered from the plague by strict quarantine. Held on the last Monday in June, it includes a procession and hymn-singing led by the local band.

Hermit of Rombalds Moor the nickname of Job Senior (born in 1780), an eccentric who eventually settled at Burley Woodhead. He lived frugally in the ruins of what had once been his cottage, wandering about to earn his living by his remarkable ability to sing bass, alto, tenor or soprano. He was also a soothsayer, weather-forecaster and heavy drinker. He died aged seventy-seven, and is commemorated by the Hermit Inn at Burley Woodhead.

Herriot Country popular name for the area made famous through the books of James Herriot and the TV series based on them, namely Wensleydale (Askrigg was 'Darrowby') and Swaledale (eg Langthwaite). In real life, Herriot is the pen name of Alfred Wight, whose vet's surgery was well to the east, at Thirsk.

hesp catch, latch, fastening

hessle hazel

heughed term for sheep kept on moor (see *heeaf*)

heyt! command to a horse to start (cf *gee-up!*)

hickin'-stick stick used for lifting

hickin'-barra barrow for lifting sacks of grain etc

hig, higg temper, annoyance, huff, offence; hurry *'e's takken 'igg*, he's taken offence (? ON *hoggva*)

hind farm worker; foreman on a farm (OE *hine*)

hippins baby's nappy (from its being worn round the hips)

hippin stooanes, steeans stepping stones

hiring fair (see *stattis*)

hissel, hissen himself

Hitching Stone boundary stone near Cowling, said to be the biggest boulder in Yorkshire (an estimated 1,200 tons) and to have been dropped by the wife of the giant **Rombald** (qv) who was sweeping up the moor. The stone is also supposed to have been associated with the druids.

hoaf, hooaf half NR

hob¹ (see *quoits, shoeing the hob*)

hob² part of range or casing level with fire grate

hob³ sprite, goblin, esp in Cleveland, and reflected in local placenames such as **Hob Hole** (Runswick Bay), where the *hob* was reputed to be able to cure *kincough* (qv) if this rhyme was recited there: *'Hob Hole Hob! Ma bairn's getten t' kincough: Tak it off! tak it off!'*

hobbin' foot cobbler's last WR

hocker (see *hacker*)

hod to hold *'od on!*, wait! (OE *healdan*)

hodden held

hog¹ to spy on courting couples WR

hog, hogg² male pig

hog³ young sheep before its first shearing, around a year old (OE *hogg*, prob from Celtic)

hoil hole; untidy or scruffy place; doorway (used in many compounds such as *muck-'oil* etc) *what a hoil!, put t' wood i' t' 'oil!*, shut the door! WR (OE *hol*, with Mercian vowel shift — see introduction)

Hole of Horcum (see *Devil's Punchbowl*)

Hollantide the time around All Saints Day (1st November), preceded by **Hallowe'en** (qv) and All Saints Day or **Saumas** (qv)

hollin holly

Holmfirth Anthem name given to *Pratty Flowers*, an old song sung so frequently in the Holme Valley area that it became identified with it. The title comes from the last lines: 'I will take thee to yon green gardens, Where the pratty, pratty flowers grow.' In 1914 it was arranged for four voices by J Perkin, conductor of the Holmfirth Choral Society, but it dates from the early nineteenth century, as it refers to fighting the French and Spanish.

honeycomb kind of **tripe** (qv)

hooal hole, place NER

hooam home

Hood (see **Robin Hood**)

hood end corner of large open fireplace, with space for a seat

hooin to harrass, hurt, ill-treat (OF *honnir*)

hoop circle of iron or steel trundled along by a child using a *guider* (qv)

hoose house (qv) NER

hopper basket or bag tied round the waist, containing seed to be sown by hand; in the steel industry, container for receiving ore and passing it into the blast furnace

hopple to tie together or otherwise restrain legs of an animal

hornblowing ancient custom maintained in two places in Yorkshire. The **Ripon** (qv) **hornblowing** is performed every night at 9 pm, when the **wakeman's horn** is sounded at each corner of the obelisk in the market square, and then in front of the mayor's house. Originating as a reassuring signal that the **wakeman** (qv) and his constables had taken over for the night, the custom reputed to go back to the granting of Ripon's charter in AD 886. Less well-known, but at least as old, is the **hornblowing** at Bainbridge in Wensleydale. Also at 9 pm three blasts are blown (traditionally by a member of the Metcalfe family) every night between the 28th September and Shrove Tuesday. The early **hornblowing** served to guide travellers through the Forest of Wensleydale, and may even have been connected with the Roman fort at Bainbridge.

The Ripon hornblower.

Horngarth (see **Penny Hedge**)
Hornsea Mere traditionally the subject of a violent dispute over fishing rights, when the monks of Meaux Abbey, near Beverley, and St Marys Abbey in York were reduced to hand-to-hand fighting. The York monks were victorious, but allowed their rivals to fish along the southern shore of this freshwater lake.
horse fairs (see **Barnaby, Hull, Lee Gap, Wibsey, Yarm**)
horse racing The oldest classic horse race in the county of Yorkshire is the St Leger, run at Doncaster in the second week in September, founded in 1776 by Colonel Anthony St Leger. The tradition of horse racing goes back to Roman times, and Yorkshire has nine courses, including York's Knavesmire, laid out in 1730 near the local Tyburn, where hangings took place. The training of racehorses is particularly associated with the town of Middleham in Wensleydale. (See also **Kiplingcotes Derby**.)
horseshoe As in other counties, **horseshoes** are thought lucky if fastened up with the ends uppermost — otherwise the 'luck will fall out'. In some parts of Yorkshire a nail was added for each of the first six days of Christmas. They were then taken out one by one till the twelfth day, when the horseshoe fell down — a device to keep the Devil at bay.
hosen stockings (obsolete, but occurring in versions of the *Lyke Wake Dirge* (qv))

hoss horse; Yorkshire is proverbially a county of horses, hence the saying 'Give a Yorkshireman a halter, and he'll find a horse'. The reputation for horse-stealing is reflected in the saying 'Shake a bridle over a Yorkshireman's grave, and he'll get up and steal the horse'. (See also **Yorkshire coat of arms**.) (OE *hors*, ON *hross*)
hoss-teng (see *clegg*)
hot to hurt NER
houpie small horse NR
house house, as distinct from kitchen *gu thru inter t' ahse* WR
how hill, esp if round NR
hub large heap of dried grass that is almost hay
Hubberholme land-letting New Year custom, now usually held on the first Monday in January, of holding a 'candle auction' to let land for the benefit of the sick and the poor in the parish of Hubberholme, upper Wharfedale. Held in the George Inn opposite the church, where a preliminary service is held. The vicar and his wardens occupy one room, 'the House of Lords', and the bidders, mostly sheep farmers, another, 'the Commons'. The auction must be completed before a candle burns out.
hubbleshoo tumult, commotion, confusion, jumble NR
Huddersfield Choral (see **choirs**)
huffil finger stall ER
hug, hugger to carry
huggin armful
huggins hips
hull[1] hollow; steep slope
hull[2] husk, shell (peas etc)

The church at Hubberholme, scene of the New Year land-letting.

hull³ pigsty NR; grinding shop WR (Sheffield)

Hull Fair reputed to be the largest travelling fair in Europe, this was originally a fair for horses, cattle and sheep, established by royal charter in 1299. Held each October on a special fourteen acre site in Walton Street, the fair is officially opened by the lord mayor ringing a bell.

Humber keel sailing ship of up to 57 feet long, with mast up to 50 feet tall, commonly used on the Humber and larger canals. Also known as the **Yorkshire keel**. (See **Tom pudding**.)

hummelled without horns (cf *doddy, polly¹*)

hummer! (often with the 'h' pronounced) mild curse, euphemism for hell, used esp in *'What the hummer!'* and *'to play hummer'*; also *Well, Ah'll go to hummer!*

Hummer Nick the Devil; *we ran like Hummer Nick* WR

Hunmouth fictional name for Hull in the novels of E C Booth

hunting One of Yorkshire's oldest traditions, with its own customs and folklore. As early as the twelfth century the Pope complained of the excessive hunting of the Archdeacon of Cleveland. In the thirteenth century, King John hunted deer in the Forest of Knaresborough, and in the fourteenth Edward III and **John of Gaunt** (qv) hunted boar in Yorkshire. Fox hunting was at its most popular in the nineteenth century. Yorkshire meets include Bramham Moor, the York and Ainsty, and Zetland, but the oldest is the Bilsdale Hunt founded near Helmsley in 1670 by the Duke of Buckinghamshire.

hurrier child who pushed or pulled the *corves* (qv) or tubs of coal from the coalface to the mineshaft WR

hunt t' gowk kind of April Fool's custom in places such as Skipton, whereby someone would be asked to deliver a letter, the recipient of which would in turn send the bearer on a false errand. (See *gowk*.)

hutch up to move over a little (on a seat)

Hutton Conyers This village near Ripon was once the venue for traditional meals on New Year's Day to mark the allocation of sheep-grazing rights by the manorial court. Each shepherd brought a large apple pie and a sweet cake, and a wooden spoon to eat the **frumenty** (qv) provided by the steward and bailiff.

I

i' in (before vowels usually becomes **in**) (see also **i' t'**)

ice shoggles icicles NER (ON, cf Norwegian *isjukel*)

idle lazy (ie indolent, rather than just unoccupied)

idle-back lazy person; support for rod used by anglers; scouring stone on a long handle; device attached to a kettle so it can be tilted while still over the fire

'igg (see *hig*)

Ilkla Mooar *On Ilkla Mooar baht 'at*, now well established as a kind of Yorkshire anthem, originated in the leg-pulling verses made up by members of a choir on an outing to Ilkley Moor, who sang their comic words to the hymn tune 'Cranbrook'. This had been composed by Thomas Clark in 1805, but the origin of the song seems to have been not long before 1877, when the tune was used by Heptonstall Glee Club for these words. The good-natured mockery is of a choir member who has left the party to go courting Mary Jane; since he is not wearing a hat he is likely to catch his death of cold on the breezy moors. The traditional opening verse runs: *'Wheeare wor ta bahn when Ah saw thee, On Ilkla Mooar baht 'at?'*. A later and less logical variant opening is: *'Wheeare esta bin sin Ah saw thee?'*. There have been all kinds of arrangements of the tune, the most original being Eric Fenby's overture 'Rossini on Ilkla Moor'.

ill-thriven poorly-developed ER

imber raspberry (cf German *Himbeere*)

inby miner's term for going away from the main shaft towards the coalface; passage used for this (see *outby*)

ing meadow, esp near a river (ON *eng*)

ingle-neuk corner of fireside, esp in old open-hearth fireplaces

inkle kind of coarse linen tape used for binding hooves, or fastening meat to a spit etc *as thick as inkle-weyvers*, very intimate

inoo (see *enoo*)

intak(e) land recovered and enclosed from rougher land or moorland

inther-ends poor crop of corn ER

Ivelet Bridge, Swuledale, one of many Yorkshire localities said to be haunted by a barguest.

Wolds wagon, with ivverin and shelvins to increase capacity.

intiv into
i' t' (pron 'it') in the
'ippins (see *hippins*)
Ivelet Bridge attractive hump-backed packhorse bridge over the Swale, said to be haunted by a *barguest* (qv), in this case a headless black dog which glides to the bridge, then disappears over the edge. There are also tales of a ghostly woman in black, and a donkey with eyes of brass.
ivin ivy
ivver ever
ivverin top rim round sides of a cart (see *shelvins*)

J

Jackdaw Nick alternative name for **Troller's Gill** (qv)

Jacob's join communal meal in village hall, Sunday school etc, where food is given and pooled (cf **faith tea**)

jag load ER

jagger a man who used horses or ponies to carry goods, esp the leader of a packhorse team (see **packhorse** routes)

jaggin small load of hay; (plural) bits of hay NER

jannock fair, right *it's nut jannock* (? ON *jamn*)

jarp (see *jowp*)

jart to hit

jarum out of shape or order WR

jather to vibrate NR

jaup (see *jowp*)

javvle (see *chavvle*)

jawther mixture, mess (cf *jotherum*)

jay-legged knock-kneed

jegs share; use (eg out of a piano)

jender to vibrate, rattle WR

Jenkins, Henry (see **Oldest Man**)

jenny¹ machine for spinning

jenny² turned lip at base of a tin

jenny³ gravity-operated haulage system in a coalmine WR

jenny⁴ small skate (Yorkshire coast fisherman's term)

Jenny Gallow girl who is said to have committed suicide in a circular hollow near Flamborough. The folklore belief is that those who run round this nine times raise the ghost of Jenny, who cries: *'Ah'll put on mi bonnet an' tee on mi shoe, An' if thoo's not off Ah'll be efter thoo!'*.

jenny-spinner cranefly, daddy long-legs

jerry chamber pot (from 'Jeroboam', large bowl)

jet hard, black form of lignite, found on the Yorkshire coast, the basis of the old Whitby industry of carving it into jewellery and ornaments. Said to be Yorkshire's oldest industry, **Whitby jet** was known in prehistoric times, and by 1855 the trade employed 1,400 people. It was most popular during Queen Victoria's period of mourning following the death of Prince Albert in 1861. (OF *jaiet*)

jib¹ to move backwards or sideways instead of forwards (horse), or to refuse to move

jib² face WR

jibber horse which jibs easily (see above); person who gives up easily in the face of difficulties

jibby, jippy starling NER

jig to play truant (sometimes used as a noun, as in 'to play jig')

jip severe pain *it's givin' me jip is this 'ere tooth*

jippy (see *jibby*)

job misfortune, poor state of affairs *it's a job!* (in the sense of a bad job)

A 1926 Jowett (7 horse-power tourer), made in Bradford.

jigger, jiggit twenty (in some systems of **sheep counting** (qv))

jiggered exhausted, tired out; flabbergasted

jike to squeak

jimmer hinge (of a door) NER

jimp to indent a straight edge with cuts and irregularities, sometimes in the sense of spoiling it; technical term for edging process in the cutlery trade WR

jinny spinner (see *jenny-spinner*)

jock food, esp for a workman *etten jock's sooin fergotten* WR

Joe Locke Barnsley benefactor whose statue in the park led to the expression *stood theeare like Joe Locke* (ie in a conspicuous, self-important manner)

Joe Plug imaginary character who rattles doors and windows, howls down chimneys etc ER

joggle stick stick which secures body of cart to shafts, moved when cart is tilted

John of Gaunt Son of Edward III, so named because he was born in Ghent (to Queen Philippa). One of the wealthiest landowners in England, he spent much of his time in Yorkshire, having been granted Knaresborough Castle and Forest as part of the Duchy of Lancaster in 1372. He was renowned for his hunting exploits, and is said to have killed the last wild boar in England. This took place at Stye Bank, Rothwell, and is commemorated by the John of Gaunt Hotel there. (See also **Haverah**.)

jome jaw of a pig

jonce to dance up and down, prance about (cf *joss*)

jonkin tea-party to celebrate a birth NR

jorum large quantity WR

joskin farm worker, country lad

joss to bounce up and down when seated (eg in a vehicle); bouncing a baby on the knee (cf *jonce*)

jother to quiver

jotherum quivering, wobbly-like mass NR

Jowett famous Yorkshire motor car made by the firm established by William and Benjamin Jowett of Bradford (1906), first in Grosvenor Road, then at Four Lane Ends.

jowl¹ jaw NER

jowl² sea swell (Yorkshire coast fisherman's term)

jowle to jolt, knock, bump (esp of heads being knocked together or against something)

jowp to strike together, esp containers of liquid or eggs, where **pace eggs** are rolled in an attempt to strike each other, in the manner of bowls; to beat (eggs) (see **pace eggs**)

jubberty obstacle, misfortune, annoying occurrence

Judy Barrett kind of mint humbug with chewy centre, named after its original Victorian maker who had a sweetshop in Westgate, Bradford.

jumble small cake, similar to gingerbread, covered in sugar

juntous, juntersome taciturn, morose, bad-tempered NR

K

kaggy'anded, kak-'anded left-handed

kale porridge, broth NER

kali (pron 'kay-lie') sherbet powder, sometimes sold in a **sherbert fountain** (qv) (ME, from Arabic *kali*, ashes)

kall to gossip, to chat at length

kall-'oil place where people gather to gossip

kansh ridge of rock or sand under sea forming an obstacle to a *coble* (qv) coming inshore (Yorkshire coast fisherman's term)

kay-legged with crooked legs, knock-kneed (see **Keighley**)

kay-neeaved left-handed (lit 'fisted')

kebbly, keggly wobbly

keck¹ hollow-stalked plant, such as hedge parsley or hemlock *as dry as a keck* (ON *kjot*)

keck² to tip

kecks trousers; underpants or knickers WR

kedd, keead sheep louse

kedge to fill (stomach), eat greedily NER

keeam (see *kem*)

keel to settle; to cool

kees, kex plural of *keck* (qv)

keigh key

Keighley kay-legged-uns humorous nickname for inhabitants of Keighley (pron 'Keeth-ly'). The serious side to this name is that it referred to bone deformities caused by the rickets once so common in industrial areas.

keld, kell spring, well (ON *kelda*)

kelfitt obsolete term for a kind of flooring nail ER

kelk¹ codfish spawn (Yorkshire coast fisherman's term)

kelk² heavy blow, thump

kelt(er) money, property (? OE *geld*)

kelter rubbish, litter

kelterment odds and ends, scraps lying around NER

kem to comb; to kill (in game of marbles)

kench slope, esp in coalmine

kenspack identifying mark or feature (eg on an animal)

kenspeckled with a marked peculiarity, all having the same features (of a family); unmistakably marked

kep to catch NER

Keppin' Day name for Shrove Tuesday once used in parts of the ER (eg Driffield) where it was the custom to throw and *kep* (catch) brightly-coloured balls on this day.

kern churn

kern supper harvest meal held when all crops are 'shorn' or cut, not to be confused with the **mell supper** (qv), held a little later at the time of 'harvest home'. The name comes from the custom of farmers originally providing cream for their workers in a churn or **kern**. They also provided cakes and ale, the latter being praised in traditional **churn supper** songs, and even in 1759 Eugene Aram noted that tankards of ale were 'politely preferred to the churn'.

kersey kind of coarse cloth woollen cloth once woven esp in the upper Calder Valley (name of village in Suffolk)

Kersmass, Kessmass Christmas

keslop rennet, used in cheese-making (OE *ceselyb*)

kessen, kest twisted, out of true

kessened (see *rig-welted*)

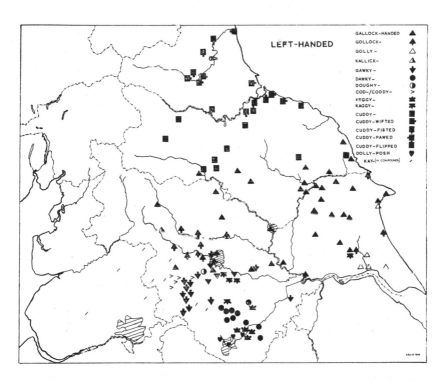

Distribution of the many dialect terms for left-handed. (Map by Stanley Ellis in the Transactions *of the Yorkshire Dialect Society.)*

kess'n to christen

kest slight squint (var of 'cast')

kested (see *cast*)

ket carrion; raw flesh, offal; rubbish

ketlock charlock, wild mustard

ketty nasty, rancid

ketty fair (see **Wibsey Fair**)

keyled leaning WR

kex (plural of *keck* (qv))

kibble[1] to grind in a mortar, for example wheat being prepared for **frumenty** (qv)

kibble[2] to sort and wash lead ore (see **leadmining**) NR

kibble tree smaller kind of *swingle tree* (qv)

Kilburn Feast The small village of Kilburn near the Hambleton Hills is notable in having not only the **White Horse** (qv) and the **Mouseman** (qv) Robert Thompson, but also an annual feast on the Sunday following the 5th July, when a mock 'Lord Mayor' and 'Lady Mayoress' are elected, a tradition possibly going back to pagan times.

Kilnsey Crag limestone outcrop about 140 feet high and about 1,200 feet long, towering above the road in upper Wharfedale, where its illusory closeness has led to the tradition of throwing stones and coins at it. **Kilsney Show** includes a fell race to the top of the crag and back, first run in 1899.

kilp pot-hook; handle of pot or cauldron (ON *kilpr*)

kilp pan pot hanging from a *kilp*, esp for making porridge

kincough whooping cough, cures for which once included a variety of strange folk-remedies, such as a child passing under the belly of a donkey, or being given frog soup or roasted mice to eat (see also **hob**[3], **tar band**[1]) (from *kink* (qv))

King Billy nickname of the equestrian statue of William of Orange erected in the centre of Hull in 1734. According to local tradition, when the clock of Holy Trinity Church strikes twelve he gets off his horse and goes for a drink.

kings! truce word in children's games (cf **barlow**)

kink to hold the breath in spasms, as in whooping cough, or with a crying baby (OE *cincian*)

kinnins cracks in the skin caused by exposure to cold and frost, painful and slow to heal WR

kinnle to give birth (of rabbits, cats etc)

Kiplingcotes Derby The oldest steeplechase horse race in Britain, this takes place over a cross-country course of 4 miles, ending at a point roughly halfway between Market Weighton and Middleton-on-the-Wolds. Held on the third Thursday in March, this remarkable tradition is believed to date from 1519. Since 1933, women have ridden as well as men. There is an official weigh-in and one judge, known as the Clerk of the Course, a position filled by the same family for more than five generations. (See also **horse racing**.)

kip-oil (see *chip-'oil*)

kippers The traditional curing of kippers, once common on the Yorkshire coast, is now confined to Whitby where the small firm of Fortunes (established 1872) still smokes kippers over wood shavings for between sixteen and twenty-four hours.

Kirby Hill Races Nothing to do with racing, but the name of a curious traditional election held every two years in August at Kirby Hill, near Richmond. This is to choose two wardens for the Hospital of St John the Baptist, an almshouse founded in 1556 by the Rev John Dakyn, who laid down elaborate rules of procedure. Names of six nominees are written on slips of paper, then sealed in wax balls and placed in a pot of water, from which the vicar draws two 'as chance shall offer them'.

kissin' bush, bough garland of evergreens hung up at Christmas, forerunner of the Christmas tree introduced from Germany in Victorian times

Kissin' Day day when it was the custom for boys to have a right to kiss any girl (once). In some parts of Yorkshire this took place on the Friday following Shrove Tuesday (**Kissin' Friday**), in others during Easter week, when it was probably a survival from the Viking festival of Hoketide.

kist large box, chest, trunk used for storage (ON *kista*)

kisted (see *rig-welted*)

kit bucket, milking pail; milk churn; pail with long handle, used for dipping

Kit familiar form of Christopher (eg Kit Calvert of Wensleydale)

kite stomach (see **Rive-kite Sunda**)

kittle[1] to tickle (ON *kitla*)

kittle[2] ticklish, tricky, tense, delicately balanced (eg a trap or trigger); easily upset **as kittle as a moosetrap** NER

kittlin kitten (ON *kettling*)

kivver stook of sheaves of corn, usually twelve

kizzened withered, wizzened NR

knacker man man who removes dead stock on a farm

knackered worn out, in a poor state (from **knacker**, a worn-out horse)

knackers testicles; bones used as castanets

knackle to do odd jobs, repairs

knackler person good at mending things

knap to snap; to knock; to take the top off (eg a protruding stone)

knapper door-knocker ER

knappers leather pads, reinforced by wood, to protect thighs during digging of peat NER

Knaresborough Bed Race the annual June bed push round the town, with a final crossing of the River Nidd, organised by the Knaresborough Round Table for charity since 1966.

knawed knew *'e knawed all aboot it* NER

knawp, knorp (see *knobble*)

knibs handles of a scythe (cf Danish *knib*)

knitting The knitting of home-produced wool was an important industry in the Yorkshire Dales, and villages such as Gayle and Askrigg, Wensleydale, had a reputation for the quality of their work. Best known of all was Dentdale, where the women were dubbed *'t' terrible knitters o' Dent'*, which was intended as a

Knitting sheath from Dentdale.

compliment to their output. A **knitting sheath** is traditionally worn on the belt to support one of the **knitting needles**.

knobble   to hit with a stick (esp on the head)

knocker-up   man who woke up millworkers on an early shift by tapping on bedroom windows with a long pole WR

knodden   kneaded

knur   hard knot of wood; wooden ball used in game of *knur and spell* (see below), usually made from holly or boxwood, and about the size of a duck's egg (cf *pot donnack*) (ME *knorre*)

knur and spell   game in which a *knur* (qv) is released from a *spell*, a spring trap fixed to the ground by four prongs. When the *knur* is released the *laiker*, or player, attempts to hit it as far as possible with a stick with a clubbed end, known as a *pummel, buck stick* or *tribbit*. A *knur* sent further than that of another player is known as a *cut*. Each player is followed round by a caddy known as a *baumer*. Although revived in recent years, *knur and spell* was at the height of its popularity in the last decades of the nineteenth century (when it was fully reported in the sports pages of certain Yorkshire newspapers), and regularly played until the 1930s.

Kompo   trade name of the well-known Yorkshire remedy for colds and coughs, registered in 1885 by the Leeds chemists J F White Ltd and sold as 'Dr White's Kompo' until 1992.

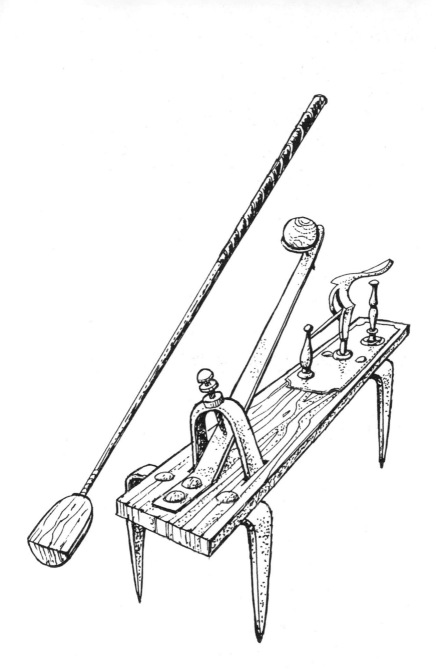

Knur and spell: a pummel (left), with the spell, holding the knur, ready to fire.

KOYLI the King's Own Yorkshire Light Infantry, originating in the regiment of the 53rd Foot in 1756, and in action for the first time at the Battle of Minden in 1759 (see **Yorkshire Day**)

kye cattle (OE *cy*, plural of *cu*, cow)

kysty fussy, difficult to please

kytle working coat of coarse linen which was worn by Dales lead-miners; coat worn by farmers NR

L

laat (see *lait*)

labber to splash, daub ER

lace to lash, beat; to add spirits etc to another drink

lace-making craft associated esp with Ripon, where lace was made of linen thread wound on **bobbins** (qv) of bone, hence the term **bone lace**

lad boy, son. Also a friendly form of address to a man, as in the WR greeting *Nah then, lad!* (cf *lass*)

lading can small vessel, with handle, used for ladling or transferring water, esp on washday (see drawing on page 164) (var of 'ladle')

lady-clock ladybird

lagged tired out NR

laggin[1] iron from a barrel, used as a **hoop** (qv)

laggin[2] apron with large pocket ER

laggy last (person), esp in a game

lahle, lahtle little

laik to play; to be unemployed or not working, esp WR (ON *leika*)

laik for warps to wait while foreman in woollen mill fastens new threads on to the existing ones

laik tally to play truant

laiker (see *knur and spell*)

laikin' toy, any kind of plaything (see above)

lair enclosure for stock NR

lait to seek, search for

laithe barn (ON *hlatha*)

lake (see *laik*)

lam to strike hard (ON *lemja*)

lambswool Christmas punch made of hot spiced ale, apple pulp and roasted apples

Lammas kind of early harvest festival held on the 1st August, when the first loaf was traditionally made from the new corn. Though still remembered in the Yorkshire countryside, the custom has died out. (See also **Yorkshire Day**.) (OE *hlaf-maesse*, loaf-mass)

land[1] to give (a blow) *sh' landed 'im a reight claht* WR

land[2] to arrive *the' landed at turned midneet*

Land of Green Ginger Various theories have been put forward as to the origin of this Hull street name, such as that it is a reference to the ginger landed here. A 1685 reference to 'ye Lands of Moses Grenehinger' suggests it could be a corruption of this. *The Land of*

Green Ginger is also the title of a novel by Winifred Holtby.

lander wooden trough, guttering of a house

lang long, esp NER (OE *lang*)

lang settle larger type of *settle* (qv), with high back (cf *squab*)

lant urine formerly collected for use in dyeworks etc (OE *hland*)

lanty person who is always late ER

lap to wrap (up)

laps woollen waste WR

larn to learn; to teach (OE *leornian*, to learn, *laeran*, to teach)

lass girl, daughter. Also a friendly form of address to a woman (cf *lad*)

Lass of Richmond Hill popularly believed to be Frances I'Anson, born in Leyburn, Wensleydale, in 1766. Her father, a lawyer, moved with his family to London in 1773, and Frances there married an Irish

A laithe, the typical Dales barn.

barrister, Leonard MacNally, in 1787. He wrote the words of the song *Sweet Lass of Richmond Hill*, and James Hook the melody. The tradition that Frances lived at Hill House, Richmond, North Yorkshire, is not supported by recent

latt   thin strip of wood, esp in a ceiling *she's as thin as a latt* (OE *laett*)

laverock   skylark (ON *laevirke*)

lay¹   to wager, esp NER

lay²   often used in the sense of 'lie', eg *Ah'll 'ave a lay dahn* WR

Leadminer's tub for carrying ore.

research — and the idea may have arisen from the fact that her grandfather and mother had lived there. There is no evidence either to connect Frances with the southern Richmond, named after the Yorkshire town. (See bibliography.)

lat   late (ON *latr*)

lea (see *ley*)

lead   to convey something in a cart *we're leadin' 'ay ter-morn* (OE *laedan*)

leadmining   This once formed an important traditional occupation in the Yorkshire Dales, going back to the Romans, whose inscribed pigs of lead have been found, for example, on Greenhow Hill near Pateley Bridge. By the end of the eighteenth century, Swaledale had as many as 2,000 leadminers, supported by women and children who **kibbled** (qv) the ore in the becks, producing about 6,000 tons of lead a year. Wensleydale also produced lead from mines such as Keld Heads. There were many fluctuations caused by flooding or worked-out veins of ore, and the industry had ceased by the end of the nineteenth century. (See **Awd Man**.)

The Leeds seal, with owls from the Saville arms.

learn　to teach, as well as to learn *Ah learned 'im 'is trade* (see **larn**)
leasin　armful of hay or corn (originally **leased** or **gleaned**)

leck　to sprinkle with water; to damp washing before ironing WR (OE *leccan*)
leckin'-can　watering can
Lee Gap　annual horse fair established soon after 1100 by a charter granted by Henry I to Nostell Priory, and claimed to be the oldest horse fair in Britain. Held on the 24th August and the 17th September, the **former and latter Lee**, it occupies a site close to the original one at West Ardsley, near Wakefield.
leeak　to look *'e leeaks a bad leeak*, he looks ill NER
leeath　(see *laithe*)
Leeds Loiner　inhabitant of Leeds; supporter of Leeds Rugby Club (the term is thought to be derived from Marsh Lane in Leeds) (see *loiner*)
　　Leeds Music Festival　first held in 1853, when Queen Victoria opened Leeds Town Hall, which is now also the venue for the Leeds International Piano Competition.
　　Leeds owls　the silver owls traditionally included in the Leeds seal and coat-of-arms were originally those of Sir John Saville (1556-1630), appointed as the first Alderman of Leeds.
Leeds Pottery　Once known throughout Europe, this often elaborate pottery was made in Jack Lane, Hunslet, from about 1770, the best work being produced between 1781 and 1800.
leet　light (OE *leoht*)
leet on　to come across, discover something by chance

leet-coloured high-pitched (voice)

leet-gi'en fickle, flirtatious, of loose morals; giddy, foolish *as leet-gi'en as a posser-'eead* (lit 'light-given') WR

leetnin'[1] lightning

leetnin'[2] lightening of an illness shortly before death, when a temporary improvement sometimes appears

leg to walk or run fast; to trip up; to throw

legger man employed to move canal boats through tunnels (eg Standedge, near Marsden) by 'walking' on the roof or sides of the tunnel

Leggin' Day old name for Easter Monday, when children *legged* or tripped each other up

leister kind of trident used in fishing

lend loan, eg *gi' us a lend o' yer bike*

lengthman person responsible for cutting grass, gritting and generally tidying-up a length of county road or lane NER

lennick, lennock supple, limp, not stiff (esp of a dead body) WR

Lent period from Ash Wednesday to Easter. Fasting was not officially required on the Sundays which were traditionally listed in the old rhyme: *'Tid, Mid, Miserae; Carling, Palm, and Paste Egg Day'*. The first three refer to the Latin liturgy. The fourth refers to **Carlin' Sunda** (qv) and the last to **Easter** (qv). (See also *pace eggs*, **simnel cake**.)

let off (see *trump*)

let on (pron with emphasis on second word) to tell, reveal; to admit, acknowledge (an acquaintance) *dooan't thee let on*, don't tell anybody

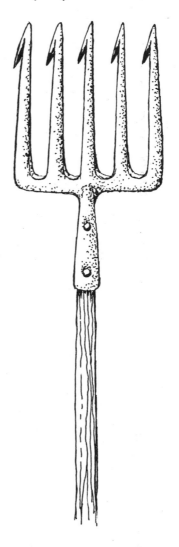

Leister, used by fishermen.

Lilla's Cross — 1,300 years old.

leuk, lewk　to look
ley[1]　scythe
ley[2]　meadow ER
leyke t'　(be) likely to NER
lief　willingly *Ah'd as lief lig i'*
bed, I'd just as soon stay in bed
(OE *leof*)
lig, ligg　to lie; to lay (ON *liggja*)
ligger[1]　branch partly cut, then
laid flat by the hedger
ligger[2]　board used by a builder
etc for mixing mortar or plaster

ligger-aht　woman employed to
lay out dead bodies WR
liggin-in　lying in (bed), esp in
childbirth
likelins　probably NER
likeness　portrait, photograph
Lilla's Cross　oldest and best-
known of the crosses on the North
York Moors, standing on Lilla
Howe, some eight miles south of
Whitby. It marks the burial mound
of Lilla, who was killed when he
interposed to save Edwin, the
seventh century Christian king of
Northumbria, from an assassin.
(See also **Ralph's Cross**.)
lillilow　flame (eg of a candle)
NER
limmers　cart shafts
linen　The manufacture of **linen**
from flax, at one time locally
grown, was in some parts of
Yorkshire, such as Leeds and
Barnsley, as much a part of life as
the woollen industry. In Nidderdale there were **linen mills** at
Glasshouses, Summerbridge,
Shaw Mills and Knaresborough,
where Waltons (established in
1785) were appointed by Queen
Victoria to provide linen for all
the royal palaces. (See *gillbox*,
heckler, tenter[2].)
ling[1]　heather, formerly valuable
for thatching, making *besoms* (qv)
and burning as fuel (see *cowls*)
(ON *lyng*)
ling[2]　long, slender sea-fish,
traditionally made into **ling pie**,
esp at Staithes (ON *langa*)
ling nail　linchpin of a wheel
lingy　springy, wiry, active; used
ironically in the ER comment

aboot as lingy as a wooden pig-trough (see also *lish*)

lip impudence, answering back

lippen to trust, count on

lish agile, active, lively, nimble

lisk groin NER (ON, cf Norwegian *lyske*)

listen at to listen to *listen at 'im!*

Listers Mill Built in Manningham, Bradford, in 1873 as the biggest silk mill in the world by Samuel Cunliffe Lister, who had made a fortune out of his wool-combing machines. The chimney, in Italian campanile style, is 249 feet high, and a famous landmark; traditionally it is said to be big enough for a coach and horses to drive round the top.

lithe to thicken soups, sauces etc

lithin thickening, usually with flour

little mesters term used for small firms in Sheffield consisting of two or three master cutlers

liver to deliver

Lizzie Leckonby comic fictional character created by J Fairfax-Blakeborough in his NR dialect tales which appeared for many years in the *Stockton & Darlington Times* and the *Whitby Gazette*.

loan, loanin (see *lonin*)

lock (see **sword-dancing**)

lofrans leggings NR

loggin' tied bundle of straw

loine lane WR

loiner person who lives in a lane (see **Leeds Loiner**)

lollicker, lolly tongue

Lonk variety of large sheep (? var of 'lank' or possibly of 'Lanc' for Lancashire)

lonnin lane, esp green lane NER

look (see *lowk*)

loomgate space between looms

loopy crazy WR

lop[1] flea *as wick (or fit) as a lop* (? ON, cf Danish *loppe*)

lop[2] choppy, with small waves (Yorkshire coast fisherman's term)

lopper to boil and bubble (said typically of porridge) WR

loppered curdled, turned sour; covered in coagulated dirt NR

loppy dirty, scruffy, verminous (from *lop* (qv))

lorry-cart (see *bogie*)

lose (see *lowse*)

loss to lose *take care, else tha'll loss it* (OE *losian*)

lotch to lap up (like a dog), drink or eat greedily

lotch ovver to move across (eg a log) in jerks, using hands and legs WR

loup (see *lowp*)

love (see *luv*)

Lovefeast Not confined to Yorkshire, but once a common practice in **Methodist** (qv) chapels here, the **Lovefeast** was a tradition borrowed by John Wesley from the Moravians. Members gathered for a time of fellowship, prayer and spiritual encouragement, centred on a symbolic communal meal of cake, with water to drink from a two-handled **Lovefeast cup**. At first, plain **sweet cake** (qv) was served, but later there developed a much richer **Lovefeast Cake** (qv) and **Scripture Cake** (qv).

Lovefeast Cake sometimes called **Lovefeast Bread**, this evolved into fairly rich fruitcake, flavoured with spices such as nutmeg, and sometimes raised with yeast. Methodists (qv) in the Dales had traditional recipes — all varying slightly — in places as close to each other as Pateley Bridge, Middlesmoor, Blubberhouses, Laverton and in Coverdale.

lover   chimney; fire-back (OF *lovier*)

Lovers' Bridge   built over the Esk at Glaisdale in the North Yorkshire Moors in 1619. The story is that Thomas Ferres was unable to cross the swollen river to say farewell to his beloved Agnes before going to join Sir Francis Drake to fight in the Armada (1588). He vowed that if he became rich he would build a bridge across the river. This he did in memory of Agnes, and later he became Lord Mayor of Hull. It is also known as the Beggar's Bridge.

lowance   break for refreshments, esp by agricultural workers in the fields (cf *drinkins*) (abbr of 'allowance', ie time or food allowed by the employer)

lowk   to weed (OE *lucan*)

lownd   calm (of sea) NER

lowp   to leap, jump (OE *hleapan*)

lowse   to finish for the day, close (school, mill etc)

lowsin'-time   time for going home after work

lucky-bod   The alternative name for the *first-fooit* (qv) referred to in the NER rhyme formerly chanted by children: *'Lucky-bod lucky-bod, chuck, chuck, chuck; Master an' mistress, tahme ti git*

up'. In the ER the *lucky-bod* sometimes came round on Christmas morning.

Luddites   The secret organisation of workers (named after Ned Lud of Leicester) whose objective was to destroy new machinery being used in the textile mills. Very active in the WR around 1812, their attack on Cartwright Mill, Rawfolds, south of Cleckheaton, being described by Charlotte Brontë in her novel *Shirley*. (See *Shirley* **Country**.)

Ludlam's dog   name of the notoriously lazy dog in a saying probably originating in the Barnsley area: *'As idle as Ludlam's dog, 'at laid itsen dahn ter bark'*, or *'. . . 'at leeaned it's 'eead agen t' wall ter bark'*.

lug¹   to drag, carry, pull (cf Norwegian *lugge*, to pull by the hair)

lug²   ear (? ME from ON)

lug³   a knot in the hair

lug-'oil   ear-hole

luggy   tangled (of hair)

luke   (see *lowk*)

lum   chimney

lump-yed   blockhead, stupid person

lunkie   (see *creep hole*)

lunt   light, flame (cf Dutch *lont*, match)

lutchet   large shovel ER

luv   the usual Yorkshire dialect spelling of 'love', to emphasise that the vowel is a short 'u' as in 'full'; *luv* is commonly used, esp in WR speech, to indicate a friendly but not over-familiar approach. It can be used by either men or women when speaking to either a child or an adult, but mostly to young children and the elderly. Commonly used by those rendering a service, eg shop assistants, bus conductors. It is sometimes tagged on to a name: *Ee, 'ello, Julie luv!*

lychgate-tying custom observed at certain churches (eg Coxwold, NR) of children tying up the lychgate during a wedding service, after which the couple must throw handfuls of coins before they can leave.

lye (see *ley*)

lyke wake vigil over a deceased person between death and burial, accompanied by lamentation such as is preserved in the *Lyke Wake Dirge* below (literally 'corpse-watch', from OE *lic-wacian*)

Lyke Wake Dirge funeral lament of great antiquity, the earliest example of Yorkshire dialect, not printed until 1686. The theme is the progress of the soul towards Purgatory and Hell, where good works done by the deceased in life help to minimise suffering. Though a Christian song, it has its roots in the pagan dread of death — and conveys an atmosphere of mystery and terror. It opens: *'This yah neet, this yah neet, Ivvery neet an' all, Fire an' fleet an' cann'l leet, An' Christ tak up thi sawl.'* (See *Brig o' Dreead, Whinny Mooar.*)

Lyke Wake Walk popular, traditional route of 40 miles, climbing 5,000 feet, over the Cleveland Hills and North York Moors from Osmotherley to Ravenscar on the coast. Founded by Bill Cowley, the first crossing (always to be completed within twenty-four hours) was made from the 1st to the 2nd October 1955.

M

mabs marbles or *taws* (qv) WR esp S Yorks

maddle to confuse, puzzle, fluster (cf *mazzle*) (var of 'muddle')

maddlin fool, silly person

mafted stifled, flushed

mag to chatter ER (cf **magpie**)

maiden clothes-horse WR

mair more NER

maister master, boss; schoolmaster (OF *maistre*)

mak kind *all maks an' manders*, all kinds

mak, mek to make

makker forger in cutlery trade WR (esp Sheffield)

Malham Cove This awe-inspiring limestone cliff, 280 feet high, was reported in about 1830 to produce a 'five-fold echo' — but this has subsequently proved to be mysteriously elusive.

Malton Sheep Sale held each year at Michaelmas, this is one of the largest and oldest fairs in the county, with as many as 14,000 sheep, and is still officially opened by the Malton town crier.

mander (see **mak**)

mank to play tricks WR

manky scruffy

mannerly good, respectable, admirable NR

mannishment application of manure or fertilisers NER (var of 'management')

mappin'-aht mopping and cleaning, esp doorsteps and windowsills, whose edges were then scoured with coloured stone WR (see **scahr**, **ruddlestooane**, **donkey stone**)

mar pond NER (OE *mere*, cf F *mare*)

March higgs stormy weather with hail and sleet (see **higg**)

mardy spoilt (child); easily upset, moody, sulky WR esp S Yorks (var of 'marred')

mardy-arse mean person S Yorks

Market Weighton Giant nickname of William Bradley (1787-1820) of Market Weighton, who was 27 stone, 7 foot 9 inches tall, and wore shoes 15 inches long. He was exhibited at fairs all over the country, and presented with a gold chain by George IV. Said to be the tallest Englishman ever recorded, he was apparently outmatched by another Yorkshireman, Harry Cooper, miner of iron ore at South Skelton around 1850, who was 8 feet 7ʃ inches tall.

marlock to frolic, play pranks (see *mullock²*)

marrer mate, friend; twin, something exactly like somebody or something; equal *tha'll nivver see t' marrer tiv 'im*

marrer ter Bonny identical (to), perfect match; awkward in behaviour, equally bad. Originally this may have been 'as marrow is to bone', ie intimately connected, but later it was influenced by 'Bonny', ie Napoleon Bonaparte, a byword for ambition and aggression in the early nineteenth century. This explains why the phrase was sometimes used in a perjorative way.

marrish marsh, land liable to flood NER (OE *merisc*)

Marsden where they *'put pigs on t' wall ter listen ter t' band'*

Martelmass (see Martinmas below)

Martinmas The Feast of St Martin (11th November) was once of great importance in the countryside, as around this time farmworkers and servants were taken into employment at hiring fairs or the *stattis* (qv). Traditionally a time of feasting, **Martinmas** took on a new significance after 1914, when the 11th November became Armistice Day.

mash to infuse, make tea (ME *masc*)

Masham breed of sheep produced by crossing a **Dalesbred**

(qv) ewe with a **Wensleydale** (qv) or **Teeswater** (qv) ram

Masham Sheep Fair Established by a charter in 1250, this ancient September fair once had as many as 40,000 sheep for sale. Though it died out after the First War, it was revived by Mrs Susan Cunliffe-Lister in 1986. (See **Bishop Blaize**.)

mashin' box containing tea and sugar taken to work WR

maslem, maslin mixture of crops such as wheat and rye, oats and beans; the term also refers to a kind of brown bread made from mixed corn, and which was once quite common in Yorkshire. (OF *mesteillon*)

maul hammer, mallet (cf *mell*)

maul abaht handle roughly WR

maunce muddle, fuss; whining complaint

maund basket, esp type once used by bait-gatherers

Maundy Thursday (see Royal Maundy)

maunsell dirty, lazy woman

maupin pointed top of the kind of haystack known as a **pike** (qv)

mawgrams whim; antics, grimace *stop makkin' mawgrams!*, stop pulling a face! (related to F *migraine*)

mawk¹ maggot; surly, unfriendly, complaining person *as fat as a mawk* (cf *cob* (qv)) (ON *mathkr*)

mawk² to become too warm *Ah s'll mawk i' this 'ere thick jumper*

mawkin effigy; scarecrow ER (see *molly-mawkin*) (? var of familiar form of Maud)

mawky full of maggots; surly etc

mawngy surly, uncooperative, complaining WR

May goslin' similar to April Fool, but term used for those on whom tricks were played on the 1st May ER

maypole The setting-up of a **maypole** — originally a freshly-cut tree — and the decorating and dancing associated with it, is an ancient spring festival which survives in several parts of Yorkshire, notably Long Preston, Aldborough, Gawthorpe and Barwick-in-Elmet. In Gawthorpe the **maypole celebrations** take place on the first Saturday in May, with a procession following a four mile route into Ossett and back before the crowning of the **May queen** and dancing round the **maypole**. The Barwick triennial tradition claims to have the oldest and tallest **maypole** in England (about 88 feet). It is lowered and re-painted every three years on Easter Monday, ready for Spring Bank Holiday. **Maypoles** were traditionally 'stolen' — that of Burnsall, for example, by the villagers of Thorpe.

mazzen to daydream ER

mazzle to daze, bewilder, confuse (cf *maddle*)

med made

meeare mare NER

meeast most NER

meeastlins mostly NER

meemaw grimace; affected manner; unnecessary fuss, or delaying tactics

meeterley moderately

meg halfpenny

Mell.

melch mild, gentle, soft (OE *melsc*)

mell¹ to meddle, interfere, molest (OF *meler*)

mell² large mallet (OF *mail*)

mell³ harvest supper (see **mell supper**, **mell shaf**) (probably derived from meal in the sense of the flour itself, or the *mell* or mallet used to pound the corn)

mell cakes (see **mell supper**)

mell doll (see below)

mell shaf the last sheaf of corn to be cut — traditionally by the farmer himself — and usually made into a **mell doll** or corn dolly, which was kept for a whole year after being given pride of place at the **mell supper** (qv)

mell supper Sometimes preceded by the **kern supper** (qv) or churn supper, held when the crops had all been cut, the **mell supper** was held at the end of the harvest,

Corn dolly made from the mell shaf.

when all was 'safely gathered in'. The tradition goes back at least to biblical times (eg *Leviticus 23:39*). The supper was often heralded by the ceremonious lifting of the **mell doll** (qv) or corn dolly onto a cart to the cry of: *'We've getten t' mell'*. Farmers usually provided generous suppers of cold meat, tarts and cakes, including specially-baked **mell cakes**. The meal was normally held in a large barn and followed by singing and dancing.

Meltham singers choir of Meltham, near Holmfirth, who once had the reputation of setting off in the wrong key and having to start again, hence the WR saying: *'Begin ageen, like t' Meltham singers'*. The choirmaster, Matthew, is supposed to have complained about their false start by saying *'Yer wrang! Yer wrang all ter hell!*. This gave rise to another jocular Holme Valley saying: *'Tha'rt wrang all ter Math!'*.

mend to improve (in health) *Ah'm mendin', on t' mend*; to replenish a fire by adding coal *mend t' fire!* (OF *mender*)

mengle (pron with silent 'g') mangle, wringer (cf Dutch *mangel*)

mengle-'oil communal mangle-house, used by many who could not afford a wringing machine of their own

mense[1] decency, neatness, tidiness (ON *mennska*)

mense[2] to tidy up (see above)

menseful decent, neat, thrifty

menseless unseemly, lacking in decency, neatness etc

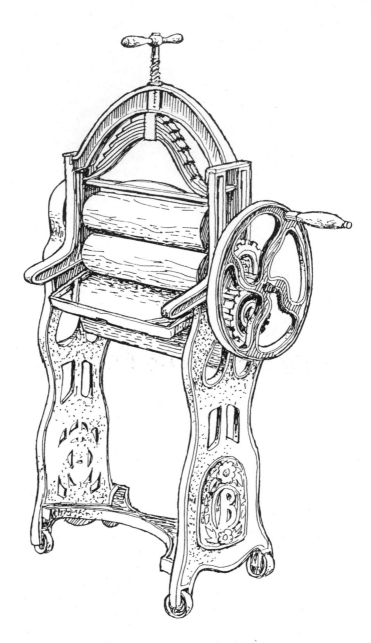

A mengle or wringer, with wooden rollers.

mention a small amount, esp of food *Ah'll 'ave just a mention* WR

merrils ancient game going back at least to 1,400 BC, introduced here by the Vikings or the Normans. It is based on a board marked with three concentric squares, with nine playing pieces for each of the two players. When a player has formed a mill or row of three, one of the opponent's pieces is taken. The winner is the player who blocks the other's moves or reduces him to two pieces. Also called Nine Men's Morris, **merrills** was once very popular in Yorkshire, and is kept alive by the Ryedale Folk Museum at Hutton-le-Hole, where the World Champ ionships are held each September. (OF *marelle*, token, counter)

mester (see *little mester, maister*)
Methodism This revivalist movement — at first within the Church of England — was particularly strong in Yorkshire, with hundreds of recorded visits by John Wesley (1703-91), and Methodist chapels (see **Octagon**) resounding to the hymns of his brother Charles. ('Methodist' was a nickname given to the society organised at Oxford University by the Wesley brothers.)
mew[1] stack (of hay, corn), esp if loose; place where hay is kept
mew[2] mowed NER
mewstead barn, hayloft; stands or supports raising hayrick from ground
meyas mouse WR (esp Holme Valley area)
meyt meat (in earlier times, food in general) (OE *mete*, food)

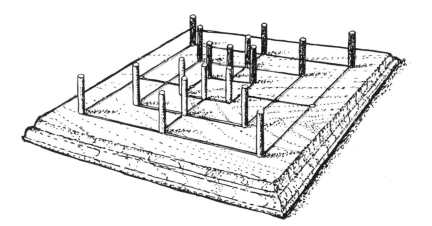

Merrils, showing two sets of nine pieces.

meyt-whooal not as ill as is made out, because the patient can still eat WR

mich much

mickle much; greater NER (ON *mikkel*)

Micklegate Bar gateway in the walls of York on which it was the custom to display the heads of executed traitors and other notable malefactors. After the Battle of Wakefield (1460) the head of Richard, Duke of York, was placed here so that 'York may look upon the town of York'.

middin dungheap; rubbish tip; dustbin (ON *myki-dyngja*)

middlin moderate, average, esp of health *Ah'm nobbut middlin'*

mig muck, manure (ON *myki*)

mill-band rope formerly used in WR woollen mills which, because of its greasy nature, smouldered well, and could be used to light fireworks at **Plot** (qv). Sometimes kept cupped in the hands, or whirled above the head to make it glow. Also called **wheel-band** in some parts of WR.

miln mill

mind! pay attention! out of the way! etc

mind to look after, pay attention to; to remember, take care (to do something)

minnin'-on term similar to *drinkins* (qv); snack which staves off hunger until the main meal WR (? ON *minna*, remind)

mint to intend, aim; to feign (a blow)

mint pasty currant pasty flavoured with leaves of garden (spear) mint

mipe to sneak; to move stealthily WR

Mischief Neet Observed in certain parts of Yorkshire, more particularly in the south-west of the county, this appears to have originated in a transfer of tricks associated with **Hallowe'en** (qv) to the 4th November, the night before **Plot** (qv). Pranks played by children range from harmless fun such as window-tapping with a button on cotton, doorhandles smeared with treacle, or the removal of gates, to the dangerous misuse of fireworks and acts of vandalism.

missel, missen myself

misslippen to disappoint

mistal cowshed (related to *mig* and *mixen* (qv))

mistetched spoilt through bad training or handling; not properly broken in (horse); fallen into bad habits. (OE *mistaecan*)

mistle (see *mistal*)

mistletoe Yorkshire maintains a unique tradition concerning this ancient symbol of healing and fertility. Though widely used as a Christmas decoration, originally in the kissing bough, forerunner of the Christmas tree, **mistletoe** has never been used amongst evergreen decorations in churches because of its association with Celtic paganism, ceremonially cut by druids at the winter solstice. In York, however, there is the tradition of placing **mistletoe** on the high altar of York Minster on Christmas Eve. In medieval times it was carried there in procession,

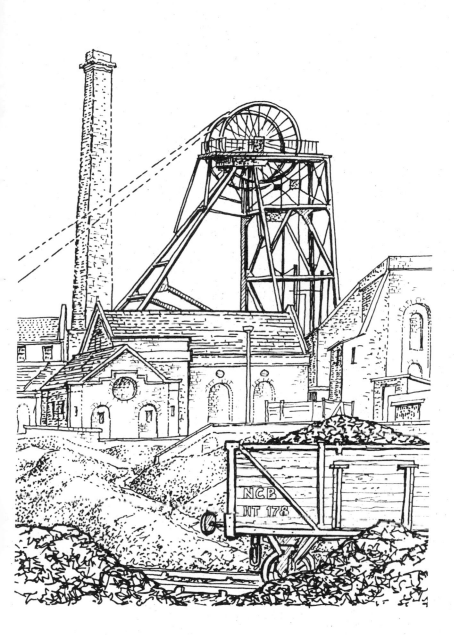

When Yorkshire coal was king: the mine pit-head with its familiar gantry.

and left on the altar throughout the Twelve Days of Christmas. This may have been a symbolic token of the victory of Christianity over paganism in Yorkshire, the clusters of three berries being said to represent the Holy Trinity.

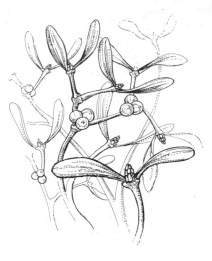

Mistletoe for York Minster.

mither, moider (see *moither*)
mixen dunghill (OE *myxen*)
mizzle[1] to drizzle (? combination of mist and drizzle)
mizzle[2] to mislead, swindle, slink away
moak donkey
mobs (see *blinnders*)
moggie[1] kind of gingerbread made with treacle (ON *mugi*, corn)
moggie[2] cat
moggy mouse (term used in certain Yorkshire coalmines)
moil toil, drudgery

moit speck of dust, grit, esp in eye WR
moither to fluster, muddle, overwhelm, pester
moke (see *moak*)
molly-mawkin an overdressed woman ER
monny many
mooant (see *munt*)
mooast most; almost
mooastlins mostly NER
mooed aht wi having too much left over (eg food) WR
mooild turmoil, confusion, mood, temper; mischievous child WR
mooinie somebody whose behaviour is supposed to be affected by the moon WR
mooit to grumble
moorcock common name for male red grouse
moor-jock moorland sheep NR
moor The moorland so characteristic of Yorkshire includes both **white moor**, containing coarse grasses, and **black moor**, consisting of heather and peat. Though the OE *mor* referred to wasteland and marsh, the **moors** support many species of flora and fauna, and have traditionally provided fuel (see *cowls*, **peat**, **turf**) as well as unspoilt terrain for walking. (See also *tewit-grund*.)
moos mouse NER (OE *mus*)
mop small codfish (Yorkshire coast fisherman's term)
mort abundance, a great deal (? OE *mergth*)
mosker canker, rust
moss peat bog (see **peat**)
moss-crop cotton-grass

moss up to keep out draughts *moss t' dooar bottom up* WR

mot, motty marker used when ploughing; projecting object (eg stem of clay pipe stuck in ground) aimed at in game of *quoits* (qv); also used figuratively to mean an interfering remark, an uncalled-for opinion *Dooan't thee put thi motty in!*, Keep out of this! WR (cf F *motte*, mound)

mother-dee campion; hedge parsley. The term seems to be derived from the superstition that if certain plants were not picked, some evil would befall that person's mother.

Mother Shipton largely mythical Yorkshire witch and prophetess, first mentioned in a pamphlet of 1641 containing her prediction that Cardinal Wolsey would never

Moak, carrying milk at Castle Bolton, Wensleydale.

Mother Shipton moth   Mouseman

Mother Shipton, as portrayed in 1648, predicting the downfall of Wolsey.

reach York (1530). A fanciful pamphlet by Richard Head (1667) claimed that **Mother Shipton** had been born in a house in Knaresborough in 1487 as a result of her mother being seduced by the Devil. Head attributed various fabricated prophecies to her, all dealing with events that had already taken place. More prophecies were invented by Charles Hindley, a Victorian bookseller of Brighton, including the prediction of the end of the world for 1881, later changed to 1991. Until about 1908 a Knaresborough cottage was shown as her birthplace, but it is now promoted as a cave near the **Dropping Well** (qv).

Mother Shipton moth A small moth with markings on its forewings resembling the traditional profile of **Mother Shipton** (qv). Formerly known as the species *Euclidia Mi*, it is now classified as *Callistege Mi*.

Mothering Sunday (see **simnel**)

mountain blackbird another name for the ring ouzel

Mouseman the name given to Robert Thompson (1876-1955), the world-famous woodcarver of Kilburn in the NR, from his custom of carving a small mouse as his emblem. He first added a mouse when carving a beam in a church roof in about 1925, following the remark of a fellow craftsman

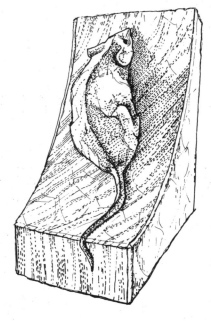

Mouse carved by Robert 'Mouseman' Thompson of Kilburn.

The Mother Shipton moth.

about being 'as poor as a church mouse'.

mow (see *mew*)

mowdiwarp mole (ME *moldewarpe*, earth-thrower)

muce square wooden tunnel in a rabbit trap which gave access to food. When the rabbits were used to the *muce* the wedge was removed from a tilted board in the floor, and they were trapped. (OF *musser*, to hide)

muck dirt; manure (? ON *myki*)

muck or nettle no turning back, between the devil and the deep blue sea

muck-lather profuse sweat

muck-leadin' taking cartloads of manure to spread on the land

muck-pluggin' loading manure into carts

muck-rawk dirty line (eg on neck) showing limit of where it has been washed

muckment rubbish, dirt, anything worthless or disreputable

muck-'oil dirty, squalid room or house WR

mucky dirty

mud might *it mud 'a' bin wahr*, it might have been worse

muff the slightest sound *dooan't mek a muff!* WR

muffin small round cake, plain and spongy, originally made on a *bakst'n* (qv), toasted and buttered. In Yorkshire, **muffins** were commonly sold in the streets by the **muffin man**, who advertised his wares by ringing a bell.

muffler scarf, neckerchief

Mule breed of sheep produced by crossing a **Swaledale** (qv) ewe with a Blue-faced Leicester

mullock[1] mess, blunder, something badly managed *tha's med a reight mullock on it, it's all of a mullock*

mullock[2] to mess about, fool around; behave clumsily (cf *marlock*)

mummers groups of actors, usually disguised and sometimes with blackened faces (see *guisers*), involved in open-air traditions such as the **Richmond Horse** (qv) and **pace egg plays** (qv) etc, or who perform the old **mumming plays** in places such as Bellerby and Knaresborough (see **Redmire**). (OF *momeur*)

mun must

Munda Monday

mungo[1] mongrel dog WR

mungo[2] cloth similar to *shoddy* (qv) in that it is made from waste, but from tougher material, such as rags from old suits and tailors' clippings, opened up by a machine called a *garnet* or *dule* (qv). The resulting *mungo* is usually of better quality than *shoddy* and produces a close-knit felt ideal for army greatcoats etc. It was manufactured from about 1813 in the Dewsbury area. In an attempt to explain how the term originated, it is sometimes claimed that a foreman once said to the millowner that it wouldn't go (ie sell), to which millowner retorted *'But it mun go!'*. It is more likely that *mungo* was borrowed from the name used for dogs in Yorkshire, the idea being that both the dog and the material were mongrel.

munk fit of sulking *'e 'as a munk on*, he's sulking WR, esp S Yorks

munt musn't WR

murl to crumble NR

muss mouth (esp when talking to young children) WR

musweb cobweb, gossamer, when floating in the air NER (from 'mouse-web') (see *femmer*)

mystery plays Yorkshire has two sets or cycles of these ancient plays, all including a good deal of dialect — the York cycle, from the late fourteenth century (48 plays), and the Wakefield or Towneley cycle (32 plays). They enact the biblical account of the history of humanity from the creation to doomsday, with special emphasis on the crucifixion and resurrection of Jesus. Originally each play in the cycle was performed by the guild of a particular craft or trade, their stage being the wagon they pushed round the city — a tradition recently revived in the streets of York. (NB. The term 'mystery' is derived not from the religious content, but from OF *mestier*, trade.)

N

nab promontory, end of hill

nabbins term of endearment to a child ER

naff hub or nave of wheel (OE *nafa*)

naffle to idle about, trifle NER

nague (pron with long 'a') to annoy constantly (eg toothache) (var of 'nag')

nail-making traditional craft located esp in Silsden, where the 'Cobbydale nail-makers' once boasted 200 small forges. The introduction of machinery led to the craft becoming extinct and being replaced by the making of clog-irons.

Naked Man name of a former inn, now a café, at Settle — apparently a nickname for the figure carved in stone in 1663 with the initials of the owner, 'I C'. The man was not intended to appear naked, as buttons, sleeve ends and stocking tops can just be made out. The name may have been a shrewd comment on the effect the figure has, especially because the board is held as though to cover nudity. There was also said to be a **Naked Woman Inn** at nearby

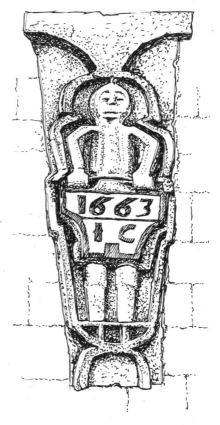

The 'Naked Man', identity still unsettled!

Langcliffe. Folklore has provided various explanations, including the theory that it is a man in a coffin, a satire on fashion, or a protest against local taxes on clothes, such as that of a halfpenny for wearing a new hat at Settle market.

nakt (pron with long 'a') naked

names It was customary, esp in the WR, to identify people by where they lived (eg Judy o' t' Wood, Tahn-end Betty) or by who they were related to (eg Susy o' Nan's) or both (eg Nelly o' Bob's o' t' Crowtrees). Yorkshire also had a high proportion of names from the Bible, including some rare today such as Hiram and Leah, and several that could be mistaken for titles, such as Squire, Duke, Major, Colonel and Prince. (See also **Dooady, Kit**.)

nang to be troublesome, painful

nangnail ingrowing toenail, corn; loose piece of skin at base of nail (cf *anger-nail, stepmother blessing*) (? ON *angr*, pain)

nanpie magpie

nantle to move slowly and feebly; to dawdle, potter about

napper head

natter[1] to irritate, annoy *yon loose floooarboard natters me*; to grumble repeatedly; to talk, chatter

natter[2] conversation, longish chat *they were 'avin' a good natter*

nave (see *nieve*)

navvy labourer employed in the contruction of **canals** (qv), roads or **railways** (qv), the latter also being sometimes known as *navvy tracks* (from 'navigator')

nawpin free handout, tip, something cadged WR

nawther neither WR (OE *nawther*)

nay no (but stronger than an ordinary negative, contradicting etc), eg *'As 'e plenty o' brass? Nay! 'E's next ter nowt* WR (ON *nei*)

nazzart rascal, villain NR

near tight-fisted, careful with money

neb nose, beak; front, projecting part, esp of a cap (OE *nebb*)

nebber flat cap WR (ie with a *neb* or peak)

neea no NER

neean none NER (OE *nan*)

neeave (see *nieve*)

neet night (OE *neaht*)

neet-rake one who stays up or out late

neet soil soil used in *privy* (qv) or earth closet

neggy-lag next to the last shot (eg in games of marbles or **conkers** (qv)) WR

nelly umbrella WR

ner than *wahr ner nowt,* worse than nothing

nerks chips WR

nesh delicate, squeamish, easily feeling cold etc (OE *nesce*)

nessy outside lavatory, esp earth closet (cf *privy*) (contraction of 'necessary house')

net steeaks stakes used with netting or wire when sheep are gathered into a fold

nettle beer fermented drink made from young nettles

nettle porridge gruel made from nettles boiled with oatmeal

Nevison's Leap Sometimes called **Nevison's Nick**, this refers

Nessy, petty, privy, closit, donnakin . . . and less polite names.

to the legendary escape of the Yorkshire highwayman John Nevison, who is supposed to have avoided capture by making a horseback leap from the top of Giggleswick Scar. (See **Swift Nick, Walton Rag Well**.)

Newburgh Priory traditional resting-place of the headless skeleton of Oliver Cromwell, said to have been given secret burial here in 1660. The priory, near Coxwold, was the home of Mary Fauconberg, who was Cromwell's daughter.

nibs (see *knibs*)

nicely quite well (of health) (ie used as adjective) *"Ow are ye' keepin'?'* *'Nicely'*

nick groove in a pully (see *band in t' nick*) *'e's goin' dahn t' nick* (said of someone thought to be deteriorating in health or dying) WR

nicker-pecker file-cutter (used in cutlery trade)

nieve fist (OE *neve*, ON *nefi*)

niff smell — usually unpleasant

nimm to skip along lightly, briskly; to walk with quick, short steps NER (related to 'nimble')

nimm to filch, steal by snatching (? OE *niman*)

nip-curn miser, mean person; cf the phrase probably originally said of a grocer keen to give no more than the exact weight, *'e's that mean 'e'd nip a curn i' two* (lit 'nip-currant')

nip-screw, nip-scrote miser, mean person

nither (pron with short 'i') to shiver with cold

nithered feeling very cold, perishing (? OE *nitherian*, to bring low)

nivver never

nobbut only (OE *nan-beutan*)

nogs knees, when in a kneeling position *dahn on mi nogs* WR

noils short pieces and knots of wool discarded during **wool-combing** (qv) (see also *tops*) (OF *noel*, from Latin *nodellus*, knot)

noit[1] difficult or confused situation; predicament; *we're at a bonny noit* (said ironically) WR

noit[2] period during which cow gives milk

nominy rhyme, jingle; prepared speech NER

nont aunt   WR (esp towards Pennines and Lancashire border, as in the name of **Nont Sarahs Inn**, see below) (from earlier *min ont*, my aunt)

Nont Sarah's inn on the high moorland road from Huddersfield into Lancashire. Popular as a stopping place and renowned for ham and eggs, it was originally known as the Coach and Horses. The name was changed in 1870 because it was already well-known as **Nont Sarah's** after the Aunt Sarah of the previous landlord, who had lent him money to extend the premises.

nooa no WR

nooan not, none WR (OE *nan*)

nooinin-scawp rest period for workman after lunch WR

nook part, share (of work etc) WR

noolies marbles (parts of WR)

noppit (see *nuppit*)

noppy head (young children)

nor (see *ner*)

noration commotion, disturbance, fuss

Norton Conyers sixteenth century house near Ripon, containing 'Mad Molly's Room'. As Charlotte Brontë once visited the house, it may have been the model for Thornfield Hall, with its incarcerated mad woman, in her novel *Jane Eyre* (1847).

North York Moors National Park Created in 1952, this covers 554 square miles of beautiful countryside, with the main information centre at Danby. Its symbol is **Ralph's Cross** (qv). The correct term for the area is the North *York* Moors, not North Yorkshire. (See **Yorkshire Dales National Park**.)

noss nurse NER

nowt (pron 'no-oot' rather than 'now-oot' in most of WR and much of NER) nothing *nowt o' t' sooart*, nothing of the kind (OE *no-whit*)

nowts (see *taws*)

nub'dy nobody WR

nuggit nougat (Provençal *noga*, nut, and influenced by 'nugget')

nuppit simpleton; mischievous child

Nunnington Worm mythical dragon, said to have been killed by Peter Loschy who is supposed to be buried in the 1325 tomb of Sir Walter de Teyes in Nunnington Church. Each time Peter wounded the dragon it was instantly healed, but he finally defeated it when he hacked it to pieces, and his dog carried off each piece to bury.

nut not (OE contraction of *na-whit*)

Nutty-Crack Neet (see **Hallowe'en**)

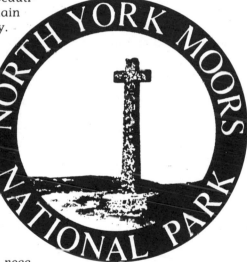

O

Oak Apple Day commemoration on the 29th May of Charles II entering London in triumph on that day for his restoration to the throne in 1660. Earlier, in 1651, he had avoided capture by hiding in an oak tree after the Battle of Worcester. Once observed all over Yorkshire, the children used to go to school wearing sprigs of oak leaf and, if possible, oak apples (ie galls). It was also the custom to beat anyone not wearing a sprig with a bunch of nettles, and to chant: 'Royal Oak Day, the 29th of May, If you don't give us a holiday, we'll all run away!'.

oard old ER

oatcake Once the staple bread of poor families, this was either made from a stiff dough, when it was known as **haverbread** (qv), or from a mixture including yeast which was poured or tossed onto a **bakst'n** (qv) and also known as **riddlebread**. The **oatcake** was hung up to dry on a **breead-fleg** (qv) by the housewife, but large quantities were made by commercial bakers, esp in the WR.

ochin (see **urchin**)

ocker to hesitate (cf **hacker**)

Octagon the chapel built at Heptonstall by John Wesley in 1764, the oldest **Methodist** (qv) chapel in continuous use, popularly said to be octagonal so there were no corners for the Devil to hide in.

'od (see **hod**)

Oak apples — galls caused by weevils.

odshin   (see *urchin*)

off   going; this is now used more commonly than the earlier *bahn* in the WR, eg *Ah'm off ter t' match*

offald   tired and dirty, in need of a bath   WR

off-comed-un   person from elsewhere, from outside Yorkshire

off-ender   third horse, when two are in double harness   ER

oft   often (OE *ift*)

'oil   (see *hoil*)

Old Amos   philosophical old Yorkshireman who has appeared as a cartoon character in the *Dalesman* since 1953, created by Rowland Lindup as *'Owd Amos'*

Old Amos.

Old Boots   nickname of Thomas Spence, boot boy of the Unicorn Inn, Ripon, famous because his nose almost touched his chin. **Old Boots** earned tips by holding a coin between the two, and also attempted to kiss the girls. He died in 1762, aged seventy.

Old John Mealy Face   nickname of a man (b1784) in Topcliffe, near Thirsk, whose reputation for niggardliness rests on his custom of pressing his face into the flour at the top of a bin before leaving home — then on his return checking to see that the impression remained undisturbed.

Oldest Chemist's   Yorkshire has the Oldest Chemist's Shop in England. Situated in Knaresborough market place, it has been in continuous use as an apothecary's and pharmacy since at least 1720, making lavender water to a traditional recipe.

oldest inn   The oldest inhabited public house in the UK is at Bardsey near Leeds. The Ellis family were landlords here from AD 953 until 1780, when the name was changed from the Priests Inn to the Bingley Arms by the new owner, Lord Bingley of Bramham Park.

oldest man   The record for longevity is attributed to Henry Jenkins, of Bolton-on-Swale near Catterick, the oldest man in Yorkshire, and possibly in the UK. Said to have been born in 1500, he died at Bolton on the 6th December 1670, supposedly aged 169. His earliest memory was of being sent as a boy to take a horse-load of arrows to Northallerton, from where they were taken by an older boy to the Battle of Flodden (1513). He worked as farmhand, butler, thatcher and river-fisherman, and was often called as a witness in legal cases because of his long memory. Though the precise figure of 169 cannot be substantiated, there is good documentary evidence to suggest that Henry lived to a phenomenal age.

The oldest Yorkshireman — Henry Jenkins.

'ollin (see *hollin*)

olmenac common dialect spelling of **almanack** (qv)

ommost almost

on of *two on 'em, what's it made on?*

once ovver once (upon a time), formerly WR

onnly (pron with short vowel) only (esp WR)

onny any

onny-bit like acceptable, tolerable

onnyrooad anyway, however (used esp when introducing a statement)

onnywheears anywhere NER

'ooal (see *hooal*)

ooast hoarse

'ooin (see *hooin*)

'ooined depressed, tired out, under pressure

'oose (see *hoose*)

oot out NER

oot o' fettle not fit, well or useable (see *fettle*)

ootgang way out

oot'n out of NER

oppen to open

oppen-band blunt, blabbing, coarse (in speech) WR (from a bag with the string loose and the mouth left open)

orkerd awkward

orts scraps, fragments, esp leftovers *feast terday, orts termorn* (cf Dutch *oor-ete*)

Osmotherley The fanciful folklore explanation of this village name is that the mother of the baby Prince Oswy (see **Roseberry Topping**) came to bury him here, and was herself later buried next to him, hence 'Os-by-his motherlay'. The name of **Osmotherley** is, in fact, derived from the proper name of a Viking, Asmundr, with OE *leah*, a clearing.

'oss (see *hoss*)

oss to make an attempt, set about doing something WR

'oss-muck horse manure

Ossett WR town whose inhabitants used to have their legs pulled in the saying *'Ossett, wheeare the' black-leead t' tram lines'*.

Otley Show the oldest known agricultural show in Yorkshire, officially dating from 1796, and informally held by local farmers for a dozen years before that date.

outby miner's term for going from the coalface back to the shaft; passage used for this (see *inby*)

oven-bottom cakes kind of large teacake, baked at the bottom of the oven, usually eaten hot with butter

ovver (see *ower*)

ovver agen opposite (esp WR)

ovver-, ower-face to give too much to eat etc *there wor that much t' eyt Ah wor ovver-faced* WR

ovvered wi' (see *owered wi'*)

owd old, esp WR

Owd Bartle character burnt in effigy at West Witton in Wensleydale. This takes place each year on the Saturday night nearest to St Bartholomews Day (24th August) so it has been suggested that **Bartle** once represented St Bartholomew, who replaced a much earlier pagan figure, as the custom seems to be of great antiquity. Locals say the effigy represents a man caught sheep-stealing, but there is a strange feeling of prehistoric barbarity as **Owd Bartle** is carried shoulder-high through the village (in recent years by generations of the Harker family), its eyes lit up by means of torch bulbs. There are traditional stopping-places outside homes and pubs when drinks are served to the carriers. Against a wall at Grisgill End the effigy is burnt to the accompaniment of singing and the final shouting of traditional dialect verse: *'At Pen Hill crags he tore his rags, At Hunter's Thorn he blew his horn, At Capplebank stee he brak his knee, At Grisgill Beck he brak his neck, At Waddam's End he couldn't fend, At Grisgill End we'll mak his end. Shout, lads, shout!'*. Grisgill (pron Kirsgill) sometimes appears as Grassgill.

Owd Joss pen name of Geoffrey Robinson of Pocklington, who wrote a humorous dialect column for the *Hull & East Riding Times* and later the *Hull Daily Mail* from 1974 to 1986.

Owd Lad the Devil; always used with the definitive article, ie *t' Owd Lad;* cf the saying *'A whistlin' woman an' a crowin' 'en Brings t' Owd Lad aht of 'is den'* WR

Owd Scrat the Devil WR

ower over; too; as with *ovver*, this can be used with adjectives to give the effect of 'very' or 'too', eg *ower lang*, too long

ower-anenst opposite NER

ower-kessen overcast NER

ower-nice fastidious, dainty NER

ower-set tired, exhausted, overburdened ER, esp Filey

owered wi' finished *it's all owered wi' 'im* (said when a person has just died) NER

Owls the traditional name of Sheffield Wednesday football club (from Owlerton, home of the club)

owlstock culvert, dyke going under road ER

Owd Bartle, uniquely burnt at West Witton.

owmer   shade (OF *ombre*)

own   to recognise; to acknowledge (eg in the street) *sh' knaws us, bud nivver owns us*

owsen   oxen

owt[1]   (pron 'aw-oot' in most parts of WR and in much of NER) anything *we're that pined we'll eat owt* (OE *awiht*)

owt[2]   ought *'e owt ter cahr quiet* WR

owt like   reasonable, well or fit *if 'e's owt like 'e'll mow t' lawn*

Oxenhope Straw Race   Each July teams of runners compete to carry bales of straw from pub to pub around Oxenhope near Keighley, stopping for a pint at each. Though only started in 1975, the race soon became an important fundraising event for charities.

oxter   armpit (OE *oxta*)

P

pace eggs hardboiled eggs, dyed in various colours, formerly the basis of several ancient Easter customs. **Pace eggs** are rolled down a grassy slope, either on Easter Sunday or Easter Monday (once called **Troll Egg Day**), traditionally in remembrance of the stone which rolled away from the tomb of Jesus on Easter morning. If they reach the bottom of the slope without cracking it is a sign of good fortune. Egg-rolling has been revived in many parts of Yorkshire, including Fountains Abbey. Another custom was to *jowp* (qv) **pace eggs** together in a game similar to **conkers** (qv). The custom of brightly-dressed **mummers** (qv) going round begging **pace eggs** is associated with surviving **pace egg plays** (see below). (**pace** is a form of OF *pasque*, Easter, from Hebrew *pesach*, Passover)

pace egg plays These traditional plays are still performed each Easter esp in the Calder Valley. The **Midgley Pace Egg Play**, involving St George killing Bold Slasher, who is revived by the Doctor's magic potion, is performed by the boys of Calder High School, Mytholmroyd, and taken round to Hebden Bridge, Midgley and other villages. A similar play is performed in Brighouse, and there have been revivals of **pace egg plays** in such places as Barnsley.

packhorse routes These were once vital for communications and supplies, esp in the Pennines, where tracks across the moors can still be followed (eg from the A640 to Marsden). The packmen, led by a *jagger* (qv), used as many as forty ponies or *gallowas* (qv), carrying a load in panniers on each side of the saddle.

Pack-Rag Day day following **Martinmas** (qv) when workers and servants moved to new accommodation

packin' (see *baggin'*)

paddle to walk slowly or with difficulty NER; to mess about, work to little purpose WR

padfoot malevolent apparition similar to a barguest (qv), usually in the shape of a large sheep or dog, padding silently along, but sometimes with the sound of a clinking chain

pafty cheeky ER

pahnat (see *pie-not*)

pahk (see *powk*)

pahnd pound *fower pahnd* (no plural) (see also *pund*) WR

paigle cowslip

palaver fuss, unnecessary and time-wasting formalities etc *What a palaver!* WR

palm common term for 'pussy willow', twigs with furry catkins, used for decoration esp on **Palm Sunday**

Palm Cross Day old name for Palm Sunday, when crosses made from **palm** (qv) were hung from the ceiling

Palmsun period around **Palm Sunday** when fairs were held, esp to show stallions, in places such as Stokesley and Guisborough

Palm Sunday (see **Fig Sunday, Spanish Sunday**)

Pals (see **West Yorkshires**)

panacalty dish made in a frying pan by simmering together potatoes, onions, and sausage or bacon

pancake bell common name for the bell tolled on Shrove Tuesday, summoning people to church to be shriven — to confess sins and receive absolution. As this day was the last before the fast of Lent, rich foods such as butter and eggs were used up in the making of pancakes. The **pancake bell** is still tolled, for example, at Bingley Parish Church and Richmond's Trinity Tower. Scarborough's **pancake bell**, originally in the

Hospital of St Thomas the Martyr, is now in the Rotunda Museum, where it is rung by the mayor at noon, mainly to announce the **Shrove Tuesday** skipping (qv).

panch (see *paunch*)

pancheon large earthenware bowl, used esp when dough is mixed and then left by fire to rise

parkin gingerbread made with oatmeal and treacle (from personal name, eg **Perkin**, familiar form of Peter)

parkin pigs biscuits in the shape of a pig made from a stiff kind of parkin (qv) (see also **Plot**)

parky chilly (? var of perky)

parlous difficult, dangerous, desperate; extremely (with an adjective) NER

partlins partly NER

parzle to stroll, saunter, go cautiously NER

pash shower

paste eggs (see **pace eggs**)

pate badger NR (cf Pateley Bridge)

Pateley Races title of a long dialect poem by Thomas Blackah, who wrote and published *T' Nidderdale Olminac*. It gives a vivid picture of Dales life in the early nineteenth century.

patten clog (qv) with irons on sole to lift it above mud etc *wahr ner a cat i' pattens* WR (OF *patin*)

patty fishcake (from *t' fish-'oil*) usually made with bits of fish between two slices of potato, fried in batter

paunch to clean out the viscera (eg of a rabbit)

pause (see *pawse*)

paut (see *pooat*)

pawat to catapult ER

pawky shrewd, cunning; precocious, particular, fussy

pawse to kick (? related to paw)

pawt (see *pooat*)

pay to hit, thrash, chastise

payed beaten, worn out with strenuous effort

pays (see *peys*)

peat traditional fuel of the northern part of Yorkshire, similar to, but to be distinguished from, **turf** (qv). **Peat** is dug from a **moorland** (qv) *moss* or **peat bog**, deeper and darker in appearance than turf. **Peat** or turf fires are said to have been kept burning continuously for at least 200 years at the **Saltergate Inn** (qv) (between Pickering and Whitby) and the Chequers Inn, Slapestones. (See also *torves*.)

Peculier of Masham An ancient court, presided over by the Vicar of Masham, which meets in the parish church twice a year, mainly to disburse funds to apprentices. As the **Official of the Peculier**, the vicar has the right ot issue wedding licences and to license apothecaries. A **peculier** is a body outside the jurisdiction of the bishop of the diocese. Of the original fifty-six **peculiers** in Yorkshire, this is the only one to surive. The official's seal (illustrated) is traditionally said to show a Saracen, presumably praying as a Christian convert. (See **ale**.)

peace egg (see *pace egg*)

pee-i'-bed dandelion (so called from the old country belief that picking dandelion leaves led to bed-wetting) WR

peeaked perched, settled, stuck *peeaked at 'ooam* WR

peeart brisk, lively, fit *as peeart as a lop* NR

peen thin, attenuated, fine; flat end of hammer NR

peff to cough, usually slightly, as with a tickly cough; to breathe in short gasps etc (? var of 'puff')

The seal of the Peculier of Masham.

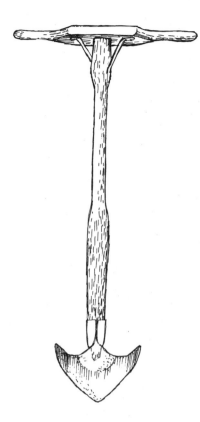

A cock-spade for digging peat.

peg frame frame holding the hessian during the making of *pegged rugs*

pegged rug (see *tab rug*)

peggy (see *dolly* and the items below)

peggy stick wooden implement for lifting clothes out of boiler or washtub

peggy tub large, barrel-shaped washtub

Penhill Giant legendary figure of great brutality and ferocity, said to have been a descendant of the Viking god Thor. He is supposed to have lived in a castle on Penhill, Wensleydale, and to have been finally defeated by an old man known as the Seer of Carperby.

penk to peer closely, peep, esp slyly; to squint

penk-eed squint-eyed

Pennine Way The first official long-distance footpath in Britain, opened in 1965, this starts in Derbyshire and ends in Scotland, but includes much of the western fringe of Yorkshire from the Calder Valley to Swaledale.

penny bazaar Stalls offering low-price items from a penny to sixpence could be found in many Yorkshire markets, but the one started in Leeds Market in 1884 by Michael Marks led to a partnership with Thomas Spencer of Skipton and to the world-famous Marks and Spencers.

Penny Hedge tradition observed at Whitby, said to have originated as a penance imposed by the Abbot of Whitby in 1159 on hunters who had murdered a hermit for protecting a wounded boar. It is probably much older, however, and may have to do with hunting rights, as the alternative name of Horngarth suggests. At 9am on the day before Ascension Day, at the water's edge in the upper harbour, a token hedge is planted, made out of eleven *stowers* (stakes) and eleven *yethers* (qv) of

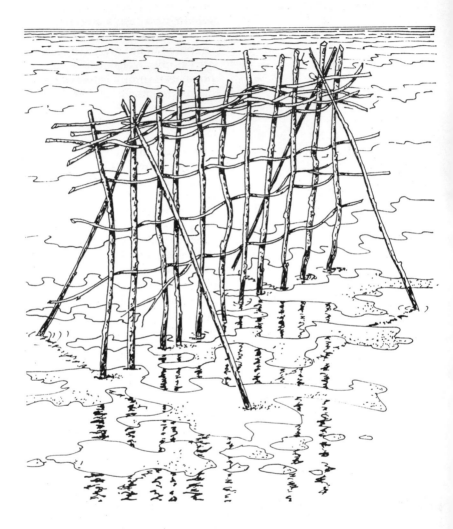

The Penny Hedge, an ancient Whitby tradition.

willow or hazel. These were supposed to be cut from Stayhead Wood with a 'knife of a penny price' — hence the supposed origin of the name. The ceremony is completed by the blowing of an ancient horn and the repeating of the words: 'Out on ye! Out on ye! For the heinous crime of ye!' The **hedge** is supposed to be strong enough to withstand three tides.

penny-'oil gatehouse of a mill where workers checked in, so called from the custom of fining latecomers a penny

pent engaged to finish piecework in a woollen mill; hard-pressed, because of the limited time to finish work WR

pepper cake rich kind of ginger-bread, so called because it included not only ginger but allspice, also known as 'Jamaica pepper'

pertic'ler hard to please, fussy *Ah'm nooan pertic'ler*, I don't mind either way

pet kittiwake gull

petty kind of *privy* (qv) (OF *petit*, ie small room)

pew spice sweets sucked during the sermon in chapel, given esp to children to keep them quiet. Mint imperials were probably the commonest. WR (The NER equivalent was *goodies* (qv).)

peys peas (see also **carlins, greys**)

pick to throw, push, esp as a term in weaving for when the shuttle is sent across the warp of the cloth; to pitch or fork hay etc

Picktree Brag A *barguest* (qv) said to take the form of *gallowa* (qv). Originating in County Durham, it is now known in the NR.

pickin'-'oil hole or door high up in the wall of a barn through which hay could be pitched WR (cf *bowel-hole*)

piece hall general name for a building designed for the display and sale of pieces of cloth, with a fine example at Halifax, completed in 1779

pie-not magpie

piecen to join ends together, esp in textile trade, when yarn breaks while being spun

pined hungry, starving

piggin small vessel, esp with handle, serving as a milking pail or **lading can** (qv) often used to fill and empty the **set pot** (qv) (cf *skeel*) (? Celtic)

piggy children's game in which a small stick pointed at both ends and resting on a stone is struck so that it flies up and is then hit as far as possible into the air

pike[1] small anvil used in making **clog-irons** (OE *pic*)

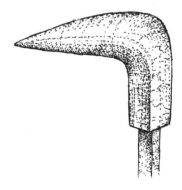

A pike.

pike² round and pointed stack of hay or group of sheaves of corn, often thatched (see *maupin*)

pike³ turnpike gate (name probably derived from spikes on gates)

pike⁴ stye, pustule WR (cf *powk*)

pike⁵ to pick up and poke about (food) WR

pikel hay-fork, pitchfork

pikelet small round cake, similar to a **muffin** (qv), not confined to Yorkshire, but well-known here (cf Welsh *pyglyd*)

pinchers pincers, pliers

pine to go hungry; to crave for food (OE *pinian*)

pissimer ant (ME *pisse-myre*, from urine smell of anthill)

pizeball type of game similar to rounders, using soft ball and hand instead of bat

plash puddle NER

plawt (see *plooat*)

pleeaf plough NER

Pleeaf Stots (see **Plough Stots**)

plean to complain

plew plough NER

plisky trick, escapade

ploo plow NER

Ploo Stots (see **Plough Stots**)

plook spot, boil, small pimple

plooat to strip, pluck off feathers NER

Plot Yorkshire term, esp WR, for the night of the Fifth of November. The failure of the Gunpowder Plot to destroy James I is celebrated with particular enthusiasm in Yorkshire as Guy Fawkes was a Yorkshireman. On **Plot Neet** the burning of a guy on a bonfire (see *chumpin'*, *proggin'*) is accompanied by fireworks and the passing round of roasted potatoes, **parkin** and **parkin pigs** (qv) and home-made **Plot toffee**. There once were several local dialect rhymes associated with **Plot**, most of them beginning 'Please to remember, the fifth of November...'. (See **Guy Fawkes**.)

plotter to wade through mud

Plough Monday the tradition of marking the return to work on the farms after the Christmas and New Year break, normally the first Monday after Epiphany. A plough is blessed during a church service on the Sunday before **Plough Monday**, then pulled by a team of **Plough Stots** (qv) round the villages. In earlier times it was customary for the *stots* to ask for gifts of drink or money and to threaten to plough a furrow in front of inhospitable houses. An important part of the tradition is a series of dances performed with longswords (see **sword-dancing**). Though the custom had died out, it was successfully revived at Goathland on the North York Moors from 1923 (by F W Dowson at the suggestion of Cecil Sharp) and more recently (from 1983) by the Claro Sword and Morris Men at Knaresborough on Plough Sunday.

Plough Stots a team of male dancers in colourful costume who perform the traditional dance — usually a **sword-dance** on **Plough Monday**. Representing *stots* (bullocks), they pull the plough round the villages or town. The **sword-dances** require great skill, but the *stots* are essentially lively, clownish characters. At Goathland they are led by Isaac (*t' Awd Man*) and Betty (*t' Awd Woman*). At Knaresborough the plough is pulled by Dobbin, a dancer disguised as a black horse. (See **Plough Monday**, sword-dancing.)

Ploughing Day former custom of farmers meeting to welcome a newcomer by giving a free day's ploughing

pluf plough NER

milk, given to children, invalids or old people (? var of 'porridge')

podged, pogged full, replete WR

poddish porridge

poich hive, esp one where bees are taken after they have swarmed

poise (see *pawse*)

poit poker (? abbr and contraction of **firepoint** (qv))

poke sack, bag, esp for flour (OF *poque*, ON *poki*)

polesmitten crazy WR

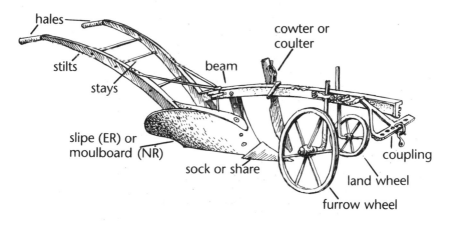

hales, stilts, stays, beam, cowter or coulter, slipe (ER) or moulboard (NR), sock or share, coupling, land wheel, furrow wheel

Pleeaf, ploo, pluf or plough.

plug to load carts by forking in manure (cf *muck-pluggin'*)

pluther sludge, semi-liquid dirt NER

po chamber pot, placed under bed (OF *pot*)

poak (see *poke*)

pobs, pobbies soft food, esp bread soaked in warm, sweetened

pole to walk, usually quickly WR

poll (pron with short 'o') to cut, lop

polly[1] cow without horns (see *doddy*, *hummelled*)

polly[2] head (term used with young children)

pollywasher reflection from metallic or other objects dancing about on walls or ceiling

polony kind of pork sausage popular in Yorkshire, with red skin and finely-minced white contents (? sausage from Bologna or Poland)

Pomfret early form of Pontefract

Pomfret cakes liquorice sweet-meat in the form of small round cakes stamped with a design showing Pontefract Castle. Known as **Yorkshire Pennies**, they were first made by a local chemist, George Dunhill, in 1760. As liquorice is a Mediterranean plant, various legends attempt to explain its introduction into the Pontefract area. It is said to have been brought here by the Romans, by a schoolmaster who had visited Spain, by another who found branches of it on the Yorkshire coast, washed up from a wrecked Spanish galleon from the Armada. He is supposed to have beaten his schoolboys with it, and they noticed how sweet the bark tasted. A more likely story is that liquorice was introduced by friars who grew it for medicinal purposes. Though Pontefract still produces liquorice, the roots — usually about three years old — are now imported, the extract being obtained after they have been crushed, ground and boiled. The last commercial crop in Pontefract was in 1966. (See *spanish*.)

pooak (see *poke*)

pooat to kick gently or move with the foot, touch with a stick (eg an

A Pomfret cake, showing the old seal of Pontefract Castle.

animal, to see if it is dead); to paw the ground; to walk or tread heavily NER

popalolly name given by children to **spanish water** (qv)

pork Pork products have a special place in traditional Yorkshire food. Families used to depend on the killing of a pig, every part of which was used, it was said, except the squeak. When pork butchers' shops became established, the excellence of their pies and sausages was contributed to in some places by butchers who were German immigrants. (See **black pudding, faggot, haslet, polony, scraps, stand pie, York ham**.)

porriwiggle tadpole ER

posnit iron saucepan, usually with three feet, used for making porridge etc (or *pocenet*)

poss¹ purse ER

poss² to push down and squeeze clothes in a washtub

posser washday implement consisting of concave, circular copper head, with holes, attached to a long wooden handle

posser-'eead (see above) (see also *leet-gi'en*)

possit a hot drink, esp milk flavoured with treacle, sugar, spices, wine etc; milk regurgitated by a baby

possit pot pot used esp at wedding breakfasts, when it was filled with hot ale and rum *possit*, into which the bride traditionally dropped the wedding ring, the idea being that the drinker who managed to get it out would be the next to be married.

posskit washtub NER

postcards Comic seaside postcards have a long association with Yorkshire, being produced by Bamforths (established 1870) of Holmfirth, where there is a Postcard Museum.

pot donnack *knur* (qv) made of pot WR

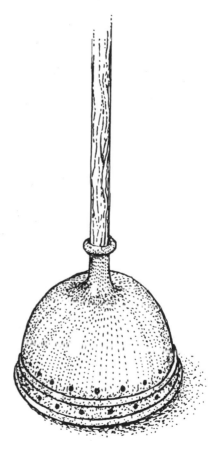

The posser — a copper head on a long pole.

141

pot o' one person not fond of company; independent, individualistic. The term originated in the early 1800s when hand **woolcombers** (qv) used to keep their combs warm in a pot on the stove. Sometimes as many as four would thus share *a pot o' fower*. (There is also a Halifax pub named the Pot o' Four.) WR

pot-setten (see *burnt on*)

pot-side *set pot* (qv) (term for this used in Sheffield area)

pots term commonly used for all kinds of crockery *ter do t' pots*, to wash up

Potter Thompson legendary character said to have come across a cleft in the rock below Richmond Castle, with a tunnel leading to an underground chamber. Here he found the sleeping King Arthur and his knights surrounded by treasures, including the sword Excalibur. When he tried to remove this from its scabbard, he disturbed the knights and fled. On returning he could find no trace of the cleft in the rock. (See **Drummer Boy**.)

powk stye, pustule (on eye)

powlin' very short haircut WR (see *poll*)

powpy horse (term used with young children) WR

Pratty Flowers (see **Holmfirth Anthem**)

prich weak or sour (home-brewed) beer

Prims Primitive Methodists, a branch of Methodism founded by Hugh Bourne in 1810, united with other Methodists in 1932, but a name still seen on Methodist chapels. (See **Methodism**.)

privy outside lavatory, esp earth closet (OF *privé*, private)

proddle (see *broddle*)

prog food, esp when eaten outside

proggin' collecting wood, esp for a bonfire or **Plot Neet** (qv) (cf *chumpin'*)

pubble soft, plump and round ER

puckly cloudy, dull ER

puddock term of reproach WR (? originally a bird of prey)

pudjack cat WR

Pudsey featured in various humorous jibes (see *ducks²*), including the delightful quip from coalmining days: *'Pudsa, wheeare they've all bald 'eeads, cos the' pull 'em aht o' t' pit wi' suckers'*.

Pudsey Pudding made to celebrate the repeal of the Corn Laws in 1846, this steamed fruit pudding was cooked by twenty local women in a Pudsey mill. It weighed twenty stones and took three days to steam. (Cf **Denby Dale Pie**.)

pulleys in the phrase *get t' little pulleys goin'* (from textile mills) the meaning is 'to speed up'

pulls short straw produced by threshing NER

pummel (see *knur and spell*)

pun', pund pound *fower pund* (no plural form) (see also *pahnd*)

put on to keep (somebody) sufficiently sustained until a proper meal can be eaten *this'll put mi on while ter-neet* WR

putten put (past participle) *'e's gooan an' putten 'putten', when 'e owt to 'a' putten 'put'*!

Q

quarrel square pane of glass; stone *flag* (qv) (OF *quarel*, square)

quart to plough a field a second time, going across the first furrows

Quay term used by Yorkshire coast fishermen for Bridlington harbour

Queen of Song Mrs Susan Sunderland (1819-1905). She was born in Brighouse, where she was also first taught to sing by a blacksmith, then by Dan Sugden of Halifax. Her beautiful soprano voice contributed to the Huddersfield Choral Society and was acclaimed everywhere. At a command performance in 1858, Queen Victoria said to her: 'I am the Queen of England. You are the Queen of Song.' In her honour was started the Mrs Sunderland Musical Competition in 1889, still flourishing today, based on Huddersfield Town Hall and locally known as *'T' Sunderland'*.

Queen of the Watering Places unofficial title of Scarborough (see spa)

queasy upset (stomach), esp when this is caused by emotion

Mrs Susan Sunderland

queer as Dick's 'at-band odd and morose, strange and sullen in behaviour or attitude. Although known in other counties, this phrase was once very common in Yorkshire. The origin of the saying is obscure and debatable. Some have seen it as an allusion to the crown assumed to have been

143

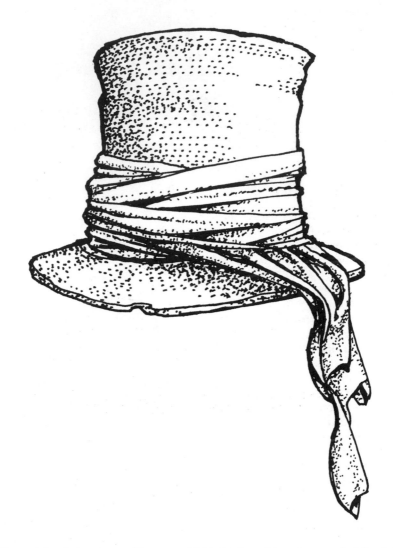

The origin of the phrase 'Queer as Dick's 'at-band' is unknown, but it might have looked like this.

sought by Richard Cromwell after his father's death (cf the alternative *'as tight as Dick's 'at-band'*), but it is more likely to be based on some unknown character with an eccentric or flamboyant hat-band of excessive length. The earliest version seems to be: *'As queer as Dick's 'at-band 'at went nine times rahnd an' still wouldn't tee'*. WR

queer-stick odd sort of person (cf *buck-stick*)

quicks thorns, esp unwanted hawthorn NR

quid[1] pound (sterling); commonly used in Yorkshire dialect, with no plural form, ie *three quid* (cf *pahnd, pund*)

quid[2] lump (of tobacco)

quishin cushion (cf *wishin*) (OF *cuissin*)

quoits game played in certain parts of Yorkshire, including the villages of Castle Bolton and Redmire, Wensleydale, Keld in Swaledale, and Ugthorpe near Whitby. At Ugthorpe two teams of nine players throw the *quoits*, heavy metal discs with a hole in the centre, a distance of eleven yards, aiming to get them on the 'pin', which projects three or four inches above the clay in which it is set. Prizes are presented at the annual supper of the Ugthorpe Quoits Club. (See *mot, shoeing the hob*.)

R

rack bend in a river almost at right angles to the main course NER

rack o' t' ee phrase used when an experienced eye, rather than implements, is used to judge size, levels etc (eg in **drystone walling** (qv)) (var of 'reckoning of the eye')

rackapelt an unruly boy ER

raddle to beat, thrash ER

raff confusion; bad temper NER

raffle to entangle, jumble, lead a wild, riotous life NER

raffled knotted, in a muddle (cf *smock-raffled*)

rag rug (see *pegged rug, tab rug*)

raggalds villains, ruffians; an old Norse word surviving in the name of Ye Old Raggalds Inn near Denholme (see **Withens**)

Railway King nickname of George Hudson, three times Mayor of York, who was one of the earliest and most prosperous investors in the building of railways in the 1830s and 1840s, by 1848 controlling almost a third of all railways in Britain.

railways an important traditional industry in Yorkshire, dating from 1811, when Matthew Murray of Leeds invented the first commercially successful steam locomotive, which was a forerunner of Stephenson's. Even before the latter's famous Stockton & Darlington Railway (1825), Murray's engine pulled coal from Leeds to Middleton in 1812. The major centres of industry have been Doncaster and York, where the National Railway Museum was established in 1975. Steam railways in Yorkshire have been revived at Middleton (Leeds), Embsay, Keighley & Worth Valley, and the North York Moors Railway (Pickering), and steam trains run, for example, on the Settle-Carlisle line over the famous Ribblehead Viaduct. (See **Railway King**.)

raitch white line or streak down the face, esp of a horse

Ralph's Cross ancient stone cross on Castleton Rigg, Rosedale, North York Moors, on top of which it is the custom to leave money for the benefit of walkers who may be in need. **Ralph's Cross** is the symbol of the **North York Moors National Park** (qv). (See also **Lilla's Cross**.)

ram, rammy with a strong or foul smell

Ramblers' Church name given to the small twelfth century church, originally a private chapel, at Lead, near Towton Moor, where the notorious battle of the same name took place in 1461 (see **Towton**). The church was restored by Leeds and Bradford ramblers in 1931, and special services have been held there ever since by the Ramblers' Association.

Rammalation Day popular name given to the day during Rogation Week when it was the custom to **beat the bounds** (qv) (var of 'perambulation')

rammel rubbish; brushwood

rammle to wander, stroll, idle about; to climb NER

rammle-rags tomboy ER

rannel bauk beam across a fireplace from which the *reckan* (qv) and vessels can be hung

rannock old, toothless sheep NR; spendthrift ER; straying animal; restless child

Ranter term sometimes applied to an old-style hell-fire preacher (originally name of a seventeenth century sect)

ranty wild, excited, boisterous, bad-tempered

ranty-pole seesaw; boisterous child

raspberry vinegar made of raspberries, vinegar and sugar boiled together, an old Yorkshire remedy for colds and sore throats, also used as a flavouring

rasselled withered (eg fruit) ER

ratch¹ small piece of land ER

ratch² to stretch; to exaggerate

ratcher tall story

ratten rat (OF *raton*, small rat)

Raven Hall This house (now a hotel) built at Ravenscar in 1774, and commanding a view of the whole of Robin Hood's Bay, is traditionally supposed to have been used as a retreat by King George III during his periods of insanity.

rawk¹ mist; drizzle

rawk² line, scratch (eg across furniture) (see also *muck-rawk*)

rawky cold, damp and misty

razzle to cook quickly over a fire ER

real splendid, wonderful (esp WR)

reckan iron bar attached to the *rannel bauk* (qv), drilled with holes to take hooks for hanging kettles etc over fire; sometimes a kind of crane

reckan-creeak hook suspended from a *reckan*

reckle to poke, stir (fire) NR

recklin weakest of the litter, outcast (cf *greck* (qv)) (ON *reklingr*)

reckon to pretend; to think, consider **Ah reckon nowt to it** (with emphasis on *to*) (? ON *reikna*)

reckovee (see *rack o' t' ee*)

Redmire Cheesecakes curd tarts (qv) once specially baked for Redmire Feast, Wensleydale, traditionally begged for by villagers in fancy dress, with blackened faces, known as the **Redmire Cheesecake Gatherers.**

reeafshaft handle (shovel, axe, hammer etc)

reeak reek (see *rick*)

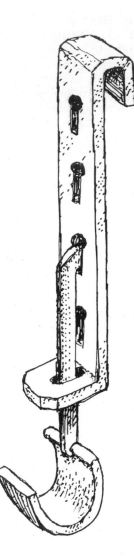

The reckan — adjustable for kettle or cooking pot.

reeast to rear up, *jib* (qv) (of horse) S Yorks

reeaster horse making less effort than the others in a team ER

reeasty rancid

reed kind of **tripe** (qv)

reet right; very (OE *riht*)

reeveshaft (see *reeafshaft*)

Refreshment Sunday (see simnel cake)

reight right; very *Ah'm reight glad* WR

relievo children's catching game in which prisoners taken by one side are kept in a den until released by the other side by touching and the shout of '**Relievo!**'

renny fox (OF *renard*)

renny tails foxgloves

reservoy reservoir (WR pron)

rewel hole made through the dewlap of cattle, kept open with rolled-up cloth soaked in turpentine, which was believed to help cattle which were not thriving NR

reng wrong WR

reyk to reach (OE *raecan*)

rheeubub rhubarb, esp WR (OF *rubarbe*) (see also *tusky*)

rhubarb charity annual social event organised mostly by chapels in the **rhubarb triangle** (qv), which included entertainment centred round a tea of home-made items, esp rhubarb pie.

rhubarb triangle term for the area between Morley, Wakefield and Leeds, where once as many as 5,000 acres of rhubarb were grown, locally known as *tusky*. Cheap coal meant that 'forcing' in heat and darkness could start in mid-November, with young shoots ready for Christmas. Now production is only on a small scale.

Ribston Pippin famous apple raised on the estate of Ribston Hall, between Knaresborough and Wetherby. In about 1707 Sir Henry Goodricke received three pips from an orchard near Rouen. From one of these came a tree which bore an abundance of apples and led to the propogation of the **Ribston Pippin** and the development of the Cox's Orange Pippin.

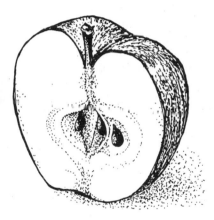

The Ribston Pippin, showing the three original pips.

Richmond Horse *'T' poor aud 'oss'* is the central figure in a **mumming play** (qv) performed in and around Richmond from the week before Christmas till New Year's Eve. The horse, accompanied by red-coated huntsmen, dies and comes back to life again. The part — probably dating from

pagan times — is played by an energetic dancer in a disguise which includes a horse's skull.

Richmond Meet not a hunting meet, but a Spring Bank Holiday gathering at Richmond, originally for cycling clubs, but now with a variety of sport and entertainment

rick¹ smoke (OE *rec*)

rick² to smoke (OE *reocan*)

rick³ heap or stack of hay, corn (OE *hreac*)

rickle to heap (peat etc); to put coal on a fire NER

riddlebread (see *oatcake*)

Riding Soon after their conquest of York in AD 867 the Vikings divided Yorkshire into three parts, each a *thriding* or third, namely the **North Riding, East Riding** and **West Riding**, with the addition of the **Ainsty of York** (qv) (**riding** is an abbr form of *thriding*, the latter from ON *thrithjungr*). (See also **South Riding**.).

Riding the Stang former custom of holding up a person to public ridicule, esp a wife-beater or an adulterer. Originally he was placed astride a *stang* or pole, and carried around to the accompaniment of whistling, the banging of bin lids and loud singing, including dialect verse about his misdemeanours. For example: *'Here we come wi' a dan, dan, dan! It's neither for my cause nor thy cause I ride this stang, But for* [name of culprit] *his wife he did bang'*. Later a *mawkin*, a straw effigy dressed in old clothes, was tied to the *stang*, taken round in

The three Ridings (from top): NR, WR and ER.

a cart and then carried round the village church three times before being taken to the culprit's house. This was done on three successive nights, and on the third night the effigy was burnt in front of the house by the ***stang-master***.

rift   to break wind; to belch

rig   ridge; back (of person or animal) (see also ***rick³***)

rigged   (see ***rig-welted***)

riggin   ridge of roof

riggot   half-gelded horse; horse that refuses to work NR

rig-welted   description of a sheep or other animal on its back and unable to get up (see also ***cast, kessened, kested, kisted***)

Ripley Boar   A boar's head surmounts the crest of the Ingilby family of Ripley, as it does in the Bradford coat-of-arms (see **Bradford Legend**). The origin is said to be an occasion in 1355 when Edward III, hunting in the Forest of Knaresborough, was about to be attacked by a wounded boar. It was killed by Thomas Ingilby, whom the grateful king knighted, also granting a charter to the village of Ripley.

Ripon Mayor-Making   Though Ripon's first charter was granted by King Alfred in AD 886, the office of mayor, replacing the original **wakeman** (qv), dates from the charter of James I in 1604. Because of the tradition that mayors are reluctant to take office, a mock search has to be made before the new incumbent is installed. Then the civic procession, led by the sergeant-at-

150

mace, moves from the town hall to the cathedral, where the service includes three blasts on the Ripon horn. (See **hornblowing**.).

Ripon rowells (see *rowells*)

rist to rest NER

rive to tear (ON *rifa*)

Rive-kite Sunda the Sunday following the *stattis* (qv) or hiring fair, when farmworkers and servants were given a splendid meal before leaving home for their year's employment (lit 'split-stomach Sunday')

rizzom tiny scrap, particle (esp WR)

Robin Hood Yorkshire has many traditional associations with the semi-legendary **Robin Hood**. It has been claimed that he was a Yorkshireman, born in Wakefield in about 1290. Several hills, towers, and wells and other topographical features are named after him, including the village of Robin Hood near Rothwell. As a wandering outlaw it is probable that he moved from Sherwood to Barnsdale Forest, north-west of Doncaster, and also to the Forest of Knaresborough, near which area he is said to have met Friar Tuck at Fountains Abbey. Other legends connect him with the Yorkshire coast, including one claiming that he went to sea with Scarborough sailors, another that he and Little John stayed at Whitby Abbey, and another that he took refuge in what came to be known as **Robin Hood's Bay**. He is certainly associated with Wakefield, and especially with Kirklees

Priory, where he is said to have taken refuge, and been bled to death by the prioress. The grave at Kirklees, said to be where his last arrow fell, is marked by a stone with an inscription beginning: *'Here underneath dis laitl stean . . . '.* This is only eighteenth century, however, and the date it gives of Robin's death (1247) is probably a hundred years too early.

Robin Hood — a Yorkshireman?

Robin Hood's Bay In spite of the name there is no historical evidence to connect **Robin Hood** (qv) with this attractive fishing village, or with **Robin Hood's Butts**, burial mounds to the south. There may, however, be truth in the tradition that he took refuge here. The village itself, called Bay Town, became 'Bramblewick' in the novels of Leo Walmsley, who lived here from 1894 to 1913.

Robin Lythe's Hole cavern with two entrances in the cliffs at Flamborough, said to be named either after a pirate whose lair this was, or a shipwrecked sailor who took refuge here.

Robinson Crusoe This story (1719) by Daniel Defoe, often regarded as the first modern novel, is said to have been partly written while the author was staying at the Rose and Crown in Halifax. The eponymous hero of the book is born in York and begins his adventures from Hull.

roister lively, noisy child

roke (see *rawk*)

Rolle of Hampole hermit and mystic, born about 1295 at Thornton-le-Dale, finally settling at Hampole, near Doncaster. One of the first churchmen to write in English rather than Latin, he influenced his fellow Yorkshireman John Wycliffe. His eccentricities included publishing fifteen signs of the end of the world, commemorated by a window in All Saints, North St, York.

Romany popular name of the Rev G Bramwell Evens, a Methodist minister of Yorkshire gypsy origins, born in Hull, famous for his talks on country life in the 1930s and early 1940s, both on BBC radio and in Methodist chapels, where he was often accompanied by his spaniel Raq.

Rombald legendary giant whose name has since been given to **Rombald's Moor**, which includes Ilkley Moor, where he is supposed to have tripped and broken the Cow from the Calf and his wife is said to have dropped the Skirtful of Stones nearby. (See **Hitching Stone**.)

romtom strong beer from the first brewing

ronce to climb up

rooad way *aht o' t' rooad!*, *look at it this rooad* (OE *rad*)

rood traditional unit of measurement used in **drystone walling** (qv) to indicate seven yards

rooar to weep, esp loudly

room front room or best room, sitting room

roond-'eead cobble, round stone (see also *tommy roond-'ead*)

roop auction sale

roopy hoarse ER

ropemaking a traditional Yorkshire trade originally associated with the linen industry, esp in Nidderdale, where there were several rope walks. **Ropemaking** in the traditional way can still be seen at Outhwaites in Hawes.

rops entrails, guts, belly (of an animal), but occasionally used humorously of a person (OE *rop*)

Roseberry Topping distinctive hill between Guisborough and Great Ayton. Weather-lore predicting heavy rain or a storm says: *'When Roseberry Topping wears a cap, Let Cleveland then beware a clap!'*. **Roseberry** has been a favourite site for beacons and bonfires, such as the one for the coronation of Edward VII. Locals

A contented-looking cow in a mistal, attached to her rudstake or boose-stake, behind which is the boskin dividing her stall.

have traditionally assumed it to be far higher than it is (1,051 feet). In 1761 it was described by a character in a play: *'It's t' biggest hill i' all Yorkshire. It's aboon a mile an' a hawf heegh, an' ez caud ez ice at t' top — on t' yattest daa i' summer, that is'*. The Anglian prince Oswy was supposedly drowned as a baby in a spring until recently flowing near the summit. **Roseberry** comes from Newton-under-Oseberry, originally *Odinsberg*. (See **Osmotherley, White Rose Walk**.)

rote   to moo loudly (esp calling to calf)

rovins   small lengths of wool ready for spinning WR

rovven   torn NER

rowan   (see *wiggin*)

rowels   spurs, formerly synonymous with Ripon, where they were made to a high standard, hence the saying: *'As trew as Ripon rowels'*.

Royal Maundy   The first known instance of this traditional almsgiving took place in Yorkshire, at Knaresborough, on Maundy Thursday 1210, when King John gave money, food and clothes to thirteen paupers of the town. The **Royal Maundy** has been held in Yorkshire in 1969 (Selby), 1972 (York) and 1985 (Ripon). (Maundy is derived from Latin *mandatum novum*, the 'new commandment' to love and to serve given by Jesus during the Last Supper.)

ruddle   red powder for marking sheep *as red as rud* NER

ruddlestooane   soft red stone

used for colouring edges of doorsteps and windowsills, quarried esp near Braithwell, S Doncaster. (cf **donkey stone**, *dooarst'n, scahrin'-stooane*)

ruddock   robin NER

rudstake   wooden post in a cattle stall, to which a chain is attached, sliding up and down (see also *boose-stake*)

Rudston   one of Yorkshire's most remarkable prehistoric monoliths, 25 feet tall and weighing about 80 tons, situated adjacent to the church at Rudston, near Bridlington. It is the tallest standing stone in the UK. Legend asserts that it was thrown by the Devil in a vain attempt to destroy the church. (The name may be derived from OE *rod*, cross.)

rue   to regret *tha'll live ter rue it!* (used more commonly than in SE)

rugby   Yorkshire played a historic part in the evolution of rugby football when, on the 29th August 1895 in the George Hotel, Huddersfield, a meeting decided to break away from the existing Rugby Union and form the NRFU, known since 1922 as the Rugby Football League. The split came about partly because, in the North, miners or factory workers lost wages if they played on Saturday. The new Rugby League paid each player six shillings per match as compensation. There were also changes in rules, such as teams reduced from fifteen players to thirteen (from 1907). Though rugby union is the traditional game in many Yorkshire schools, rugby league has an enthusiastic following which justifies the 1895 breakaway.

ruiz to carouse, drink heavily *'e'll ruiz 'issen ter deeath*

rully dray, low-sided cart; under-carriage of wagon

runch wild mustard, charlock

runty short, thick-set ER

rushbearing annual procession of children to the parish church carrying rushes, originally strewn thickly over the stone floor. Though the custom had died out

Rushbearing at Sowerby Bridge.

in Yorkshire, it has recently been revived in Haworth and Sowerby Bridge. On the first weekend in September a procession leading a **rushcart** pauses for a **rushbearing service** at St Peters Church, Sowerby, where the pulpit carries a permanent shield decorated with rushes.

rush-bob   tuft of rushes

ruttle   to rattle, esp sound of mucus in air passages

S

sackless ineffectual, lacking in energy or effort, simple-minded (originally harmless, innocent of wrong intent) (OE *sacleas*, from ON *saklauss*)

sad not properly risen (of bread, cakes etc)

sad cake kind of *fatty cake* (qv) with a centre filled with currants and sugar

saig saw WR (OE *saga*)

saigins sawdust

saim lard; dripping, fat

St Aelred Abbot of Rievaulx from 1147, his theological writings earning him the nickname of 'the English St Bernard'

St Alkelda said to have been strangled at Middleham by two pagan women in about AD 800, she is commemorated in the churches of both Middleham and Giggleswick, but lack of historical evidence suggests she may be a mythical figure associated with holy wells. (cf ON *kelda*, spring)

St Enoch affectionate nickname given to Enoch Priestley of Wibsey, a **Methodist** (qv) alderman, whose campaign for a new road linking Wibsey with Bradford resulted in St Enoch's Road, named in his honour.

St Hilda's Serpents fossil cephalopods (ammonites) found in the rocks of the Yorkshire coast, popularly explained by the legend that St Hilda of Whitby (AD 614-680) once turned a plague of serpents into stone.

St John of Beverley Founder of a monastery at Beverley, where he later retired, John was renowned for his scholarship and sanctity. After his death in AD 721 many

St Hilda's Serpents are in fact ammonite fossils.

miracles were attributed to him, including the restoring of sight to a blind man and the victory of Agincourt, following which Henry V ordered his feast day (7th May) to be kept throughout England.

St Leger (see **horse racing**)

St Robert the twelfth century hermit, Robert Flower, born in York, who eventually settled in a cave on the River Nidd, near Knaresborough. Here he became renowned as a holy man and friend of the poor, and legends tell of his miraculous powers of healing and ability to tame stags to pull his plough. In 1216 he was visited by King John who granted him land on which was later built the Trinitarian Priory of St Robert. After Robert's death in 1218, pilgrims came from all over the county to visit his tomb, from which healing oil is said to have flowed.

St Wilfrid's Feast (see **Wilfra Feast**)

St Wilfrid's Needle passage in the Anglo-Saxon crypt of Ripon Cathedral (dedicated to St Wilfrid) through which women tradition-ally passed, proving their chastity if they could 'thread the needle' by being slim enough to get through.

St William famous twelfth century Archbishop of York to whom thirty-six miracles are attributed. Born William Fitz-herbert, of noble parents, he became chaplain to King Stephen, canon and treasurer of York Minster, then archbishop in 1142.

Accused of financial irregularities, he was deposed five years later, but restored in 1154. On his triumphant return to York the wooden bridge across the Ouse collapsed, but it is said that the crowd was saved from drowning as William miraculously changed the river to solid ground. His tomb (built in 1284) behind the high altar of the Minster was the site of further miracles, such as the restoration of eyes to a knight who had lost both. The miracles are commemorated in the St William window of 1422.

Saltaire Unique to Yorkshire's industrial heritage, this model village was built by Sir Titus Salt, pioneer of alpaca wool fabric, in 1853. As well as the mill on the River Aire, he provided a splendid Congregational chapel, schools, hospital, institute etc, and also homes, including forty-five alms-houses, and a fourteen acre park — but no pub, as he was a tee-totaller.

Saltaire lions four stone lions, eight feet in length, in the centre of Saltaire, originally sculpted for Trafalgar Square by Thomas Milner, but considered too small. The local tradition is that, when midnight strikes, they come to life and go down to the Aire to drink.

Saltersgate Inn an isolated pub on the Pickering to Whitby road, famous for its fire which is supposed to have burned contin-uously for at least 200 years. Originally called the Waggon and Horses, it is said to have been a meeting point for smugglers who secretly salted fish when salt was heavily taxed. Legend claims that an excise officer was killed here by smugglers and buried beneath the fireplace. Because of conservation measures, wood and coal are now kept burning instead of the traditional peat.

sam to gather, pick up, bring together *we're sammin' up*, we're collecting our things (OE *samnian*)

samcast land ploughed in five or six yard breadths

sark shirt; vest (OE *serce*)

sarra, sarrow to supply, feed (pigswill etc) (OF *servir*)

sarrowins slops and waste used to make pig swill

saumas loaves square cakes or loaves containing dried fruit, formerly made on All Souls Day (2nd November), similar to soul cakes in other parts of the UK (see *Cakin' Neet*) (from 'soul-mass')

savoury pudding baked in a tin and served with beef, like **Yorkshire pudding** (qv), but made of breadcrumbs, oatmeal, suet and onions, and flavoured with sage

scahr to scour, clean up (esp doorstep) (cf *mappin'-aht* (qv))

scahrin' stooane stone used to rub doorsteps and windowsills clean and leave a coloured finish at the edges (see **donkey stone**, *dooar-st'n, ruddlestooane*)

scale[1] metal frame in a penknife, carrying the blades WR (Sheffield area)

scale[2] to spread or rake out (manure etc) (? from the idea of measured distribution)

scale-boose (see *skelbeease*)

scallion shallot; spring onion; young onion with long neck and small bulb (OF *eschalogne*)

scar, scaur cliff or rocky outcrop on a hillside (ON *skera*, to cut)

Scar temporary village built for workmen and their families during the construction of Scar House Reservoir (1921-1936). The huts or hostels had electricity and flush toilets, and there was a large recreation room, cinema, bakehouse, laundry, hospital and church, as well as the services of the Nidd Valley Light Railway.

Scarborough Fair Originating in a charter of 1161 granted by Henry II, the fair was last held in 1896. It is commemorated by an old cross in the harbour and the folk song 'Are You Going to Scarborough Fair?'.

Scarborough Lily evergreen houseplant (*Vallota speciosa*) with trumpet-like red-orange flowers in late summer. Said to have originated in bulbs washed ashore near Scarborough from a wrecked ship on its way from South Africa. Alternatively it has been suggested that the bulbs were introduced from South Africa by a sea captain named Purnell in the nineteenth century.

Scarborough skipping (see **Shrove Tuesday**)

Scarborough warning This is usually defined as 'a punch first, then the warning'. In the seventeenth century it was described as 'a sudden mischief, felt before it is expected' and said to be derived

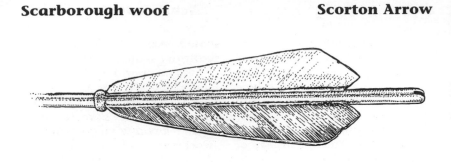

The Scorton Arrow, a silver trophy.

from the sudden, stealthy taking of Scarborough Castle by Sir Thomas Stafford in 1557. The phrase is older, however, and may have arisen because Scarborough, like Hull and Halifax, had a reputation for swift and summary treatment of law-breakers. (See **beggars' litany**.)

Scarborough woof kind of catfish landed esp in Scarborough and used in various Yorkshire dishes such as **woof pie**

scarpy dry, stony (soil) ER

scoddy meagre, poor (esp food)

scollops (see *collops*)

scopperdiddle (Sheffield area form of *scopperil* — see below)

scopperil small top, sometimes made from a button and a small peg, set spinning by finger and thumb; a lively child; small wheel used to impress a design into butter; small tube inserted in diseased animal's skin to drain off fluid; squirrel (Icelandic *skoppara-kringla* suggests ON origin, but could be related to OF *escureul*, from Latin *scuriolus*, squirrel)

Scorton Arrow silver arrow presented as a trophy, first competed for on the 14th May 1673 at Scorton near Catterick, and now the chief prize at the annual meeting of the Society of Archers,

Scarborough Lily

the oldest body of archers in the UK. The contest opens with the blowing of the Thirsk Bugle, after which any archer who swears is traditionally fined a shilling. The distance to the target is 100 yards. (see **archery**.)

Scott motorbikes much-prized motorbikes manufactured by the Shipley firm of Alfred Angus Scott (1884-1923), who built his first bike in 1906. The **Scott Trial**, run at Arkengarthdale each October, is said to be the toughest event of its kind in the world.

scouring process of washing wool to remove dirt and grease (see also *scahr, scahrin' stooane*)

scraffle to move with difficulty (eg through a crowd) NER

scran[1] food

scran[2] to gobble up

scrannel poor quality, worthless ER

scraps small remnants of pig meat, usually ready-cooked; scraps of batter, given free by fish and chip shops

scrat to scratch; to struggle to make a living

scrawm to scribble, scrawl; to scramble

scray low wooden frame on which cloth or produce is laid; low table (cf Dutch *schraag*, trestle)

scrimshaw whalebone, ivory etc ornamented by carved designs. Though not exclusive to Yorkshire, the craft was associated with sailors on the whaling ships of Hull and Whitby from as early as the seventeenth century (? from a surname)

Scripture Cake This was popular amongst the **Methodists** (qv) of the Dales, eaten at **Lovefeasts** (qv), anniversaries and open-air

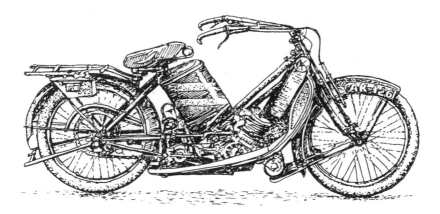

A Scott motorbike, made in Shipley.

'fruit banquets'. The ingredients of this rich fruitcake were all found in the Old Testament, and recipes consisted of texts. For example: 4 cups of 1 Kings IV 22 (flour), 1 cups of Judges V 25 (butter), 2 cups of Jeremiah VI 20 (sugar), 2 cups of 1 Samuel XXX 12 (raisins), and so on.

scrogs stunted bushes ER

scrow muddle, upheaval, rough and tumble; rubbish

scruffle, scuffle to hoe, esp between rows (eg of turnips), break up surface of rough ground

scruffler horseshoe hoe

scuff glancing blow, esp on back of head, with hand

scutch to strike, esp with thin stick or whip (OF *escoucher*)

scutters (see *skitters*)

scuttle basket for holding meal etc; metal receptacle for coal (ON *skutill*)

seam kind of **tripe** (qv)

Seamer Fair Established by Richard II, the fair at Seamer, near Scarborough, continues to be proclaimed, even though the fair itself has lapsed. Each St Swithins Day (15th July) the lord and lady of the manor read the charter under an old oak tree on the village green, then scatter coins to be scrambled for by local children.

season pudding savoury pudding baked in a similar way to **Yorkshire pudding** (qv), containing sage and onion (cf **savoury pudding**)

seck sack

seckaree kind of smock formerly worn by farm labourers ER

seea so NER

seeaf safe NER

seeaminla apparently

seean soon NER

seeap soap NER

seear sure NER; *Ah seear*, I'm sure ER

seeat[1] seat WR (ON *saeti*)

seeat[2] soot NER (OE *sot*)

seeaves rushes NER (ON *sef*)

seed saw (esp NER)

seemin'-glass mirror

seet sight; a great deal (OE *sihth*)

seg[1] small metal stud hammered into the sole or heel of a shoe to minimise wear — probably an extension of the original meaning of a piece of hard skin or callus (ON *sigg*)

seg[2] animal which has been gelded; old bull

seg[3] sedge, reed

seggie second (in children's games) (cf **ferrie**, **laggy**)

segrams ragwort NER

seizure stroke (usually used in the sense of a less severe stroke)

selled, sellt sold

Semerwater said to be Yorkshire's only true natural lake. According to legend, beneath its waters lies a submerged city, flooded as a result of a curse made by a mysterious beggar who had been denied shelter there, and found hospitality only in a humble cottage on the hillside. The huge Carlow Stone on the shore, said to have been thrown at the inhabitants by a giant, is supposed to bring prosperity when touched by couples about to marry. In 1956 the tradition was started of holding a lakeside service on August Bank Holiday Sunday, conducted from a boat to commemorate the preaching of Jesus from a boat on the Sea of Galilee. (See **Gormire**.)

semmanty slender, graceful NER

sen self (*missen*, *thissen* etc)

Sessay Giant mythical being associated with the village of Sessay, between Thirsk and Easingwold. He is said to have had one eye, the mouth of a lion, and to have carried off cows under his arm. He is supposed to have been killed by Guy Dawney from S Yorks, after he had been stunned by the sail of a windmill.

set to lay (table); to sow (seed)

set on (see *burnt on*)

Set'day-neet voice affected speech, with dialect features suppressed (probably because Saturday night social gatherings meant more contact with '*off-comed-uns*' (qv))

set pot (pron with emphasis on second word) large copper for boiling water, fixed in a corner of the living room, usually next to the fireplace *Ah've an 'eead like a set pot*, I've a very bad headache (see *pot-side*)(OE *settan*, to place)

setten up placed; provided for NER

settle wooden seat, usually with high back and sides, and sometimes a chest underneath; couch, sofa (cf *lang settle*, *squab*) (see drawing on page 42) (OE *setl*)

sewer sure

Sexhow Worm the mythical dragon-like serpent associated with the village of Sexhow, which once stood near Hutton Rudby. It was said to feed on the milk of nine cows every day — until it was finally killed and its skin hung up in the church at Hutton Rudby. (See **worms**.)

shackle wrist

shaht to shout WR

shahve (see *shive*)

shak to shake (OE *scacan*)

shakked shaken

shakked i' bits falling apart; crazy WR

shambles name given to streets in York, Wetherby and Kirbymoorside, but not confined to Yorkshire. Originally this term referred to food stalls, esp those used by butchers.

shape to get organised, make an effort; to show promise (cf *frame* (qv))

sharn cow dung

sharp quick *bi sharp, mak sharp!*, hurry up!

Shat Skellmanthorpe (nickname said to refer to those who 'shattered' Pontefract in Civil War)

shedder passageway with gate at one end enabling sheep to be separated

sheddler swindler WR

sheepdog trials These are held at various times all over the county. The Yorkshire Sheepdog Society, for example, usually holds its championship Open Sheepdog Trials in early May at locations varying from year to year. One of the best-known trials takes place in June at Harden Moss on the

The set pot, with a piggin or lading can, and a voider full of washing.

moors above Holmfirth. First held in 1908, it involves more than 200 working dogs.

sheep counting Also known as sheep-scoring, this system of numerals is said to go back to the Ancient Britons, and in its structure is similar to the ordinal numbering in Celtic languages, eg Welsh. Rarely heard nowadays, except for the first few numbers, **sheep counting** numerals were nevertheless in use here and there during the first half of the twentieth century, and were in standard use until around the middle of the nineteenth century, when most systems were written down. These vary from place to place. As an example, here is the Wensleydale one: 1 *yan*;.2 *tean*; 3 *tither*; 4 *mither*; 5 *pip*; 6 *teaser*; 7 *leaser*; 8 *catra*; 9 *horna*; 10 *dick*; 11 *yan-dick*; 12 *tean-dick*; 13 *tither-dick*; 14 *mither-dick*; 15 *bumper*; 16 *yan-a-bum*; 17 *tean-a-bum* 18 *tither-a-bum*; 19 *mither-a-bum*; 20 *jigger*

Sheffield Plate copper plated with steel, by a process accidentally discovered in Sheffield by Thomas Boulsover in 1742

shelvins additional sides to increase capacity of a cart when used for carrying hay (see drawing on page 88)

shenk dish with small holes used for skimming cream off milk

shent ower overcast ER

Shepherd Lord nickname of Henry Clifford, son of Lady Anne Clifford of Skipton, who sent him to Cumberland to train as a

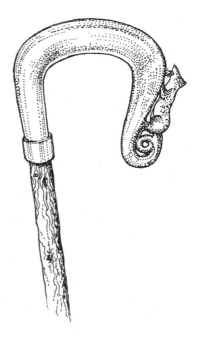

A shepherd's crook.

shepherd, to avoid capture during the Wars of the Roses. He returned to Skipton Castle, but was said to be happier hunting in the Forest of Barden, where he built Barden Tower in about 1485.

shepster starling (? from the bird's habit of standing on the back of sheep, looking for ticks)

sherbet fountain cylindrical packet from which the *kali* (qv) is sucked up through a tube of liquorice

Shevvilder inhabitant of Sheffield

shibband shoelace (from 'shoe' and 'band', string)

shift to move, to get a move on etc *shift aht o' t' rooad!* (OE *sciftan*)

shim Dutch hoe ER

shippen, shippon cowshed (OE *scypen*)

shippy (see *shepster*)

Shipton (see Mother Shipton)

shirl (see *guider*)

Shirley **Country** name sometimes given to the Spen Valley parishes of Birstall, Batley, Mirfield, Dewsbury and Hartshead, in which Charlotte Brontë set her 1849 novel *Shirley*. (See Luddites.)

shive thick slice (of bread, meat)

shiver very thin slice

shockle (see *shoggle*)

shoddy cloth made from shredded rags, discarded woollen goods and waste from spinning and weaving, mainly in the mills of Dewsbury, Ossett and Batley, the process having been invented by Benjamin Law in 1813. Softer and generally of poorer quality than *mungo* (qv).

shoe-cross sign of the cross made with a wetted finger on toe of boot or shoe to bring luck or ward off cramp NR

sho'el shovel NER

shoeing the hob early form of *quoits* (qv) in which a horseshoe was thrown on to an iron pin called a *hob*

shog to walk in a slow, uncertain manner, as with extreme tiredness or old age WR

shoggle icicle; stalactite, stalagmite NER (abbr for 'ice-shoggle')

sholl to slither, slip, slide

shoo she (Note that it is usually pron with a very short vowel, and is best represented as *sh'*)

shoon, shooin shoes (OE *scogean*)

shooit to shoot WR

shoot to shout NER

shop place *all ovver t' shop* WR

shot rid *wi mun get shot on it* (cf 'get shut of')

showther shoulder

Shrove Tuesday (see *barring-out*, pancake bell, whipping tops and below)

Shrove Tuesday Skipping an old Scarborough tradition, possibly originating in the practice of fishermen discarding worn rope when they changed from line-fishing to potting around **Shrove Tuesday**. The skipping is accompanied by traditional rhymes, and takes place on the foreshore in the afternoon, having been heralded in at noon by the ringing of the **pancake bell** (qv).

shun to ignore a person, not speak to them (OE *scunian*)

shutten shut NER

shutter to fall down in disorder (eg out of a container); to fall heavily (rain etc) *it's shutterin' dahn* WR

shygram shawl NR

sich such

sickened emotionally upset WR

sickened off repelled, put off WR

side[1] to clear (eg dishes etc from a table); to put away *side them pots*

side[2] superior attitude because of status etc *ther's no side on 'im*

side by to bury ER

sider person who clears table etc

sike (see *syke*)

sike(n) such

sile[1] to strain, pour, as through a sieve; to rain heavily *it's silin' dahn* (cf Norwegian dialect *sila*)

sile[2] strainer, sieve, esp in cheese-making

sile[3] young herring NER

siller silver (OE *seolfor*)

silverwhips wild cabbage NER

simmeron primrose NR

simnel cake rich fruitcake, including a layer of marzipan inside and on top, decorated with eleven balls of marzipan representing the Apostles, without Judas. Traditionally eaten the fourth Sunday in **Lent** (qv), Mothering Sunday, which was also known as **Refreshment Sunday** or **Simnel Sunday**. On this day, farmworkers and apprentices visited their mothers, bringing flowers and simnel cake. (OF *simenel*, from Latin *simila*, wheaten flour)

sin since

sind to rinse, wash down (see Castleford)

sipe to ooze, drain slowly (OE *sipian*, to soak)

sippet wooden shovel used for grain ER

sitha! sither! look (here)! (originally *see thee/thou!*)

sitting-up This refers to the custom of children sitting on a platform at the front of a chapel for the Sunday School Anniversary, dressed in their best clothes, facing the congregation. Their recitations and singing formed an important part of the service.

skahme (see *skyme*) NER

skeeal school NER

skeeath disc for cutting grass, which is fixed to the front of a ploughshare

skeel wooden pail used for milking, with one section extended to serve as a handle

skeets skids for launching *cobles* (qv) NER

skeg to glance, peep

skelbeease division within a cowshed (ON *skelja*, to divide)

skell(er) to warp, twist, esp of wood

skell up to upset, overturn

skellered warped, crooked

skelp to beat, thrash

sken to squint at; to look intently

sken-eyed having a squint

skep, skip basket; coal bucket; wheeled container used to charge a blast furnace; wicker tray used for carrying baited lines (Yorkshire coast fisherman's term) (ON *skeppa*)

skerrick small amount, tiny bit *Eyt it up — ivvery last skerrick*

skew-whiff aslant, cockeyed

skift (see *shift*)

skillet small iron pan (? OF *escuelet*)

skillie[1] thin gruel WR

skillie[2] skylark WR

skimmer to shine brightly, sparkle NR

skipping (see **Shrove Tuesday**)

skitter to scamper off, hurry along

skitters diarrhoea (ON *skita*)

skive to split, pare, leather or hide (ON *skifa*)

skrike to shriek (ON *skraekja*)

Skull of Burton Agnes skull of Anne Griffith, said to be bricked up in a wall of seventeenth century Burton Agnes Hall near Bridlington. Anne, mortally wounded by thieves, begged her two sisters to keep her head in the home she loved. After her burial in the churchyard, the hall was subjected to ghostly disturbances until the skull was brought back there.

skyme to glance sideways, furtively or scornfully NER

slaape slippery NER

slack[1] depression in the ground, small valley, dell, hollow in a hillside (ON *slakki*)

slack[2] coal dust and very small bits of coal

slack[3] with little work or business

slack-jack lazy person

slack-set-up careless, ineffectual, casual (textile term originally referring to belts too slack on the pulleys, or to warp too slack for weaving)

slack-wun'-up (see *slack-set-up*)

slaht to splash, splatter with mud etc; to spill or dribble liquid

slammack to loiter ER

slape (see *slaap*)

slapstone (see *slopstooan*)

slart (see *slaht*)

slasher kind of bill-hook used for trimming hedges and cutting undergrowth

slate to set, encourage to attack (dog); to scold, rebuke effectively *a reight slatin'*, a real telling-off

slatter to spill, splash, slop WR

sleck (see *slack*)

slifter space between flagstones, crack in a wall

Slingsby Serpent the mythical dragon-like serpent or **worm** (qv) associated with the village of Slingsby near Malton in the fourteenth century, said to have encircled the fair damsel Helena before being killed by Sir William Wyville.

slippy slippery

slipe to shave off; to cut peat NER

slive to move stealthily ER

slob to slip (of loose-fitting shoes) (cf *slotch*)

slocken to slake, quench (thirst)

slop smock WR

slops trousers; trouser legs

slopstooan stone sink, usually a shallow one, in which buckets were stood to drain after being filled

slotch to move about (of shoes etc) because too loosely fitting; to eat noisily or greedily

slotch person of slovenly appearance; drunkard

slought (see *slaht*)

slowdy soft, flabby ER

Slowit Slaithwaite, one of the places which earned the jibe *'wheeare the' raked t' mooin aht o' t' cut'* (qv)

slowp gulp *'e supped it at yah slowp* NER

sloyd elementary training in woodwork and carving (named after a Swedish system, originally *sloejd*)

sluffed, sluffened disheartened, low in spirits (see *heart-sluffened*)

slug to destroy (esp a bird's nest)

slummery soft, slimy etc, because undercooked (eg an egg)

slummocky dirty, untidy (of a person)

sluthery slimy, slippery (eg of path) (? var of 'slither')

slutter (see *shutter*)

smallest church the church at Upleatham, near Saltburn, is said to be the smallest church, not only in Yorkshire, but in England. It has, however, been reduced from its original size.

smeeak smoke NER

smiddy¹ smithy, esp S Yorks

smiddy² hive or swarm of insects ER

smit to mark sheep (OE *smitan*, to smear)

smittle to infect (with a cold etc) (cf *smit*)

smock-raffled out of routine, muddled

smooat-'ole hole through hedge made by rabbits and hares; hole made to let sheep through NR

smoot hole in which a sheep shelters NR (see also *thirl*)

smopple brittle, crisp ER

smow to smirk, chuckle to oneself WR

snaffle to talk through the nose NER

snap¹ packed lunch, originally as used by coalminers in the WR, and by leadminers in NR

snap² crisp, brittle kind of ginger biscuit, for example **brandy snap** (qv)

snape to check growth (of plants) NER

snattle to fritter (away); to delay

sneck door latch — strictly speaking the bar or part of the latch which is lifted by pressing

on a thumb lever

sneck-lifter gift, as inducement, to wife or girlfriend; single drink (in a pub) bought in the hope of being made welcome WR

sneel snail NR

snell cold and wet (weather) WR

snew snowed NER

snicket passageway, esp when this is a short cut (cf *ginnel*)

snickle to tie a noose for a snare

snickleway term specially coined in 1983 by M W Jones to describe the narrow passages between the buildings of old York (combination of *snicket*, *ginnel* and alley)

snig to haul, drag out, esp timber on ground; to tow hay to the barn

sniggle (see *snickle*)

snirkled shrivelled with drought NR

snirp¹ to scorch NR

snirp² so cold the grass is frozen NR

snitch nose (see below)

snite to blow or wipe the nose, esp without using a handkerchief (OE *snytan*)

snizy bitingly cold and damp NR

snob cobbler

snod smooth, sleek; short (sheep's fleece) (? ON *snothin*, bald)

snook to sniff (up nose)

snotters cold in the head, with runny nose etc WR

snubbits projecting parts at rear of a cart on which it rests when tilted up

sny sneaky (of a wind etc)

Society of Yorkshiremen in London name of the once prestigious society which first met on the 3rd December 1678, and in

1688 commissioned the **Yorkshire Feast Song** (qv). An inaugural dinner of a later society was held in 1899, when it was estimated that 14,000 Yorkshiremen lived in London. (See **Yorkshire Society**.)

sock ploughshare (OF *soc*)

sodger soldier (OF *soudier*)

soft weak, cowardly WR; foolish NER (OE *softe*)

sooalin', sooavin' huge ER

sooart kind *t' first o' t' sooart, nowt o' t' sooart*

sooth south NER

soss[1] to drink, lap up; to splash

soss[2] to fall wearily or heavily into a chair or onto a bed

soul cakes (see *saumas* and *Cakin' Neet*)

South Riding fictitious Riding created by Winifred Holtby in her novel of that name (1936), set mainly in Holderness. There cannot, of course, be a fourth Riding, since by definition each is a third (see **Riding**)

spa Formerly often spelt **spaw**, the name comes from Spa in Belgium, and was first applied to the Tewit Well in Harrogate, described in about 1594 as 'the English Spa'. People came to 'take the waters' at Yorkshire **spas** including Ilkley, Skipton, Aldfield (near Ripon), Malton, Askern (near Doncaster) Whitby and Boston Spa, but the best-known were Harrogate (1571) and Scarborough (1620), the latter becoming 'The Queen of the Watering-Places'. (See **Stinking Spaw**.)

spadger sparrow WR

spand dappled with red and white (eg calf)

spak spoke

spane (see *speean*)

spane off to return to normal meals after superior meals (eg on holiday) WR

spang to throw, esp violently; to spring NR

spanish liquorice. Liquorice root, chewed and sucked, used to be popular amongst Yorkshire children, as did all kinds of sweets made from *spanish* (so called from the country of origin). Concentrated liquorice sold by chemists was widely used to make a simple drink, known as *spanish water*, usually carried round in a medicine bottle and *swigged* from time to time. (See below and also **Pomfret Cakes**.)

Spanish Sunday Spanish water was, in some areas, drunk on Good Friday or Palm Sunday, hence the name **Spanish Sunday**

sparable (see *spav*)

spaulder to sprawl, spread out

spav small headless nail made esp for **clog irons**

Spaw Sunday the first Sunday in May, formerly the traditional time for drinking water from a local spring or **spa**, esp in the Calder Valley. (See **spa**, *spawer*, **Stinking Spaw**.)

spawer visitor, tourist NER (from 'spaw', early spelling of **spa**)

spawin' visiting the seaside or other watering places; to take out visitors for pleasure trips in boats NER

spawlder (see *spaulder*)

speead spade NER

speean¹ to wean an animal; to separate lambs from ewe

speean² spoon NER

spelder to spell NR

spelk¹ thin piece of hazel or willow used in thatching, split down the middle and pushed in to hold the thatch (cf *spell²*)

spell, spelk² small splinter of wood in finger etc; rail, bar, rung (cf German *spellen*, to split)

spell³ spring trap used in game of *knur and spell* (qv)

spenged pied, esp red and white (of cattle) (cf *spand*) NER

sperrins (see *spurrins*)

sperrit spirit

spetch¹ to patch WR

spetch² sticking plaster WR

speyk¹ to speak

speyk² saying or story in Yorkshire dialect, usually known as a *'Yorkshire speyk'*; sometimes used in a perjorative way

spice sweets *you can't 'ave t' spice an' t' 'awp'nny*. The term was originally used of gingerbread etc, then applied to all confectionery, as some of the early sweets were spice-like, eg peppermints, aniseed balls, clove balls etc. (see **Yorkshire mixture**.) (OF *espice*)

spice cake rich fruitcake, esp Christmas cake, traditionally eaten with cheese. Each portion is supposed to bring the eater a 'happy month' in the New Year. It is also considered unlucky to cut spice cake or **Yule cake** before Christmas Eve.(See **Yule cake**.)

spink chaffinch

spit long, thin spade used esp for digging drains in fields (OE *spittan*, to dig with a spade)

spittle small, flat wooden shovel used to handle bread etc in the oven

A spittle, used for handling dough and bread.

splart, splurt to spray out or sprinkle (water) WR

splatter-footed knock-kneed WR, esp S Yorks

splauder to spread out NER

sploats catapult

spogs (see *spice*)

Spon Spurn Head

sporn to spur

sprag¹ strong piece of wood or metal used to place between spokes of wheels to stop trucks etc moving; support used to prop up roof

sprag² to tell tales, reveal secrets WR

sprag³ young codfish (Yorkshire coast fisherman's term)

spraggy bony ER

sprat sixpenny piece WR

spretch to crack (of hatching eggs)

A sprag, for jamming wheels.

spriggets fresh new growth of heather

sprodden spread

sprog¹ to spit

sprog² young child, baby

sprottle to struggle, esp with little effect; to struggle to keep balance or get up after a fall (term used mostly of animals); to spread oneself out WR

sprottle-fooited splay-footed WR

spuggy house sparrow

spurrins banns of marriage (OE *spyrian*, to ask)

spurtle stick for stirring (cf *thible*) NER

squab kind of *lang settle* (qv) with cushion; couch

stack mill chimney; vertical part of a blast furnace

staddle, staddling foundation of a haystack, frame of posts and beams NER

stag young gelding NER

staggers disease of animals, esp sheep, affecting ability to walk

staggarth stack yard (of a farm)

stagnated taken aback NER

staith, steeath landing stage, quayside (cf **Staithes**) NR

Staithes bonnet distinctive cap traditionally worn by the women of Staithes on the East Coast, originally by all the wives and womenfolk of fishermen. The design shows Viking influence, and similar bonnets were once worn in Norway. The **Staithes bonnet** protected the head when women carried baskets of bait or fish, the flap at the back stopping water dripping down the neck.

stale (see *steyl*)

stalled fed up (with), tired (of), satiated (? from cattle fattened up in a stall)

Stamford Bridge Pie Less familiar than the **Denby Dale Pie** (qv), these pear pies were baked and shared by the community every 25th September. This was said to commemorate a vital turning point during the Battle of Stamford Bridge in 1066, when an English soldier sailed under the bridge in a malting tub and speared the Viking who was guarding it. The pies were made in the shape of a boat, or tub, with a skewer to represent the spear. Though the custom died out, it has been revived, for example, in 1966.

stand pie large pork pie, popular at Christmas, so called because such pies were originally made with a hand-raised pastry crust standing without the need of a dish. (See *growler*.)

The Staithes bonnet — symbol of the Yorkshire coast fishing communities.

*Three birds common in Yorkshire: shepster (above),
spuggy (below left) and stoggy (below right).*

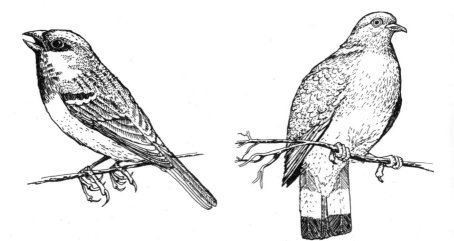

stang pole, shaft, stake, wooden bar (see **Riding the Stang**) (ON *stangar*)

starnel starling (see also *shepster*)

starved very cold (of person), perishing with cold *wi wor fair starved aht theeare, starved ter deeath* (OE *steorfan*, to die, suffer intensely)

starved-un person who easily feels cold

stattis This was the annual hiring fair for farmhands and domestic servants, commonly held in November, usually at **Martinmas** (qv). Those seeking work would line up in the centre of a market town, waiting to be taken on for a year and a day, the transaction being confirmed by the mutual exchange of a 'God's-penny'. (Corruption of 'statutes', laws first framed for the engagement of labourers in the reign of Edward III.)

statute (see above)

stawpins holes in muddy ground made by cattle or horses; hoof marks (see also *stowp²*)

steddin farm building

stee ladder; stile (ON *stige*)

steeanchecker stonechat

steeane stone NER (OE *stan*)

steeap (see *stoup*)

Steeas Staithes, once well-known for its inhabitants making a living by collecting *flithers* (qv) for bait., and for the ancient fishing community symbolised by the **Staithes bonnet** (qv) (see drawing on page 173)

steg gander (ON *steggi*, male bird)

stell hole gutter, drain in farmyard

stem to leave a cow unmilked

stepmother blessing sore piece of skin at root of fingernail

stevvan to shout lustily, bawl; to order, reserve; to speak beforehand (OE *stefn*)

stey (see *stee*)

steyl handle, esp of a brush or broom

stick an' stivver everything, completely (cf 'lock, stock and barrel')

stiddy (see *stithy*)

stilt handle of a plough

stingo strong beer from the first brewing

Stinking Spaw the Old Sulphur Well in Low Harrogate, notorious for the stench of its mineral water containing hydrogen sulphide and smelling of bad eggs. For fifty-six years (until 1843) it was presided over by Betty Lupton, 'Queen of the Harrogate Wells'. (See also **Harrogate headache**, spa.)

stint right to pasture on a common (eg a **stint for ten kye** — ten head of cattle)

stirk bullock or heifer of about a year old (OE *stirc*)

stithy anvil (ON *stethi*)

stob piece of wood pointed at one end; stump of a tree NER

stoddy foolish, inept *as stoddy as a yat-stowp* ER

stoggy wood pigeon (ie ring dove or stock dove)

stood standing

stook a group of sheaves of corn (ME *stouk*)

stoop (see *stoup*)

stoor (see *stower*)

stop it off! stop! (doing something) WR

storken to set; to stiffen as it cools *t' bacon an' eggs 'as storkened* (ON *storkna*, to coagulate)

stot bullock; sword dancer (see **Plough Stots**)

stoup post, gatepost, mile post; standing stone (see **Two Stoups**) (ON *stolpi*)

stour, stower rung of a ladder; stake, pole (ON *staurr*)

stower mist, blizzard, driving rain, cloud of dust, so it is difficult to see ahead *it's stowerin' an' we can't see owt* NR

Stowksla Stokesley

stowmer horse which is a good worker NER

stowp[1] (see *stoup*)

stowp[2] deep footprint of cattle NR (see also *stawpins*)

strackle to struggle against odds

stracklin person who tries hard, but is ineffectual

strake part of the iron rim of a cartwheel

strang strong NER (ON *strangr*)

strap credit WR

straw to spread, esp hay

stray common land, originally for pasture, esp the **Stray** in Harrogate (OF *estrayer*)

streea straw NER (OE *streaw*)

strickle[1] whetstone for a scythe etc (OE *stricel*)

strickle[2] to sharpen, hone (a blade, scythe etc)

Strid narrow passage between the rocks where the River Wharfe forces its way through in Bolton Abbey Woods. Though it looks easy to jump across, many have been drowned here in the turbulent water, notably the Boy of Egremond, or 'young Romilly'. The legend is retold by Wordsworth in *The Force of Prayer*. The boy, hunting with his greyhound, jumped across the Strid 'perhaps for the hundredth time'. The poem goes on: 'But the greyhound in the leash hung back, And checked him in his leap. The boy is in the arms of the Wharfe, And strangled by a merciless force.' Bolton Priory is said to have been built in his memory — though his name appears next to his mother's in

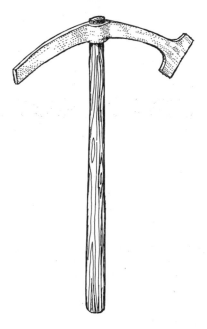

A stubbin' dig.

176

The Swaledale tup, used as the logo of the Yorkshire Dales National Park.

the charter. (See also **White Doe of Rylstone**.) (OE for 'stride', but probably originally from OE *strith*, turmoil, because of the turbulent water.)

strinkle to scatter, sprinkle

strunt first few inches of a horse's tail (nearest the body) NER

stubbin' dig implement for digging out roots of bushes etc ER

study to turn things over in the mind, meditate, think hard (often with implication of anxiety) *Ah lay awake studyin'* (extension of standard use, cf SE 'in a brown study')

stunt obstinate NER

stupid obstinate, stubborn (cf 'as stupid as a mule')

suckshin liquid manure NR

sud should

suited pleased *'e's reight suited wi 'is new car* (OF *siute*)

summat something (var of somewhat)

Sunderland *t' Sunderland*, the Huddersfield music festival (see **Queen of Song**)

sup to drink (OE *supan*)

swad pod (peas etc)

Swadil Swaledale

swage ornamental bevel on top edge of knife blade; die for use on an anvil; tool for bending metal WR

swale, sweeal to burn, blaze, melt away (candle); to throw away, waste

Swaledale breed of sheep, the rams of which are the most highly

177

valued. Predominant in the NR, they have black faces with white at the nose end (cf **Dalesbred**). This is the sheep used as the symbol for the National Park. (See **Yorkshire Dales, Tan Hill**.)

Swaledale cheese As in the case of **Wensleydale cheese** (qv) this was once made only in farmhouses, but since 1987 it has been made commercially by the Swaledale Cheese Company of Richmond.

swang bog; long oar NER

swape cross-bar of wooden gate; handle of mangle; pump handle

Swardill Swaledale

swarf, swarth[1] grit worn from grindstones when blades etc are ground; mixture of grease and grit, on axles etc (S Yorks) (see *yaller-belly*) (ON *svarf*, file-dust)

swarf, swarth[2] bacon rind, pork crackling, fat (OE *swearth*)

swarth, swath[3] lowland grass WR

Swastika Stone inscribed stone, dating from the Bronze Age or early Iron Age (2,000-500 BC), on the edge of Ilkley Moor near the top of Hebers Ghyll. Similar to designs found elsewhere in Europe,

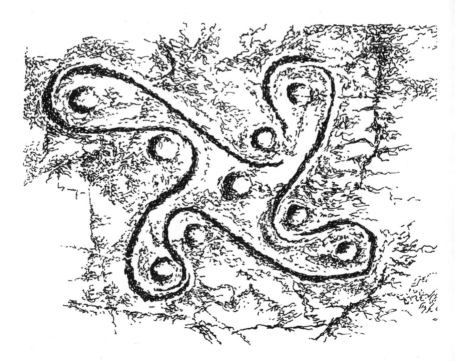

The Swastika Stone, Ilkley Moor.

this may symbolise fire or the sun. The name is derived from the Sanskrit for 'good fortune'.

swatch   sample, pattern book (of cloth) WR

swathe   originally the breadth of grass or corn cut down by one sweep of the scythe; area of cut grass ready for haymaking

sweet cake   plain (sweet) cake, as distinct from **spice cake** (qv)

swidden   area of moorland where the heather has been *swiddened* or deliberately burnt off to encourage new growth or *spriggets* (qv), and so help the grouse population

Swift Nick   popular name of the highwayman John Nevison, born in 1648 at Wortley, near Pontefract, where his brother was schoolmaster. Like Robin Hood he is supposed to have robbed the rich to give to the poor. Hanged at York in 1684, his legendary exploits have contributed to the mythology surrounding **Dick Turpin** (qv). (see **Nevison's Leap, Walton Calves.**)

swig   drink, often a quick gulp that is cadged *Gi' us a swig!*

swingle tree   pivoted bar to which horse traces are fastened

swipple   short bar or a flail, the latter used when corn was threshed by hand

swite   to sharpen wood or a pencil to a point WR

swithen   (see *swidden*)

swittle   small poker, heated to bore holes NR

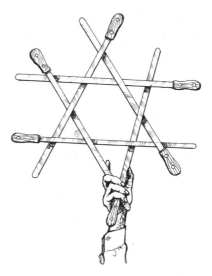

The lock held aloft at the climax of a longsword dance.

swizzen   (see *swidden*)

sword-dancing   a tradition dating from pagan times, as is indicated by the climax of certain of the Yorkshire dances, when the swords are skilfully woven into a **lock** and held aloft, perhaps to symbolise the sun. The **longsword dancers** of Grenoside place the lock over the head of one dancer and lift off his fur hat to symbolise beheading. Yorkshire teams or 'sides' mostly use longswords of 30-40 inches in length. (See **Boxing Day, Plough Monday** and **Plough Stots.**)

syke   small stream, gully, gutter

Sykes family   (see **Wold Rangers**)

T

t' The definite article 'the' is pronounced as a glottal stop before consonants, or as **t'** before vowels. West of Halifax it is sometimes pronounced as **th'** before vowels. In the ER, esp in Holderness, it is sometimes not pronounced at all.

ta, tha you (familiar form) *What's tha doin'?* WR

tab end originally a textile term referring to the first woven end to which the strips of the warp are attached; the discarded end of a cigarette

tab rug sometimes called a *rag rug* because it is made from odd bits of material (*tabs* or rags) pushed through hessian backing on a frame by means of a **brod** (qv) or peg — hence the other name of *pegged rug*

tabs waste ends from piece of cloth WR; ears WR, esp S Yorks

tack food, esp if of inferior quality *poor tack*

tackler weaving overlooker, loom *tuner* (qv) WR

ta'en taken

taffled tangled, knotted

tahme time

tahn town WR

tak, tek to take

tak off, tek off to imitate

tak on, tek on to make a fuss *Deean't tak on seea!* NER

tak up, tek up to improve (of weather)

tale account of something not necessarily true *It's a tale!*, It's not true, *awf a tale*, not the full story

tallacky messy, loose, flabby

tally living together without being married *they're livin' tally* (see also **brush**, **daytal**)

tang projecting part of knife etc fixed into handle (ON *tange*)

Tan Hill Inn name of the highest inn (1,732 feet) not only in Yorkshire but in England. It was built in 1737 to serve local miners, and passing drovers and packhorse traders on their way to County Durham. Today it serves as a base for the annual Swaledale Sheep Fair.

tanner sixpenny piece

tantattlin fancy cake, small tart, dainty food

tantle to dawdle, loiter, idle time away; to do odd jobs NER

tap-'oil opening through which molten metal runs out in a blast furnace

tar band[1] strip of black material, usually velvet, worn by older women round neck, sometimes with small cameo broach attached. It was traditionally thought to protect the throat, warding off infection. The smelling of tar was thought to cure coughs, esp *kincough* (whooping cough), and children were often taken to breathe in the fumes when roads were being tarmacadamed.

tar band[2] string dipped in tar to stop ends fraying

tarrant badly-behaved child NR

taws marbles, once the basis of the popular game of ring-taws. The players each placed the same number of marbles in a circle drawn on the ground, then took turns to drive out marbles, the order being determined by the nearness of each player's marble to a large marble rolled some distance from the ring. The

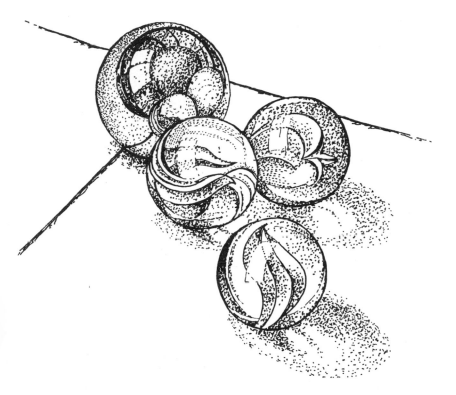

Taws — marbles of glass or metal.

various games were known by terms such as **plonkers**, **'oily** and **ringy**. Marbles, kept in special cloth bags, were won and lost, unless the players agreed to play **nowts**, when none changed hands. (See **alley-taws, blood-alley, bollie, dobby¹, mabs**.)

teagle crane; tripod of poles with chain and pulley for hoisting (var of 'tackle')

ted to turn and spread (hay); to rake into heaps

tee to tie (OE *tegan*)

teea¹ toe NER

teea² tea WR

teead toad NER

teeafit (see *tewit*)

teeak took NER

teeap (see *tup*)

teeave¹ (see *tew*)

teeave² to paddle NR

teem to pour (out); to unload (a cart); to rain heavily   *it wor teemin' it dahn* WR (ON *toema*)

teemer man who pours out molten metal from a blast furnace

Teeswater breed of sheep indigenous to Teesdale, with esp good fleece, used in cross-breeding

teg sheep in its second year (see also *hog*)

tekken taken

telled, tellt told (not ungrammatical, but an older form)

tell-tale-tit tale-bearer, revealer of secrets — used esp in children's rhyme beginning: 'Tell-tale-tit, Your tongue'll split' (originally **tell-pie-tit** from 'pie', magpie)

temse sieve, esp for sieving flour (OF *tamis*)

teng to sting (OE *stingan*)

teng-lether dragonfly NR

tent to watch over, to look after (eg grazing animals) (var of 'attend')

tenter¹ cowherd; the man who watches over engines and machinery in a mill WR

tenter² wooden frame for stretching and drying cloth (OF *tendre*, to stretch)

ter-morn tomorrow *ter-morn i' t' morn*, tomorrow morning (ME *morwen*)

ter-neet tonight

Terriers nickname for Huddersfield Town Football Club

testril badly-behaved child NR

tetchy peevish, irritable NER

tew to toil, work hard, struggle to accomplish (? OE *tawian*, to treat badly)

tewit lapwing

tewit grund marshy area of moorland (see **moor**)

Tewit Well (see **spa**)

tewtle to snow just a few flakes NR

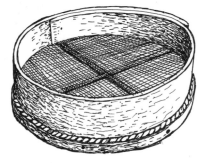

Temse.

A thacker or theeaker, climbing a stee.

tha, thi you; your (familiar form)

thack, theeak to thatch (OE *thaec*)

thack-brod (see *brod¹*)

tharf cake oatmeal bread or cake, usually thick, made with lard and treacle (cf *watti cake*) (OE *theorf*, unleavened)

that so *'e wor that 'ungry*; also used as a tag for emphasis, eg *it is that!*

theatres Yorkshire has a long tradition of itinerant acting in **mummers** (qv) and **mystery plays** (qv), and several theatres dating from the eighteenth century, such as the Theatre Royal in York built in 1744 and later to flourish under Tate Wilkinson. Richmond's small but authentic Georgian Theatre was built in 1788 (restored in 1962), and, under the management of Samuel Butler, became part of a circuit which included Guisborough, Ripon, Harrogate and Pontefract.

theet   watertight, closely woven *as theet as a bottle* (said of Staithes fishing boats) ER (prob not var of tight, but from OE *thiwan*, to smear with pitch)

them   those *them 'osses*

thible   wooden implement for stirring, esp porridge; stick for stirring washing (cf *spurtle*)

thick   on very friendly terms, in collusion

thills   shafts of a cart ER

thimmle   thimble (OE *thymel*)

thine   yours (familiar form)

think on   (pron with emphasis on second word) to remember, esp to do something *Think on! Tha mun fetch t' brass termorn*

thirl   hole through wall used by sheep NR (OE *thyrel*)

Thirsk Bugle   (see **Scorton Arrow**)

thissel, thissen   yourself

thivle, thivvel   (see *thible*)

thoddy   third person (in a team or on a farm)

thoil   to be willing to give; to afford; to endure, tolerate, put up with, allow (usually in the negative) *Ah can't thoil it*; a person who has no *thoil* or who will not *stand 'is thoil* is lacking in generosity WR (OE *tholian*)

Thible.

Thomassing custom once observed on St Thomas's Day (21st December) of poorer women and children going round begging, originally mainly for pearled wheat which was used to make frumenty (qv)

thondil plot of land for ploughing, roughly three-quarters of an acre

thosty thirsty

thra from

thrang (see *throng*)

thrave a stook of corn, originally consisting of two groups of twelve (ON *threfi*)

Three Laps nickname of William Sharp of Laycock, Keighley, who inherited the name from his miserly father, who had used this phrase when ordering a suit. Because of his father's quarrel over the marriage settlement, William's engagement was broken off. He was so upset that he took to his bed, where he is said to have stayed for forty-nine years until his death in 1856. (See also *laps*.)

Three Peaks popular traditional fell race, starting and finishing in Horton-in-Ribblesdale, and taking in the summits of Penyghent, Whernside and Ingleborough. The race was first recorded in 1887. Those invited to join the **Three Peaks of Yorkshire Club** must have completed the twenty-five mile route with its 5,000 feet of ascent in a minimum of twelve hours.

threeap to argue, grumble, complain, contradict, esp obstinately and persistently (OE *threapian*)

threeap dahn to bully (verbally)

threng (see *throng*)

threpple-throited with three throats (said of an immoderate drinker) WR

throit throat WR

thropple windpipe; throat

Throp's wife Yorkshire housewife of whom no details are known except that she was proverbially busy, giving rise to the saying *'as throng as Throp's wife'*. To this was once added *'. . . 'oo brewed, weshed an' baked on t' same day, then 'enged 'ersen wi t' dish-claht'.* WR (? var of Thorp)

throssie, throstle song thrush (OE)

throit throat WR (OE *throte*)

throng busy (see *Throp's wife*)

throttle (see *thropple*)

thru through, often used in the sense of 'from', eg *'e's thru Leeds*, he's from Leeds (OE *thurh*)

thruff through NER (see *thru*)

thrummly awkward, untidy, muddled

thrums ends cut from the warp while on the loom, used esp to make mops and floorcloths (ON *throemr*)

thrussen thrust

thrussen (up) overcrowded, pushed in too close together

thrutch pushing, jostling *there's allus mooast thrutch wheeare there's t' leeast room* WR

thummleteea big toe NR

thump local feast, fair (see **Halifax Thump Sunda**)

thunner thunder (OE *thunor*)

thunner pash sudden heavy shower NR

thwart mark line based on landmarks used to check the progress of a ship (eg in the Humber estuary)

thwitel kind of knife esp made in Sheffield

ti, tiv to, esp NER

tide fair, usually linked to a place name, eg **Bowling Tide** (qv)

tidgy tiny, very small WR

tidy-betty ash-pan; guard to prevent ashes from falling out into hearth

tig to touch lightly

tig, tiggy children's chasing game sometimes called *tiggy touchwood*, bescause a child was 'safe' after touching a tree or wood (see also *catchins*)

Tigers nickname of Hull City Football Club

tighten to get a move on; to clear off WR (textile term, from the tightening of belts on pulleys, which made them move faster)

til to

timpy-toed walking with feet turning inwards

tin can squat children's game in which one who is 'it' finds another person hiding and races him or her to be the first to kick a tin can

tingalary kind of street piano, worked by turning a handle, once commonly heard in the industrial WR

tip-cat (see *piggy*)

tipple to fall or knock down, tumble, topple

tipple dahn to rain heavily WR

tipple-tails somersault

tit small, lively horse

titmoos bluetit

tivvy chase, run about, run quickly

toathri several (usually used as a noun, with 'a') *there wor a toathri 'osses* (form of 'two or three')

tod fox (ME)

toffee Home-made toffee used to be common in Yorkshire, and the famous Halifax firm of Macintosh started in 1890 when John and Violet Macintosh sold toffee made from a recipe found in their family album. There is a similar origin for Thorntons toffee in Sheffield in 1911 when Norman Thornton, later joined by his brother Stanley, sold their home-made toffee at sixpence a bag. Other Yorkshire toffee firms have included Thornes of Leeds and Rileys of Halifax. (See also **butterscotch, Harrogate toffee, Plot**)

toit hobby, absorbing occupation, having the attention fully engaged, keeping occupied, in practice, in trim *keepin' i' toit* WR

tolther to hobble, totter (OE *tealtrian*)

tommy rubbish, nonsense ER esp Hull

tommy-box lunch tin used by foundry workers, esp in Middlesbrough (from *tommy ticket*, an early kind of food voucher)

tommy-owt lad doing odd jobs ER

tommy roond-'eead huge rock or boulder in a field NR

tommy-spinner (see *jenny-spinner*)

Top Withens — the inspiration for Wuthering Heights?

Tom Pudding nickname of short, rounded barges used on the River Don and S Yorks canals, replacing the earlier **Humber keel** (qv) at the end of the nineteenth century

tom trot kind of **Plot toffee** (qv) made with black treacle and demerara sugar

tonn to turn NER

tonnup turnip NER

tonty something very small (originally a term for a small marble)

tooan one of two WR

toon town NER

top-coit overcoat WR

top-maker manufacturer or mill specialising in **tops** (qv)

Top Withens sometimes known as Far Withens, a ruined farmhouse on the moors near Haworth, thought to have been the original

of Emily Brontë's **Wuthering Heights** (qv)

Tophams Column erected by Edward Topham to mark the spot where a meteorite fell near Wold Newton, ER, in 1795. Said to be the largest meteorite recorded in Britain, it is in the National History Museum in London.

tops longer fibres of wool after combing, ready for spinning. They are distinguished from **noils** (qv), and many Yorkshire woollen mills specialised in **tops** and **noils**. WR

torves top part of **peat** (qv), with heather roots (var of 'turves')

touch (see **mill-band**)

towter peeping Tom WR (Sheffield area)

Towton site of the bloodiest battle on English soil, fought on Palm Sunday 1461, when the army of the House of York defeated that of the House of Lancaster, the latter fighting with a snowstorm in their faces. The battle lasted ten hours, estimates of those killed ranging from 20,000 to 38,000. It is said that nearby Cock Beck ran red with blood for two days. (See **Towton Rose** below, and also **Rambler's Church**.)

Towton Rose white rose with a red centre, which formerly grew on the site of a battlefield (see above), said to be tinged with symbolic blood, probably the burnet or Scotch rose (*Rosa spinosissima*)

trackless trolley bus WR (so called to distinguish it from a tram which ran on a track)

traipse to walk wearily

trams Once an important feature in Yorkshire towns and cities, in the early years they were drawn by horses. Leeds, for example, had horse buses in 1839, horse trams from 1871, and electric trams from 1897. Inclined cliff tramways have been in use in Scarborough since 1875, and in Saltburn since 1884. The popular 'toast-rack' tramway from Saltaire to Shipley Glen was opened in 1895. No longer regarded as obsolete, modern trams have reappeared in cities such as Sheffield.

traps belongings *fetch all thi traps ovver 'ere* (abbr of 'trappings') WR

traycle treacle (ME *triacle*)

traycle possit (see *possit*)

Treasurers House one of the oldest buildings in York, and built on the site of Roman barracks, the **Treasurers House** has become famous for the ghosts of marching Roman soldiers in the cellars, convincingly reported by Harry Martindale.

treat children's party, often held in the open air, mainly organised by Sunday schools (see **Whitsuntide**)

tret treated

tribbit long pliable stick with clubbed end used in game of *knur and spell* (qv)

trig to fill (to capacity), esp stomach

tripe Tripe was a cheap, nutritious food for the poorer people of the industrial WR, with many **tripe shops** selling little else. **Tripe** is eaten cold or traditionally stewed with onions. (See also *elder*, *honeycomb*, *reed* and *seam*.)

tripe-'ound fool S Yorks

trivit (see *tribbit*)

trod footpath (OE *trod*, track)

Troll Egg Day Easter Monday (cf **pace eggs**, *trolling*)

Troller's Gill Notorious for being haunted by a *barguest* (qv), this is a grim ravine, some 500 feet long and 60 feet deep in the limestone near Parceval Hall, Wharfedale. The *barguest* of **Troller's Gill** is said to be a large spectral hound, and various accounts refer to its blazing eyes, one claiming it had a single eye burning right in the middle of its forehead. An earlier spelling was Trowler's Gill, and it has also been known as **Jackdaw Nick**.

trolling the custom of rolling

hardboiled eggs down a slope on Troll Egg Day (qv) (see **pace eggs**)

trollop slovenly woman (cf *trull*)

trones scales, esp for weighing pigs (OF *trone*)

troosies trousers NER

trull immoral woman (cf *trollop*)

trump to break wind WR (OF *tromper*)

trunnel pie pie containing mainly **tripe** (qv), served hot with peas (possibly so called from *trunnel*, a hole in the top of a furnace)

tul to

tumril wooden feeding trough, usually square with legs (originally a cart) (OF *tumberel*)

tundish funnel; vessel used for pouring molten metal into moulds in steel industry WR (shortened from 'tunnel-dish')

tuner textile term for a loom mechanic who tuned or adjusted the machinery in a woollen mill

tup male sheep, ram; huge iron weight used by quarrymen to break up stone (ME *tupe*)

tup lump large piece of stone in a quarry (see above)

turf fuel similar to **peat** (qv), but cut from a dry surface, and containing roots, being lighter in appearance than **peat**

turf cakes cakes such as *fat rascals* (qv) made over a fire of turf (qv)

turkeys The first turkeys to be brought back from the New World were introduced by William Strickland of Boynton Hall, near Bridlington, who had sailed with Sebastian Cabot in the sixteenth century, settling at Boynton in 1549. The Stricklands included the turkey in their family crest, and the bird features in Boynton Church.

Turpin (see **Dick Turpin**)

tusky rhubarb (qv) WR, esp Morley and S of Leeds

tussy-peg tooth (term used with young children)

tu'thri (see *toathri*)

Twelve Apostles traditional name of the Bronze Age circle of stones on Ilkley Moor not far from the path from **Dick Hudsons** (qv); also the nickname of the twelve engineers selected by A A Scott to work on his 'Scott Sociable' (see **Scott motorbikes**)

twilt to beat, thrash, clip *Ah'll twilt thi lug-'oil* WR

twind to turn, twist *she wor twindin' t' mengle* (var of 'wind')

twined angry (eg of a wasp) WR (? the idea of being 'wound up')

twinder person who turns the rope while others skip, esp at Scarborough (see **Shrove Tuesday**)

twinge earwig WR (see also *forkin'-robin, twitchbell*)

twister textile worker who twists together strands of wool in spinning, winding yarn from one *bobbin* (qv) to another

twinter sheep which has lived for two winters

twitchbell earwig (see also *forkin'-robin, twinge*)

Two Stoups local name for Yorkes Folly, at Guisecliff high on the moors near Pateley Bridge, built around 1740 by John Yorke of Bewerley Hall, Bewerley, to

Turkeys were first landed and bred in Yorkshire.

provide employment for the local population during economic hardship.

tyke dog, cur, esp small mongrel terrier used for catching rats etc. From the common sight of a Yorkshireman owning such a dog, the term came to be used to apply to anyone born and bred in Yorkshire. At first used perjoratively, the nickname is now generally accepted by Yorkshire people, who proudly apply it to themselves. (ON *tika*, bitch)

Tykes nickname of Barnsley Football Club

U

'ug, 'ugg, 'uggins (see *hug, hugger, huggins*)

uggrum pig ER

ullot owl (dim of OE *ule*)

Ulph's Horn ivory drinking horn made from a two foot long elephant's tusk, one of the treasures of York Minster, said to have been presented by the Danish chief Ulph in the eleventh century when he gave land to the church. It was restored and beautifully ornamented at the expense of Lord Henry Fairfax in 1675.

'ummer (see *hummer*)

umpteen a lot (of) (used more commonly in WR) *umpteen on 'em*

unbethink to think again, or change one's mind *Ah unbethowt missen* WR

unbeknown unknown (to)

'und behind, posterior (short for *be-hund*)

under being dealt with by (used more than in SE in phrases like *sh' wor under t' doctor*)

under-'and to have something *under-'and* is to be dealing with it, to have it in mind etc

underdrawing loft, space between ceiling and roof

undergang underground archway, tunnel

understand to hear, to be told *Ah understand 'e's poorly, Ah've been given to understand*

uniform holiday week shared by several mills WR

unkers haunches, thighs ER

unmenseful untidy or badly-dressed; ill-mannered

unsneck to unlatch

upgang uphill road or track ER

An urchin or ochin.

191

Ulph's Horn, an eleventh century treasure.

up-mooden heaped up, as in a spoonful of sugar, which contains a generous amount, rather than being levelled off WR

uppins upper part of shoe

upshell, upskittle to overturn, upset; to tilt up (a cart)

urchin hedgehog (OF *herisson*)

us (pron 'uz') us; our *we want us dinner* WR, esp S Yorks

us-sen ourselves

uvvil covering for finger end, finger-stall

uzzle blackbird NER (OE *osle*)

V

Valley of Desolation ravine near Bolton Abbey so called because of damage caused by a disastrous storm here in 1826

varmint vermin (var of OF *vermin*)

varra, varry very

vast o' a lot of *a vast o' muck, a vast o' fooals* NER

Vendale name given to Littondale in Charles Kingsley's *The Water-Babies* (1863). Kingsley stayed at Bridge End House in Arncliffe, which in the novel became the dame school. Under the bridge near here was the place where little Tom met the Water Babies.

vennel drain, gutter, sink

vessil cups small lidless boxes containing a doll representing the baby Jesus lying in the manger, or sometimes two dolls representing the Virgin and Child. Taken from house to house at Christmastime by children, who sang a dialect verse and carols begging for money. A traditional Cleveland rhyme ran: *'God bless t' maister of this 'oose, An' t' mistress also, An' all yer lahtle bonny bairns 'At roond yer table go'*. (See **Christmas**, *wessle bob*.)

vetnary vet (veterinary)

viewly, viewsome pleasing to the eye, good-looking

voider wicker clothes-basket (see drawing on page 164) (OF *voideor*)

W

waak weak NER

wad would

Wade name of the semi-legendary giant, said to be an Anglian chieftain, who, with his wife Bell, built the castles of Mulgrave and Pickering respectively. They built these at the same time, according to legend, and had only one hammer between them, which they tossed back and forth the eighteen miles across the moors. They lived in Mulgrave Castle, and built a road from Lythe to Pickering, known as **Wade's Causeway**. As in the case of the giant **Rombald's** (qv) wife, stones on the moors are said to have fallen from Bell's apron. (See **Devil's Punchbowl**.)

wae's t' 'eart! obsolete expression of grief (lit 'woe is the heart')

waff oatmeal cooked with treacle and milk WR

waffly unsteady; shaky, dizzy

wag¹ man in charge of horses on a farm (from waggon)

wag² to play truant (sometimes used as a noun in *to play wag*)

wahr¹ worse *whar ner nowt* WR

wahr² war WR

wahve! turn to left (horse)

Wainhouse Tower curious folly, originally built as a chimney in 1871 by J E Wainhouse, owner of a dye-works near Halifax. In 1875 he completed it as an observation tower 253 feet high, with 403 steps. Sometimes called 'Spite Tower' because of the belief that Wainhouse wanted to outdo a rival and overlook his property.

wait on! (pron with emphasis on second word) wait!

waits those going round singing Christmas carols, esp when accompanied with instruments. This used to be the standard Yorkshire term for **Christmas singers** (qv), and in Pickering, for example, the *waits* were accompanied by a shouter who roused householders to come to the door or window in the early hours of Christmas day.

Wakefield pudding kind of moulded bread-pudding filled with stewed apples

wakeman watchman; chief magistrate of **Ripon** (qv), until 1604, when the office became that of mayor. The Ripon motto is: 'Except ye Lord keep ye Citie, ye Wakeman waketh in vain' (Psalm 127).

wakken (see *wekken*)

Walking Parson nickname of the Rev A N Cooper of Filey (b 1850) who often walked thirty miles a day, and walked from Filey to Venice (653 miles), and from Filey to Rome (741 miles), the latter in six weeks. He was in the tradition of Foster Powell of Horsforth (b1734) who walked from York to London and back in five and a half days.

Walkington Hay Ride annual procession of horse-drawn farm carts on the third Sunday in June between Walkington and Beverley, originating in the traditional **hay ride**, and revived in 1967 to raise money for charity. It includes other vehicles, such as the Holderness stagecoach, and participants wear Victorian costume

wall capes stones finishing off the top of a wall

wallop blow, beating; approximate amount, as in *bi t' wallop*, by rule of thumb.

wallops game similar to ninepins, but instead of rolling a ball the players try to knock down the nine wooden skittles by throwing a stick. The game is associated with certain villages, such as Castle Bolton, Wensleydale, and is sometimes played at country shows.

Walton calves faint-hearted men (see below)

Walton Rag Well Named from the custom of tying strips of cloth as votive offerings following cures, this well at Walton, near Wetherby, was reputed to have water beneficial for eye diseases. The highwayman Nevison (see **Swift Nick**) was

surprised here by local men who then ran away, hence the nickname **Walton calves**.

wame stomach; belly (OE *wamb*)

wang to throw, esp with violence; *Wang it ovver 'ere!*

wang tooth molar, back tooth or side tooth (OE *wange*, jawbone)

wankley weak, unsteady; weakest of litter

wapentake division of a shire in areas of Viking influence. (ON *vapnatak*, referring perhaps to a show of weapons in voting)

warf tasteless; musty (of food) (cf *wolsh*)

wark[1] work (OE *weorc*)

wark[2] ache, pain **belly-wark**, **teeath-wark** etc (OE *waerc*)

warp[1] lengthwise threads in weaving

warp[2] sediment from river deposited after flooding

warp[3] group of fish (eg *a warp o' 'errins*) NER

warril quarry NR

warridge withers, shoulder-bone (of horses)

wart charms folk remedies for making warts disappear include stroking them with a snail, which is then impaled on a thorn. Other folk remedies are touching with meat, bean pods, peas, elder and **wart stones**.

washin' day Monday is the traditionally the day for washing clothes, with Tuesday reserved for ironing.

Washington stars The original stars eventually included in the American flag are said to be in the Washington coat-of-arms depicted in a window in the eastern clerestory of Selby Abbey.

wassailing Originally the custom of wishing good health (from the OE greeting *Wes hal!*) it centred round the *wassail bowl* and communal drinking at Christmas. Later the term was used for going round with *vessil cups* (qv) and singing carols. Some *wassailers* included the line *'Here we come a-wassailing'*, and others wished country families: *'A pooakful o' money an' a cellar-full o' beer, A good fat pig an' a new-cauven coo'*.

wathsteead ford

watter water (OE *waeter*)

watter wallops dumplings boiled in water S Yks

watter wolf fabled creature said to be swallowed by those who drank out of dirty streams or wells, and which lived in the stomach on the food the person ate, causing discomfort and loss of weight until it was regurgitated.

watti cake similar to *tharf cake* (qv)

Wauds the Yorkshire Wolds ER

wayant keen

ways (see *come thi ways*) NER

weasen windpipe (OE *waesend*)

weatherglass barometer

Weatherman William Foggitt of Thirsk, famous for his weather forecasts based on traditional sayings and observation of the plants and creatures of the Yorkshire countryside. His interest was inspired when he saw the total eclipse of the sun at Giggleswick on the 29th June 1927.

web piece of cloth being woven

wed to marry (OE *weddian*, to pledge)

wed married

weeak to cry out (in pain or fear) WR

weeam (see *wame*)

weean child NER (contraction of 'wee' and 'one')

weeant wont

weearish irritable ER

weeks corners NER

weel well

weel-bushed well off, wealthy

weet wet (parts of WR)

weft crosswise threads in weaving

wekken to wake (up); to waken (OE *waecan, wacian*)

well-dressing Although now essentially a Derbyshire tradition, the floral decoration of wells and springs, to placate the spirits that were thought to inhabit them, has been revived at Cragg Vale near Hebden Bridge, and introduced at other places in South Yorkshire, such as Dore near Sheffield.

welt to hit, beat, esp as punishment

welted (see *rig-welted*)

wemmle to overbalance *t' cart's wemmled ower* NER

wemmly wobbly

wengby cheese that is old and hard (from *whang, wheng* (qv))

Wensleydale variety of sheep, large, hornless and long-coated, bred in central Wensleydale, with a characteristic blue tinge in the skin of the face and ears.

Wensleydale cheese justly-prized Yorkshire cheese, probably first made in Wensleydale by the Cistercian monks of Jervaulx Abbey, founded in 1156, who used milk from their large flocks of ewes. For centuries made in farmhouses, the production of **Wensleydale** is now mainly in the factory between Hawes and Gayle, started in 1897, and later developed by Kit Calvert. Though mostly white cheese, the traditional **blue-veined Wensleydale** is sometimes available. (See also **Coverdale, Swaledale.**)

Wensleydale Heifer pedigree shorthorn bred by Thomas Willis of Carperby between 1861 and 1871. In its honour the inn in West Witton, which had been called the **Craven Heifer** (qv), was renamed the **Wensleydale Heifer.**

Wensleydale Lad title of a comic song in NR dialect, written around 1800, describing the visit of a Dales lad to Leeds.

wer our

wersel, wersen ourselves

wesh to wash (OE *waescan*)

Wesleyan member or chapel belonging to the Wesleyan **Methodists** (qv) (cf **Prims**)

wesp wasp NER

Wessies people from the West Riding NER

wessle bob This term (and the var *Wesley bob*) has been used in two different ways. It sometimes refers to the *vessil cup* (qv), and sometimes to a *wassail* (qv) *bough* or to glass baubles used to decorate a Christmas tree. (See *kissin'-bough*.)

West Yorkshire's regiment originating in the Prince of Wales Own (1685) which recruited in the WR, esp in the First World War, when men from the same area were known as the 'Bradford Pals', 'Leeds

Pals', 'Sheffield Pals' etc because they joined up and trained (and were often casualties) together.

wether lamb that has been castrated (OE *withar*)

weyve to weave (OE *wafan*)

wey-ya! command to a horse to stop

wham swamp, marshy land (ON *hvammr*)

whang, wheng tough leather, thong, bootlace (see *wengby*)

whap to flip over NER

whapcock small heap of hay NR

Wharton Bibles presented to generations of Yorkshire children through Sunday schools on condition that they learn by heart certain psalms specified by Philip, Lord Wharton (1613-1696), who made provision for Bibles to be paid for from his estate.

what for severe punisment or retribution *Ah'll give thi what for!*

wheea who NER

wheear(e) where

wheel-band (see *mill-band*)

wheel-'eead hub, central part of a wheel *as drunk as a wheel-'eead* (ie because it wobbled) WR

while until *they'll be 'ere while Munda*

whinge to whine, cry, as when a baby is teething; to cringe, draw back (now accepted in SE in the first sense)

whinny gorse, furze (? ON, cf Norwegian *hvine*)

Whinny Mooar moor over which the soul must pass in the *Lyke Wake Dirge* (qv)

Whip-ma-whop-ma-gate name of York's shortest street, said to refer to the practice of the whipping and beating of malefactors, but possibly also relating to **dog-whipping** (qv).

whippet   small, elegant yet hardy dog used in racing, esp in the mining areas of the WR, where it was bred by miners as a cheaper alternative to the greyhound.

whipping tops   wooden tops kept in motion by small whips — a coloured stick with a knotted leather throng through a hole. Once a favourite pastime of children, esp girls, whips and tops traditionally appeared on the pavements at Shrovetide. Coloured chalks were used on the upper surface of the tops, making patterns which blended as they spun.

whisht   silent *'Od thi whisht!*, Be quiet!

Whitby Regatta   Started in 1840 as a competition between local rowing clubs, this traditional three day event assembles yachts and other vessels on the River Esk and in Whitby harbour, as well as holding a fair and procession of floats in the town.

White Doe of Rylstone   legend which inspired Wordsworth to write a poem of almost 2,000 lines on how Francis Norton of Rylstone was murdered, and buried at Bolton Priory. His grave was visited every Sunday by his sister Emily, accompanied by her pet white doe. After her death the deer continued to make the Sunday pilgrimage to the grave of Francis Norton.

White Horse   Yorkshire's White Horse is comparatively recent, carved out of the hillside above

Kilburn in 1857. Designed by Thomas Taylor, it was made by the village schoolmaster John Hodgson and thirty villagers. Measuring 314 feet by 228 feet, it is one of Yorkshire's most familiar landmarks.

White Mare Crag   name given to Whitestone Cliff overlooking Lake Gormire. Though the 'mare' may be derived from 'mere', referring to the lake, legends include stories of a rider leaping over it on his white mare, and the saying concerning hay growing on the *riggs* (banks) of the lake: *'When Gormire riggs shall be clothed wi' hay, T' White Mare o' Wissoncliff 'll bare it away'*. (See Gormire.)

white-ovver, -ower   with a covering of snow   *it's white-ovver this mornin'*

White Rose   The Yorkshire Rose is officially the old pure-white *Rosa alba*, said to have been plucked as his emblem by Richard Plantagenet, Duke of York, at the start of the Wars of the Roses (1455), when the House of Lancaster adopted a red rose. Though this story is used by Shakespeare, the White Rose was the symbol of the House of York long before this date. It is also the emblem of the King's Own Yorkshire Light Infantry (**KOYLI** (qv)), and appears in many heraldic designs, badges etc as the symbol of Yorkshire.

White Rose Walk   This route was first walked in 1968 by the Yorkshire Wayfarers as a north-south complement to the **Lyke Wake Walk** (qv). Starting near **Rosesberry Topping**

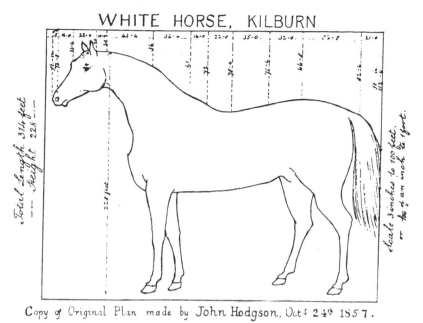

WHITE HORSE, KILBURN

Copy of Original Plan made by John Hodgson, Oct. 24ᵗʰ 1857.

The White Horse, as originally planned.

(qv) and finishing at the **White Horse** (qv), it covers thirty-seven miles (59km).

Whitsun boss flower worn in a man's buttonhole, originally at **Whitsuntide** (qv), when new suits and smart clothes appeared.

Whitsuntide This Christian festival was until recently observed by churches and Sunday schools walking round, sometimes with a banner, usually on Whit Monday, to sing hymns in the open air; the well-known *Onward Christian Soldiers* was specially written for the children of Horbury Bridge, near Wakefield, in 1865 for such an occasion. The songs were usually followed by games, races, and a 'bun fight', this being commonly known as a **Whitsuntide *treat*** (see *treat*). This has largely died out, but competitive walking survives in the **Bradford Whit Walk** (qv). **Whitsuntide** was also the time when children received new clothes, the boys proudly going round in their new suits, the pockets of which friends and relations traditionally placed a coin to bring good luck. ('Whitsuntide' is derived from the white garments worn by converts baptised at Pentecost.)

whittle knife, esp clasp knife (ME *thwittel*)

Wibsey Fair one of the oldest horse fairs in Britain, said to have been started by the monks of Kirkstall Abbey soon after their foundation (1152). Dealers used to come to Wibsey, south of Bradford, from far and wide, the horses being trotted along Folly Hall Road. The last day sometimes featured a **ketty fair** of broken-down animals. In recent years, horses have given way to the funfair.

wick¹ life; quick, base of fingernail esp NER

wick² lively, alive, eg *wick wi' mawks*

wick³ week esp WR

wicken (see *wiggin*)

wicks, wickens couch grass; weeds in general NER

widdy, withy¹ metal ring to which a cow chain is attached, moving up and down a *boose-stake* (qv)

widdy² willow

wig kind of cake containing currants NR

wiggin mountain ash or rowan tree, superstitiously believed to have the power to ward off evil spirits and protect from witchcraft. Branches of rowan were placed in cowsheds and fastened to lintels as a protection, and were most potent if gathered on St Helens Day (18th August).

wike corner of the mouth ER

Wilfra Feast popular name for Ripon's festival in honour of St Wilfrid, commemorating his return from exile in AD 686 to his monastery at Ripon. **St Wilfrid's Feast**, held on the Saturday before the first Monday in August, originally opened with an effigy of the saint being escorted into the city, but now the long-established tradition is of a man dressed as St Wilfrid, and mounted on a white horse, leaving the town hall at 2 pm to lead a colourful procession of decorated floats round Ripon. The saint is finally welcomed at the cathedral by the dean and chapter, and the mayor and council, for a service of thanksgiving.

Wilfra Pies apple pies made for **Wilfra Feast** (qv) which have slices of cheese baked in with the apple

Wilfra Tarts Specially baked for **Wilfra Feast** (qv) by Ripon housewives, these are traditionally kept by the door, handy to offer to visitors. The filling is usually made from

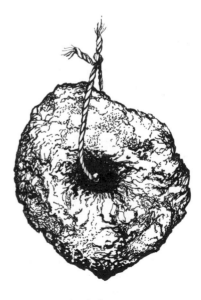

A witch stone.

breadcrumbs soaked in egg and milk, ground almonds, butter, sugar and grated lemon rind.

Willance's Leap part of Whitfield Scar near Richmond, over which a draper called Robert Willance galloped his horse in 1606 and miraculously escaped death.

willey to prepare raw wool by shaking out dirt and loosening the fibres so that they are ready for scouring

willn't won't, will not (used in certain parts of NR)

wimble gimlet, any tool for boring a hole

winder¹ window

winder² to winnow (OE *windwian*)

Windyridge This name, now given to homes all over Yorkshire, was inspired by the first novel of William Riley, *Windyridge* (1912), who used a cottage in the village of Hawksworth, north of Baildon, as the home of his heroine, Grace Holden.

winter-'edge clothes-horse

wire in to tuck into food, eat heartily; work with energy

wishin cushion (? abbr of *quishin* (qv))

wiskit small basket; tapered basket formerly used by miners to carry coal along galleries WR

witchcraft Many Yorkshire traditions concern **witchcraft** and **witches**, the latter to be kept at bay with charms such as **witch stones**, a stone with a hole in it and suspended by string. Houses were protected by **witch posts** and the planting of rowan or *wiggin* (qv). Some **witches** are anonymous, but

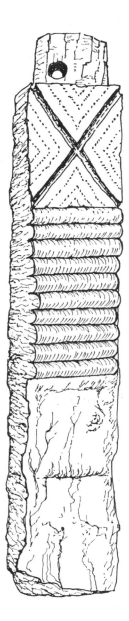

A witch post from a Yorkshire cottage.

others have a basis in history, such as Sally Carey of Kirby Hill, near Boroughbridge, Peggy Flaunders of Marske, Nan Hardwick of Spittal Houses, and the witches of Pocklington (1630, 1642, 1649), Danby Dale and Fewston, the latter described by Edward Fairfax in 1623. (See also **Awd Nan, Barrow Witch, Mother Shipton, Yatton Brigg**.)

witheret weasel NR

wivoot without NER

wizzand (see *weasen*)

wockery weak

Wold Rangers term describing unemployed workers who roamed the Yorkshire Wolds during the nineteenth and early twentieth centuries, living off the land and doing odd jobs on farms. They were befriended by Sir Tatton Sykes (1772-1863) of Sledmere, who regularly supplied them with tea and sandwiches, and by his eccentric son who handed a shilling to every **Wold Ranger** who greeted him or who brought back the coats he discarded as the day grew warmer.

wolsh tasteless, without real flavour; lacking in salt

wolt to tilt, overbalance *t' clock's off wolts*, the clock is ticking irregularly (cf *welted* (qv)) WR

woltin' day Wednesday (ie the day marking the beginning of the second half of the week, which had then *wolted*)

wom home esp WR (var of *'ooam*)

woof (see **Scarborough woof**)

woolcombing process of straightening wool fibres, separating them into *tops* (qv) and *noils* (qv) (see also *pot o' one*)

woollen industry Yorkshire has traditionally been a county of sheep and woollen manufacture, with a weaver's guild in York as early as the twelfth century, when Beverley and Hull were also centres of the trade. Later the ample coal, water and communications of the WR made it ideal for textile mills, with Bradford becoming the 'wool capital of the world' (see **Worstedopolis**), and Leeds equally important for clothing manufacture. (See *beammate, bobbin-ligger, brat, doffer, elbow-mate, mungo, noils, pent, penny-'oil, shoddy, willey,* **worsted**, and items below.)

woolsorter worker grading fleeces and wool (see **woolsorting**)

woolsorter's disease anthrax, once commonly contracted from the wool of infected sheep

woolsorting highly-skilled traditional craft requiring years of experience to grade as many as 5,000 different qualities of wool according to length, fineness and colour. The **woolsorter** is protected by a *brat* (qv) and does his work by *t' rack o' t' ee* (qv).

worm term used for a mythical creature similar to a dragon or wyvern. Like the Lambton Worm in County Durham, the Yorkshire *worms* were supposed to be capable of rejoining the severed pieces when they were attacked. (See **Handale, Nunnington, Sexhow** and **Slingsby**.) (OE *wyrm*)

worsted cloth made from best-quality yarn, spun from long-staple wool, finely combed and closely twisted, and a famed product of the

The spinning wheel, symbolic of Yorkshire's bygone cottage industry.

WR, esp Bradford. Worsted cloth generally has a smoother, less whiskery texture than woollen fabric. (Named after Worstead near Norwich.)

Worstedopolis name coined to describe Bradford, recognised as the capital of the **woollen industry** (qv)

wossup wasp

wotchet orchard ER

wots oats NER

wrang, wreng wrong (OE *wrang*)

wreet wheelwright, esp one who travelled round villages and farms mending implements

wrezzle weasel ER

wummel large corkscrew NR

wun wound

wurrum *worm* (qv) (OE *wyrm*)

wuthering wild, blustery, howling (wind). This adjective was made famous by Emily Brontë in the title of her novel *Wuthering Heights* (1847), thought to refer to **Top Withens** (qv), on the moors near Haworth. (? var of 'wither' or 'weather'.)

wuz to spin round a basket of washed yarn to remove water WR

wye young heifer, up to three years old (ON *kviga*)

Y

yacker acre NER (ON *akr*)

yackrons acorns NER

yaffle(r) green woodpecker (from the bird's call)

yah one; also used in some systems of **sheep counting** (qv) NER

yak oak NER

Yakkam Acomb near York

yal ale NER

yaller-belly grinder in the cutlery trade, from the fact that grinders were daubed with the yellow of the *swarf* (qv) S Yorks, esp Sheffield area

yam¹ home NER

yam² *hame* (qv)

yam hooks hooks on each side of a horse's collar to which traces are attached

yamley homely

yammer to chatter, esp noisily (OE *geomerian*)

yan one; also used in **sheep counting** (qv) (cf *yah, yar*) NER

yance once NER

yance ower once (upon a time) NER

yanly, yannerly alone, solitary; shy NER

yar one (cf *yah, yan*) NER

yarbs herbs NER

yark to pull, esp with a jerk *'e yarked mi tooth aht* WR; to beat NER

Yarm Fair horse fair established long before 1674, when Charles II renewed the charter, held each October at Yarm near Middlesbrough, and popular with gypsies and travellers (see **Barnaby Fair**). As in other places the horse-trading element has gradually been replaced by a funfair.

yarnut (see *yennet*)

yat¹ hot NER

yat² gate NER

yat-steead gateway; ground covered by the opening of a gate NER

yat-stoup, -stowp gatepost NER

Yatton Brigg subject of a NR dialect poem written by Richard Blakeborough, *T' Hunt o' Yatton Brigg*, which included the curse of a witch over her deadly brew, beginning: *'Fire cum, Fire gan, Curlin' smeeak keep oot o' t' pan!'*.

Yattoner inhabitant of Great Ayton, the village where Captain Cook went to school. It is said that *'Yattoners wade ower t' beck ti seeave* (save) *t' brig'*.

yawl fishing boat larger than a *coble* (qv) and with sails NER (cf Dutch *jol*)

yawd horse of inferior breeding NER (ON *jalda*, but also influenced by 'jade')

yeald heddle (of a loom)

yed, yeead[1] head

yed[2] yard (eg of a farm)

yed[3] yard (measure)

yedder (see *yether*)

yell to weep, esp loudly (cf *bawl*)

yennet earth-nut (*Conopodium majus*), an umbelliferous wild plant with an edible root about the size of a chestnut. Also known as *yeth-nut*. NER

yersel, yersen yourself

yest yeast. Yeast was once so commonly used in home baking

yat-stoup

band or strap

swape

yat-heead

hesp or sneck

yat-steead

Yat — a typical five-barred gate.

The yawl, once a common sight off the Yorkshire coast.

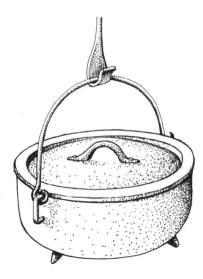

A yetling.

that it was sold from house to house by the **yeast man** or the **muffin man** (qv). (See also **barm, barmpot, barmy**) (OE *gest*, ON *joestr*)

yesterneet   last night

yeth   earth NER

yethers   osiers (branches of willow), esp those used to make the **Penny Hedge** (qv)

yetling   iron pan, sometimes on three short legs; iron pot, esp suspended over peat fire

yewer   udder NR

yitten   scared, cowardly WR

yivvin   oven NR

yocken   to eat or drink with enjoyment

yoller   yellow (OE *geolu*)

yon, yond   that, those; that person (OE *geon*, cf German *jener*)

yonder over there (OE *geond*)

yonderly preoccupied, with a faraway look (said esp of someone during serious illness, implying that death is near)

yoon oven NER

York ham traditional kind of best-quality ham, dry-cured, said to have originally been smoked with oak shavings during the building of York Minster, but possibly simply a shortened name for 'Yorkshire ham'.

York Minster fires Though fire damage occurred in 1069, 1137 and 1840, folklore surrounds the 1829 arson by the fanatic Jonathan Martin (see also below), and the 1984 blaze in the south transept — possibly struck by lightning.

York Minster Screen long comic dialogue in NR verse written in 1833 about the controversy surrounding the restored choir screen following the fire caused by Martin (see above).

Yorke's Folly (see **Two Stoups**)

yorker cricket term for a ball bowled so as to pitch just in front of or just beyond the bat

yorks string tied round trousers just below the knee, esp by quarrymen WR

Yorkshire Archaeological Society Founded in 1863 in Huddersfield, the society has had its current name since 1893, and is now based in Leeds, where it has a library and archives, and publishes its annual *Yorkshire Archaeological Journal.*

Yorkshire bite old term applied to Yorkshire dealers, reputed to be sharp and cunning (see *tyke*,

Yorkshireman's coat of arms)

Yorkshire Dales National Park This was created in 1954, and covers 680 square miles and includes all of the Dales except Nidderdale, which is nevertheless of outstanding beauty. The main information centre is at Grassington, and the park's symbol is a **Swaledale** *tup* (qv). (See **North York Moors National Park.**)

Yorkshire Day The 1st August, which is **Lammas** (qv) and also the anniversary of the Battle of Minden (1759), at which Yorkshire soldiers helped to gain the victory. **Yorkshire Day** was started in 1975 by the **Yorkshire Ridings Society** (qv), founded that same year with the aim of re-instating the **Ridings** (qv).

Yorkshire Dialect Society founded in Bradford on the 27th March 1897 by a group working for Professor Joseph Wright in the compilation of his *English Dialect Dictionary.* The first annual meeting was held in York the following September. The society holds several meetings a year in various parts of Yorkshire and publishes two annual journals, *Transactions* and the *Summer Bulletin.* (See **Christmas Crack, East Yorkshire Dialect Society.**)

Yorkshire Feast Song Commissioned by the **Society of Yorkshiremen in London** (qv) in 1688, the music was written by Henry Purcell and the words by Thomas D'Urfey. The latter are so dated as to be unuseable — except for the concluding line 'Long flourish the City and County of York!'.

A soldier of the King's Own Yorkshire Light Infantry, who fought at the Battle of Minden in 1759, the anniversary of which is also Yorkshire Day.

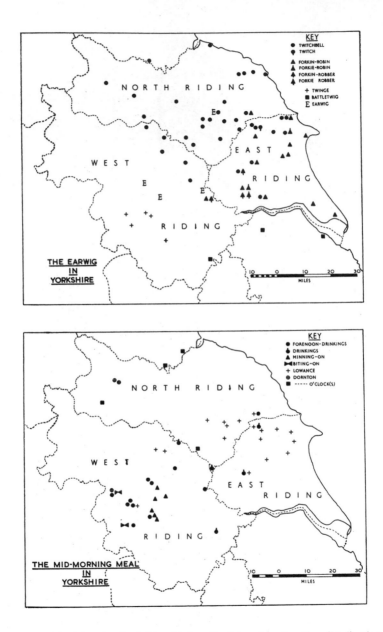

Maps produced by the Yorkshire Dialect Society, showing the distribution of certain dialect words.

Yorkshire Fog *Holcus lanatus*, a kind of quick-growing grass, found in poor pastures, given this name by early seed merchants (see *fog*)

Yorkshire grace A blunt WR grace before meals is traditionally said to be: *'God bless us all, an' mak us able, Ta eyt all t' stuff 'at's on this table'.*

Yorkshire keel (see **Humber keel**)

Yorkshire mixture assortment of hardboiled sweets of various shapes and colours, including pear drops, striped humbugs etc (see *spice*)

Yorkshire penny old name for Pomfret cakes (qv)

Yorkshire Post the county's oldest newspaper, started in Leeds in 1754 as the *Leeds Intelligencer*. In 1939 it absorbed the *Leeds Mercury* which had been founded in 1718.

Yorkshire pudding This world-famous batter pudding was originally made by placing the pudding mixture (eg 1 or 2 eggs, 4oz flour, pint milk and water, pinch of salt, thoroughly blended) in a baking tin under a joint of meat roasting before the fire. This meant that, as it cooked, the pudding absorbed juices from the meat. It also explains the reason why **Yorkshire pudding** is traditionally eaten as a first course, with beef gravy or onion gravy. Because meat was expensive, with little to go round in poorer families, the diners were encouraged to eat as much **Yorkshire pudding** as possible so they would have little room for the meat, hence the shrewd saying: *'Them 'at eyts mooast puddin' gets mooast meyt'.*

Yorkshire Relish traditional sauce with a fruity, spicy flavour, originally made by Yorkshire housewives, and first made commercially by the firm of Goodhall and Backhouse of Leeds in 1837, when Robert Goodall, a chemist, bottled and sold his wife's recipe. A decision in the House of Lords in 1897 made **Yorkshire Relish** the only 'geographical trademark' of its kind, and it was advertised as 'the most delicious sauce in the world'. It is made at Hammonds, Apperley Bridge, though the firm is based in Lancashire.

Yorkshire Ridings Society formed to promote the county and its three ancient **Ridings** (qv) in 1975, in which year it instituted the first **Yorkshire Day** (qv)

Yorkshire Rose (see **White Rose**)

Yorkshire Show Still officially known as the **Great Yorkshire Show**, this prestigious three day event in July was first held in 1837,

The Yorkshire Rose.

The Yorkshire Terrier.

organised by the Yorkshire Agricultural Society. In 1951 it moved to a permanent 250 acre showground in Harrogate.

Yorkshire Society Various societies of this name have been formed over the years in places outside the county, such as Birmingham, Edinburgh and London, the latter distinct from the **Society of Yorkshiremen in London** (qv). The Yorkshire Society in Yorkshire was founded in 1980 to encourage all things connected with Yorkshire. It awards the annual Yorkshire History Prizes and the Bramley History Prize.

Yorkshire speyks (see *speyks*)

Yorkshire teacakes teacakes, usually about six inches across, plain or with dried fruit

Yorkshire Television independent television company founded in 1968, with its principal studios in Leeds

Yorkshire Terrier originally bred by Yorkshire miners for use in underground hunting, this dog is the result of crossbreeding between the Skye Terrier, Black and Tan, and Dandie Dinmont. At first it was known as a miniature long-haired terrier, but since about 1910 has been officially named the **Yorkshire Terrier**. With its colours of golden tan and dark steel-blue, it is now an important dog in shows, for which its hair is grown long and straight.

Yorkshire toast This can be found in various humorous forms. For example: '*Ere's tiv us — all on us — an' me an' all! May wi nivver want nowt, nooan on us — Ner me nawther!*' (WR). '*Ere's tiv us — all on us — all on us ivver! May neean on us want nowt, Neean on us nivver!*' (ER).

Yorkshire, too phrase implying that the speaker is a match for the other person(s) in astuteness and skill in trading, eg *I's Yorksher, too, t' maister's Yorksher, too.*

Yorkshire tyke (see *tyke*)

Yorkshireman jocular term for a fly drowning or drowned in a glass of ale (from alleged cadging nature of Yorkshiremen)

Yorkshireman's coat of arms The earliest known design for this curious satirical comment on the character of Yorkshiremen was by Thomas Tegg of Cheapside in London, in 1818. This included a magpie, a fly and a flea (representing chattering, sponging and backbiting), a horse and a gammon ('Unhang'd they're worth nought does the gammon reveal').

Yorkshireman's motto This is usually given in the WR form, and shows the *tyke's* (qv) ability to laugh at himself and his alleged meanness: '*Ear all, see all, say nowt; Eyt all, sup all, pay nowt; An' if ivver tha does owt fer nowt — Do it fer thissen!*'.

youd to nag NER

yowe ewe NER

yucker child, youngster ER

Yule pagan winter-solstice festival, now synonymous with **Christmas** (qv) (name derived from ON *jol* — the festival around the shortest day)

Yule cake kind of Christmas cake or **spice cake** (qv), varying in shape and contents in different parts of

The Yorkshireman's coat of arms

Yorkshire. Nidderdale **yule cakes**, for example, were small and round, and contained yeast, whereas towards the East Coast they tended to be rectangular, with criss-crossed strips of pastry on top.

Yule candle   traditionally lit by the master of the house from the stump of the previous year's **Yule candle** (cf **Yule log** below)

Yule log   burnt at Christmas, and traditionally lit from a charred remnant of the **Yule log** of the previous year, the idea being to symbolise the continuity of life. (Sometimes called **clog**.)

Bibliography

Dictionaries, glossaries and dialect studies

The English Dialect Dictionary (6 vols) (1905) Joseph Wright
The Oxford English Dictionary (2nd edition) (20 vols) (1989)
Survey of English Dialects Vol 1 (1962) ed H Orton and W J Halliday
Survey of English Dialects: The Dictionary and Grammar (1993) ed Clive
   Upton, David Parry , J D A Widdowson

Dictionary of Archaic Words (1850) J O Halliwell
A List of Provincial Words (Wakefield) (1865) W S Banks
Glossary of the Cleveland Dialect (1868) J C Atkinson
The Dialect of Mid-Yorkshire (1876) C C Robinson
A Glossary of Yorkshire Words (Whitby) (1876) F K Robinson
Glossary of Almondbury and Huddersfield (1883) A Easther
Glossary of Words used in Sheffield (1888) S O Addy
The Folk Speech of East Yorkshire (1889) J Nicholson
The Dialect of the West Riding (1891) S Dyer
Yorkshire Folk Talk (NR and ER) (1911) M C F Morris
Dialect Dictionary of the North Riding (1928) A E Pease
The Dialect of the Huddersfield District (1928) W E Haigh
T' Yorksher Lingo (Halifax) (nd) J Baron
A Glossary of Dialect (Sheffield) (1936) B R Dyson
The White Rose Garland (1949) ed W J Halliday and A S Humphrey
The Minster Screen (NR dialect) (1967) ed W J Halliday
Yorkshire Dialect (1970) J Waddington-Feather
Emily Brontë and the Haworth Dialect (1970) K M Petyt
English Dialects (1972) G L Brook
Patterns in the Folk Speech of the British Isles (1972) M Wakelin
The Language of British Industry (1974) P Wright
Word Maps: A Dialect Atlas of England (1987) C Upton, S Sanderson,
   J D A Widdowson

The Dialects of England (1990) P Trudgill
Basic Broad Yorkshire (1992) A Kellett
Transactions of the Yorkshire Dialect Society (from 1898 to the present day). These contain articles on every aspect of dialect, as well as many word lists and technical glossaries of Yorkshire trades and crafts.

Booklets of dialect words, small anthologies etc

A Cleveland Anthology (1963) ed W Cowley
An Anthology of West Riding Verse (1964) ed G Wade
An Anthology of East Yorkshire Dialect Verse (1965) ed W Cowley
A Bonnie Hubbleshoo (Swaledale and Arkengarthdale) (1970) M Batty
The Muse went Weaving (1972) F Brown
The Yorkshire Pudding Olmenack (1973) ed B Dyson and S Ellis
The Yorkshire Yammer (1975) P Wright
Songs of Whitby and its Folk (1975) H Brown
Keeping Yorkshire Alive (1977) H Stone
Poems from the Yorkshire Dales (1979) G Jefferson
A Yorkshireman's Dictionary (1980) P Wright
Tales from the Wolds (1982) H Johnson
Pennine Thowts (1982) D Beer
Words throo t' Shuttle Ee (1983) ed G England
Humour from the Ridings (1985) B Dyson and G Robinson
East Riding Dialect Dictionary (1986) N Stockton
A Levelheeaded Dalesbred Lass (1988) R Dent
Dialect in and around Sowerby Bridge (1990 reprint) ed E Gledhill
Come thi Ways In (1990) R Dent
Kirkbridge Kaleidoscope (1991) M Park (based on the Radio York Series 'Tom and Seth')
The *Summer Bulletin* of the YDS also includes words and phrases, but mainly contemporary dialect verse and prose.

Yorkshire tradition and folklore

Old Yorkshire (1881) ed W Smith
The Folklore of East Yorkshire (1890) J Nicholson
Wit, Character, Folklore and Customs of the North Riding (1898) R Blakeborough
Yorkshire Notes and Queries (5 vols, 1905-9) ed C F Forshaw
Goodies (1912, reprinted YDS 1990) W F Turner
British Calendar Customs (1938) A R Wright

The White Rose Garland (1949) ed E J Halliday and A S Humpleby
The Spirit of Yorkshire (1954) J Fairfax-Blakeborough
The Lore and Language of Schoolchildren (1959) I and P Opie
Regional Archaeology: Yorkshire (1965) I H Laycock
The Brontës and Their World (1968) P Bentley
Life and Tradition in the Yorkshire Dales (1968) M Hartley and J Ingilby
You Don't Know Your Yorkshire (nd) Y E News (Doncaster)
Lang Sarmons (1974) A Jarratt
The Essential West Riding (1975) H Whone
Yorkshire through the Years (1975) I Dewhirst
Life and Tradition in West Yorkshire (1976) M Hartley and J Ingilby
Methodism in the Great Haworth Round (1978) J Dawson
Yorkshire Mill Town Traditions (1978) W R Mitchell
Reminiscences of a Bradford Mill Girl (1980) M Newberry
Know Your Yorkshire (1980) A Kellett
East Yorkshire Miscellany (1981) J Danby
Yorkshire Farming Memories (1981) S Harrison
Life on the North York Moors (1981) W R Mitchell
Mirfield: Life in a Yorkshire Village 1900-1914 (1984) J H Hird
The Lass of Richmond Hill (1986) P Wenham
Traditional Food in Yorkshire (1987) P Brears
The Fight for Yorkshire (1988) M Bradford
Food in Yorkshire (1988) J Poulson
A Yorkshire Christmas (1989) ed G Collard
Fairs, Feasts and Frolics (1989) J Smith
East Yorkshire Facts and Fables (1989) ed N Stockton
'Knaresborough Maundy', *Yorkshire Archeological Journal* (1990) A Kellett
A Haunt of Rare Souls: old inns and pubs of Yorkshire (1990) B Pepper
Folk Tales of the North York Moors (1990) P N Walker
Life in a Liberty Bodice (1991) C Burniston
Historic Knaresborough (1991) A Kellett
Drystone Walls of the Yorkshire Dales (1992) W R Mitchell
Made in Yorkshire (1993) M Colbeck
The *Dalesman* (from 1939) also contains a wealth of information on Yorkshire tradition and folklore, as do the more recently founded *Yorkshire Ridings, Yorkshire Life, Pennine* and *Yorkshire Journal.*